ELIZABETHAN LITERATURE AND THE LAW OF
FRAUDULENT CONVEYANCE

Mistress Ford and Mistress Page convey Falstaff in a buck-basket of laundry. From a painting by Rev. Matthew William Peters, ca. 1789. Photograph supplied courtesy of the Folger Shakespeare Library.

Elizabethan Literature and the Law of Fraudulent Conveyance

Sidney, Spenser, and Shakespeare

CHARLES ROSS

ASHGATE

© Charles Ross 2003

All rights reserved. No part of this publication may be reproduced, stored in a retrieval system, or transmitted in any form or by any means, electronic, mechanical, photocopying, recording or otherwise without the prior permission of the publisher.

The author has asserted his moral right under the Copyright, Designs and Patents Act, 1988, to be identified as the author of this work.

Published by
Ashgate Publishing Limited
Gower House
Croft Road
Aldershot
Hants GU11 3HR
England

Ashgate Publishing Company
Suite 420
101 Cherry Street
Burlington, VT 05401-4405

Ashgate website: http://www.ashgate.com

British Library Cataloguing in Publication Data
Ross, Charles, 1949-
 Elizabethan literature and the law of fraudulent conveyance
 : Sidney, Spenser, and Shakespeare
 1.Sidney, Sir Philip, 1554-1586 - Criticism and
 interpretation 2.Spenser Edmund, 1552?-1599 - Criticism and
 interpretation 3.Shakespeare William, 1564-1616 - Criticism
 and interpretation 4.English literature - Early modern,
 1500-1700 - History and criticism 5.Fraudulent conveyances
 - England - History - 16th century 6.Law in literature
 I.Title
 820.9'355'09031

Library of Congress Cataloging-in-Publication Data
Ross, Charles, 1949–
 Elizabethan literature and the law of fraudulent conveyance : Sidney, Spenser, and Shakespeare / Charles Ross.
   p.m.
 Includes bibliographical references.
 ISBN 0-7546-3263-6 (alk. paper)
  1. English literature--Early modern, 1500-1700--History and criticism. 2. Law in literature. 3. Sidney, Philip, Sir, 1554-1586--Knowledge--Law. 4. Shakespeare, William, 1564-1616--Knowledge--Law. 5. Spenser, Edmund, 1552?-1599--Knowledge--Law. 6. Law--Great Britain--History--16th century. 7. Law--Great Britain--History--17th century. 8. Law and literature--History--16th century. 9. Law and literature--History--17th century. 10. Fraudulent conveyances--Great Britain. I. Title

PR428.L37 R67 2003
820.9'355--dc21   2002074535

ISBN 0 7546 3263 6

Typeset by IML Typographers, Birkenhead, Merseyside, and
printed and bound in Great Britain by MPG Books Ltd, Bodmin, Cornwall

Contents

Preface ix
Acknowledgments xvii
A Note on the Text xix

Introduction 1

1. Falstaff's Conveyances 11
2. "Creditors and Others": The Purpose of 13 Eliz., c. 5 (1571) 29
3. Carried Away in Arcadia 43
4. Purchase and Consideration in *Faerie Queene* IV and V 71
5. Coke, Collusion, and Twyne's Case (1601) 101
6. Shylock's Penalty 113

Conclusion 133

Index 137

There is doubtless a lengthy story to be told of the evolution of the land law in Elizabeth's reign ... We read of fraudulent conveyances in several sessions, of fines and tenants for life, aliens' lands, corporations' conveyances and so on. In some cases the purpose of debate and legislation seems to have been to regularize and enforce a standard means of procedure, and to cut through the jungle of sharp practices which bedevilled the land market. And it must be remembered that as a high court Parliament could, and often did, take cognizance of cases of disputed title, calling witnesses and hearing counsel for the parties involved. The sheer amount of time and energy apparently devoted to all these problems demands both respect and understanding, and the record may provide varying degrees of insight into a number of problems. How far, and by what means, was the efficiency of the law advanced, and what did the lawyers themselves contribute to the progress? Why did the problem of fraudulent conveyances seem so unmanageable?
— T. E. Hartley, ed. *Proceedings of the Parliaments of Elizabeth I, I: xxiv–xxv.*

"'Convey', the wise it call. 'Steal'? foh: a *fico* for the phrase."
– Pistol

For Clare

Preface

This book began as a project in the sociology of law, a branch of jurisprudence that studies the impact of laws on the beliefs and behavior of society. The development of laws prohibiting fraudulent conveyances first attracted me, as a Renaissance scholar, because legal historians trace modern rules to a statute passed in 1571, during the Elizabethan era. I was curious why the ethical questions the law seemed to have settled – so much so that modern laws echo the wording of the statute of Elizabeth I – were still alive. Not only are US states and federal bankruptcy experts tinkering with these regulations, but the key question of when and why the law should apply did not seem obvious to me or to those people I interviewed for the project, which like most sociology of law investigations depended on attitude questionnaires. Why should not someone subject to a sudden lawsuit be able to protect his assets by putting them in another's name?

Uncertainty about the nature and working of the law raises cultural as well as legal issues. A comparison between modern and Elizabethan attitudes suggested itself, but since one cannot hand a questionnaire to an Elizabethan, I thought perhaps the literature of the period might provide clues on English thinking about the subject. It turns out that Shakespeare dramatized the issue, and its cloudy morality, in real life when he and his companions floated timbers from the old Theatre across the Thames to evade the grasp of Gyles Allen, who was claiming the building as an attachment to his land after the Burbages' lease expired. Lawyers may choose sides on this one. A literary example of evading a creditor occurs when Mistress Ford has Falstaff dumped *into* the same river to save him from the clutches of her jealous husband. She thereby evades her marital debt of loyalty, while the ethical ambiguity of her action is signaled both by Mistress Pages's language – "convey, convey him out" – and by Falstaff's sordid experience in a buck-basket of laundry – "ramm'd ... in with foul shirts and smocks, socks, foul stockings, greasy napkins" – where he successfully hides until, despite almost drowning, he escapes. Developing this theme, *The Merry Wives of Windsor* offers a trove of references to fraudulent conveyancing, most of them unrecognized by scholars practicing an older approach to law and literature, which scoured the vocabulary of Elizabethan plays for legal allusions.

Exactly why fraudulent conveyance laws dominated the discourse of the period of history covered by this book – roughly 1571 to 1601 – is not easy to answer. A modern analysis of discursive practices suggests that what everybody did, but could not admit doing, found its sanction in the official insistence that everyone talk about it. This insistence was part of the economy of power wherein a counter-pressure from below met the government's strictures against distressed Catholics, as lawyers not unnaturally found ways to respond to official policy. Power, as Foucault said, moves in all directions.

The development of fraudulent conveyancing law was part of the process of the centralization of violence in the state. Private settlements easily led to trouble, the riots that Falstaff threatens at the beginning of *The Merry Wives of Windsor* or that the defendants were found guilty of in Twyne's Case (1601), the judicial decision that did so much to clarify and solidify English law. Furthermore, the literary expression of law as the conveyance or carrying away of women that I find in the work of Philip Sidney and Edmund Spenser explains why the movement we usually think of from public to private between the medieval and early modern period is also a movement from private to public. The semantic field of fraudulent conveyancing already included the carrying away of women, thereby encouraging literature publicly to portray the private world of debt by narrating stories in which lovers or ravishers or passion carried women away. My argument for concentrating on a seemingly minor set of laws is that debt is more pervasive than sex, at least in the common law. Debt lasts all night.

If twentieth-century jurisprudence has moved from a sociological approach to an understanding of law as cultural discourse, the sociological approach was itself a reaction to earlier schools of thought. Civil societies, as Cicero said, require justice, and it is natural that one should keep promises, pay debts. But natural law does not require the power of a central authority for enforcement. Such legislation is positive law – that is, law established by the legislative power of government. Its goal, as Locke said, is the preservation of society, the maintenance of what the sixteenth century called *chevisance* or plain dealing.

Contrasting the English tradition, the nineteenth-century German school of jurisprudence regarded the passage of a law as merely an event, perhaps for utilitarian purposes, but not something eternal, not the expression of right reason or comparable to divine law, which the soul can discover for itself. This school regarded law as the product of the pulse of a nation, something everyone in the country feels, a traditional growth. This is not as silly as it sounds. There have been those who have propounded the strict rule of laissez-faire economics. If the laws of commerce are the laws of God, then nothing can be done for the poor; they must starve. But if laws are the sap that flows through the tree of a nation, then economic institutions must work towards strengthening society. Humans must create laws, not wait to receive them from on high.

Besides looking at the circumstances under which the statute of Elizabeth was passed in 1571, this study considers a similar set of laws from Renaissance Italy that happened to be legislated at the time the source story for Shakespeare's *Merchant of Venice* was written. Comparative law is the subject of what is called analytical jurisprudence, a method that leads one to believe that whatever political force may have been at work in the drafting of Elizabethan laws, a fundamental sense of fairness seems also to have been present. For if the law, as the economic interpreters believe, is the will of a dominant social class looking to its own self-interest, there are nonetheless cases, as Roscoe Pound noted, where "judicial and juristic idealism has produced and enforced ultra-ethical rules of conduct in advance of the ideas of the dominant or any other class of the lay community." Particularly in equity cases, where fraud was often an issue, idealism seems to be a controlling force in those legal systems that make unusual advances in justice.

Writing somewhat ironically against such idealism, Oliver Wendell Holmes said that law is not justice or morality but prediction based on the reports, statutes, and treatises of England extending back 600 years. To know the law, look at it as "a bad man, who cares only for the material consequences which such knowledge enables him to predict, not as a good one, who finds his reasons for conduct, whether inside the law or outside of it, in the vaguer sanctions of conscience." Perhaps in reaction to Holmes, the eminent jurist Benjamin Cardozo argued for an enlightened judiciary, one with a conception of social needs, one who responded to the "spirit" of the law by filling gaps, clarifying ambiguities, mitigating hardships. The common law must be Darwinian, sacrificing mercilessly what does not work; its method is inductive, drawing generalizations from particulars. All rules are hypotheses, not final truths.

Although Twyne's Case was decided by a group of lawyers – men like Egerton, Coke, and Anderson – who were up to their ears in shady property deals, their judicial decisions reflect some combination of idealism, practice, and powerful social custom. They understood the law methodically and considered its impact on society, and their work benefits from a comparison with American legal realism. Karl Llewellyn, the foremost theoretician of this mid-twentieth-century school of jurisprudence, posed a question that touches my subject: What use is the ability to sue, unless if you win you find that "the other party is solvent and has not secreted his assets?" Just what did Bassanio do with Shylock's 3000 ducats?

The years this study spans, then, were formative for both the law and literature of early modern England. The fifth statute passed during the thirteenth year of the reign of Queen Elizabeth, known to lawyers and historians as 13 Eliz., c. 5 (1571), was an act voiding fraudulent conveyances made to "delay, hinder, or defraud creditors and others." The legal effect and force of the law were unclear until 1601, when the chief justices of England handed down their decision in Twyne's Case. Twyne had received property – a herd of sheep – from a man named Pierce whose purpose in making the transfer of ownership – that is, the conveyance – was to keep his property away from his creditors. The creditors sued to void the transfer, claiming it had been made to defraud them. The issue in the case was how to determine whether Pierce intended to defraud his creditors when he gave his sheep to Twyne and in particular the meaning of the phrase "good consideration" in the statute. In their decision the justices listed what they called "badges," or indicators, of fraud, and these have been a feature of English and US law ever since. These badges included things like the fact that Pierce was insolvent when he gave away his sheep, that he received no real consideration or payment for them, that he actually retained possession and marked the animals with his mark, and that the piece of paper recording the transfer rather suspiciously said that the conveyance was made in good faith.

Although later law developed the notion of "constructive" fraud, where intention is irrelevant, the law under Queen Elizabeth I explicitly required that element. Since it is usually impossible to know directly what someone is thinking, however, intention had to be demonstrated by circumstantial evidence, such as the badges of fraud provide. During the period covered by this book, it came to be understood that if a fraudulent conveyancing law was to be able to "look backward," as one Member of Parliament put it, intention had to be analyzed in two parts. Let us say a man gives £5000 to his son. Three days later he declares bankruptcy. Should his creditors be able to void the gift? There is no law against giving property to a family member. The father may even claim to have received consideration in the form of love and affection. But the sudden, ensuing bankruptcy raises the suspicion that he knew that the gift would leave him insolvent. His intention at the time of the gift may be regarded as inchoate – unformed, unclear – until the second act reveals its true purpose. During the period covered by this book, the law was groping its way toward this two part analysis. A few years later, fraudulent conveyancing would become part of bankruptcy law; indeed, such a gift, if it left a debtor insolvent, would be by definition an act of bankruptcy. But this resolution did not occur until the last years of Elizabeth's reign. The literature of the period reflects not so much the question of intention as the ethical issue of when conveyances should be allowed.

During the period between the passage of the statute and its clarification by the courts, Sir Philip Sidney and Edmund Spenser lived and died as poets. William Shakespeare wrote most of his histories and all of his comedies. Moreover, these authors had reason to be aware of legal developments in the field. Like other prominent Englishmen, such as Sir Walter Ralegh or Shakespeare's friends the Burbages, they engaged in, or complained about, fraudulent conveyancing. It seems that Sidney had a sophisticated, almost visceral concern with the ethics of fraudulent conveyancing, almost as if by inheritance as a member of the higher nobility. Spenser and Shakespeare in many ways followed the example of Sidney's *Arcadia*, the most popular piece of original prose fiction for over two hundred years.

As a legal concept, fraudulent conveyancing is less unified than it appears at first. Yet its diversity gives it a cultural resonance that makes it particularly suitable for literary criticism. The major works discussed in this book – Sidney's *Arcadia*, Spenser's *Faerie Queene*, Shakespeare's *Merry Wives of Windsor* and *The Merchant of Venice* – have plots that turn on the abduction of women, a form of fraudulent conveyance, broadly defined, that allows the inclusion of references to other, narrower forms of the practice without violating artistic unity.

Perhaps because there will always be a little larceny in everyone's heart, fraudulent conveyancing is still a problem of debtor–creditor relations today. Four hundred years of advancing legal thought separate us from the age of Shakespeare when laws against fraudulent conveyances were weaker than they are today and as a result the practice was a more signal feature of the culture. Yet new laws produce new frauds, and the problem of defining limits remains. The issue has arisen in US Medicaid law, as elderly people facing enormous costs of nursing home care try to divest their assets, often by giving them to their children, in order to become eligible for need-based payments. One view regards this practice of divestiture as mere "asset planning"; another regards those who transfer for less than full value as lacking a "modicum of decency." New York has in the past taken a strict approach, drawing on fraudulent conveyance law and looking not just to recent transfers, but to one's assets over an entire lifetime to determine if patients should be denied Medicaid on the grounds that they conveyed property with the intent to make themselves insolvent and so unable to pay the enormous debts generated by modern medical care. Many people, however, regard Medicaid as a right and see nothing wrong with planning (including asset divestment) in such a way as to make themselves eligible for a program sponsored and paid for by the government. The government, it is felt, has little at stake, whereas the transferor is trying to protect his family's inheritance and the earnings of a lifetime.

Fraudulent conveyances similarly impact US state exemption standards in bankruptcy. Should a debtor be allowed to convert cash owed to a creditor to a life insurance policy – or, as in Florida and Texas, a homestead of enormous value – that an exemption statute places beyond his creditor's reach? Another, more complex example of fraudulent conveyance law arose during the merger mania of the 1980s, when it became a key issue in claims against executives who arranged leveraged buyouts (LBOs) of corporations. The point made was that the leveraged company often received nothing of value in return for yielding its assets as collateral to a lending institution. The question occurs not just in bankruptcy cases or shareholder suits against large corporations, but in family law. What about a spouse who hides earned assets in an off-shore bank account, beyond the reach of the US legal process, and then seeks a divorce? Some lawyers are calling this practice a form of fraudulent conveyancing, because it effectively defrauds the abandoned partner. The practice is disturbing, not only because it is morally unfair – usually to women – but because, legally, it works.

Fraudulent conveyances, these examples show, are often not so much fraud in the sense of deliberate misrepresentation as they are a struggle between two parties to define what constitutes fair behavior. So phrased, the issue of fraudulent conveyance is a social concern. The central role played by fraudulent conveyance law in Medicaid, bankruptcy, LBOs, family law, and debtor–creditor relations reinforces the impression that our attitudes to fraudulent conveyance tell us something important about US society today and English society during the Renaissance. In each of these rapidly changing areas, the law is torn between two functions, what some consider the urgent need to regularize and clarify right and wrong, and the opposite jurisprudential function: the need to establish laws that conform to the patterns of conduct that society works out for itself.

Even when society has not formally made up its mind about what is fraudulent and what not, many people are at least partially conscious of wrongdoing when they convey away property to avoid a creditor. Cognitive dissonance is the term psychologists use to describe what results when actions conflict with beliefs. Unconsciously, people seek ways to resolve the dissonance. In the case of fraudulent conveyance, debtors may effect this reconciliation by drawing on myths of popular culture that valorize their individual rights and depersonalize their creditors. The evil creditor can be the unfriendly bank of populist American folklore. It may be the federal government, too big to be hurt by attempts of the average citizen to protect his life's savings. It may be the impersonal "market," the faceless owners of stocks and bonds, who are regarded not as suffering losses, but as rewarding the entrepreneurial efficiency of those who prudently manage assets, as in arranging a corporate guarantee or a leveraged buyout. For the Anglo-Norman rebels Spenser knew in Ireland, the faceless and distant power was the queen of England. In *The Merry Wives of Windsor*, it is a wealthy husband.

The struggle to overcome obstacles suits fraudulent conveyancing to comedy and comic drama. In the plays of Plautus and Terence, the creditor often takes the form of a distant father or husband or brothel owner to whom a girl owes a duty that she seeks to convey to a young man, whom she will marry. In *The Ghost*, for example, Philematium is in debt to Philolaches for buying her freedom with his own money, so she pays back her debt by loving him exclusively, despite the advice of Scapha, who argues that Philematium overpays her debt, since Philolaches will certainly leave her. In other dramas of Plautus, slave girls are typically conveyed from house to house or given sanctuary to protect them from brothel keepers. Indeed, so suited is conveyancing, as a type of revenge, to comedy that, as Erich Segal observes, young men typically court bankruptcy in the Roman comedies. The lovers' insolvency – like Falstaff's (who therefore symbolically stands in for Anne Page's suitor Fenton, who has money enough but lacks the good will of Anne's parents) – allows comedy to represent the "breaking of restrictions" that is the "heart" of the genre. Like comedy, fraudulent conveyance can take many forms. In Moliere's *Le Festin de pierre*, Don Juan gets rid of his creditor Monsieur Dimanche by professing such warm friendship and sharing such solicitude for him that the creditor never gets to demand his money. In Ibsen's *Doll's House*, Nora owes money on a debt that she cannot divulge, leading her into demeaning but essentially comic strategems, like her dancing the Tarantella, to deceive her husband. Tom Wolfe's comic novel *A Man in Full* begins with a Falstaffian protagonist facing bankruptcy who seeks a way to shield his assets from an impatient bank and its hilarious hatchetman, the workout *artiste*. During my original project a local banker assured me that farmers trucked grain to distant relatives in case they could not meet their loans. Wolfe's brand of fictional realism humorously illustrates a situation bankers regularly confront when debtors like Charlie Croker try to protect what is dear to them:

> "What'll he do *next*?" . . .
> Harry [the workout *artiste*] said, "Oh, that's easy. He'll try to hide the airplanes."
> "That's a safe fucking bet," said Shellnut.
> "An ordinary human being can't imagine how tightly a shithead bonds with his airplanes," said Harry.
> "Yeah," said Shellnutt, " . . . Remember that shithead from Cybermax, Harry? Duber was his name, or something like that?"
> "Yeah."
> "Fucking hoople sells his King Air, he claims. Turns out he sold it to his sister-in-law for a piece of paper."

Comedy contrasts to the narrow genre of tragedy, because comedy has an enormous range of plots. The ways of fraud, too, are endlessly inventive.

As in the case of Elizabethan literature, however, the discourse of debt may disguise deeper concerns. Although some debts survive the grave, in the long run death wins. Wolfe's novel features a millionaire Southern real estate developer who suddenly hears time's winged chariot at his back. In Scott McPherson's play *Marvin's Room*, where AIDS is the unspoken subtext, the director of a funeral home suggests that to reduce assets and thereby qualify for government assistance, a family buy the biggest tombstone it can find. Both books create a tension between what is and is not a matter for public discourse, between private morality and public ethics.

Bibliographical Note to the Preface

Readings cited or closely paraphrased or deliberately imitated in this preface include John Locke, *The Second Treatise of Government* (1690); Oliver Wendell Holmes, Jr., "The Path of the Law," *Harvard Law Review* 10 (1897): 457–478; Roscoe Pound,

"The Scope and Purpose of Sociological Jurisprudence," Part I, *Harvard Law Review* 24 (1911): 591–619; Parts II and III, *Harvard Law Review* 25 (1912): 140–168 and 489-516; Benjamin N. Cardozo, *The Nature of the Judicial Process* (1921; New Haven: Yale University Press, 1937); Karl Llewellyn, "A Realistic Jurisprudence— The Next Step," *Columbia Law Review* 30 (1930): 431–464. My comments on the German Historical School closely track Isaiah Berlin, *The Roots of Romanticism* (Princeton: Princeton University Press, 1999), p. 125. Material from Michel Foucault can be found in *The History of Sexuality*, vol. 1: *An Introduction* (1976; New York: Vintage, 1990). References to some cases and articles on modern fraudulent conveyancing include *Randall v Lukhard*, 729 F2d 966, at 969 (4th Cir 1984) (dissent said anyone who transfers assets for less than full value and then applies for Medicaid lacks even a "modicum of decency" and has sunk to "immoral depths"); *State v Goffins*, 546 A2d 250 (Conn. 1988) (allegation that transfer of Medicaid patient's property was fraudulent conveyance); Terry Carter, "Counseling Granny Now OK: Ban on Advice on Medicaid Asset Transfers Struck Down," *ABA Journal* (November 1998): no pp.; Robert Charles Clark, "The Duties of the Corporate Debtor to Its Creditors," *Harvard Law Review* 90 (1977): 505–562; Douglas G. Baird and Thomas H. Jackson, "Fraudulent Conveyance Law and its Proper Domain," *Vanderbilt Law Review* 38 (1985): 829–855 (criticizes application of fraudulent conveyance statutes to leveraged buyouts); *Credit Managers Ass'n v Federal Co.*, 629 F. Supp. 175, 179 (C.D. Cal. 1985) ("A firm that incurs obligations in the course of a buyout does not seem at all like the Elizabethan dead beat who sells his sheep to his brother for a pittance"); Douglas G. Baird, "Fraudulent Conveyances, Agency Costs, and Leveraged Buyouts," *Journal of Legal Studies* 20 (1991): 1–24, *but* cf. Kathryn V. Smyser, "Going Private and Going Under: Leveraged Buyouts and the Fraudulent Conveyance Problem," *Indiana Law Journal* 63 (1988): 781–824 (traditional policies of fraudulent conveyance law serve to prevent individuals in control of a corporation from benefitting themselves at the expense of the corporation's creditors); *Re Kaiser Steel*, 87 B.R. 154 (1985) (court refused argument that fraudulent conveyance did not apply to LBOs because US Statutes on fraudulent conveyancing derive from sixteenth-century English law); Debra Baker, "Castaway," *ABA Travel* (October 1998): 55–59 (husband cheated wife by shipping $11 000 000 to the Cook Islands: "Estate Planning or Money Hiding?"). I have also quoted from Erich Segal, *Roman Laughter: The Comedy of Plautus* (New York: Oxford University Press, 1987), pp. 17–18; Elder Olson, *The Theory of Comedy* (Bloomington: Indiana University Press, 1968), p. 59; and Tom Wolfe, *A Man in Full* (New York: Farrar Straus Giroux, 1998), pp. 241–242.

Acknowledgments

Like any long project this one has incurred many obligations. Its proximate cause was David Funk's Sociology of Law seminar. I have benefited from Purdue University's microfilm collection of Early English Books and the Commonwealth Collection of early English case law in the library of the Indiana University School of Law – Indianapolis. My former colleague Seth Weiner first connected Shakespeare with fraudulent conveyancing. The resulting article, a version of this book's chapter on *The Merry Wives of Windsor*, appeared in *Renaissance Drama* 25 (1994): 145–169, edited by Francis E. Dolan. Patricia Parker encouraged my work by citing that article in her book *Shakespeare from the Margins* (Chicago, 1996). I want to thank Paula von Loewenfeldt for *chevisance*. CoryAnne Harrigan has been a constant and much-appreciated corrector. Paul Kahn played the role of interlocutor during a moment of crisis. David Papke gave me copies of his books. Allen Mandelbaum, as usual, read and encouraged. David Rosenthal, our local Chapter 11 Trustee, said he would read a book without footnotes; I give him this preface. Colleagues and students including Paul White, Ann Astell, Tom Adler, Vicki Scala, David Wood, Mardy Phillipian, Erica Rude, and Tara Pedersen have kept the Renaissance alive at Purdue. Michelle Parkinson brought Foucault to my attention at the right time. Mihoko Suzuki introduced me to Erika Gaffney, our editor at Ashgate, whose professionalism has been a refreshing surprise. I would also like to thank Angelica Duran, Constance Jordan, Thomas Kuehn, Dan Lowenstein, Michael Murrin, David Nirenberg, James Nohrnberg, Terry Reilly, John Watkins, Luke Wilson, and two anonymous readers. Portions of this study were presented at the Center for Humanistic Studies in the School of Liberal Arts and the Romance and Epic seminar at the Newberry Library.

Some debts can never be repaid, of course, and so this book is for Slaney, who wondered why I never left the house during her high school years; for Sam, a true artist; and, as always, for Clare.

A Note on the Text

There are many editions of English statutes and case reports, including William Rastell, ed., *A Collection in English, of the Statutes now in force, continue from the beginning of Magna Charta* (London, 1598). I have sometimes modernized punctuation and spelling of historical documents and early publications for the convenience of the reader. Translations are my own, except for Sidney's correspondence with Languet. Later editions of *The Third Part of the Reports of Sir Edward Coke* translate Twyne's Case (3 Co. Rep. 80b), which first appeared in legal French in *Le Tierce Part des Reportes del Edward Coke Lattorney generall le Roigne* (London, 1610).

Introduction

> "O, good! convey! Conveyers are you all,
> That rise thus nimbly by a true king's fall."
> *Richard II*

A fraudulent conveyance occurs when someone in debt places his or her property out of reach of his or her creditors' process. The ethical idea behind the legal concept of a fraudulent conveyance is that integrity is preferable to generosity.[1] A person should not give away property until all debts are paid. Both ethical and the legal concerns occur in Ben Jonson's play *Epicene*, when the character Truewit describes the conveyances some women make before marriage. "This, too, with whom you are to marry, may have made a conveyance of her virginity aforehand, as your wise widows do of their states before they marry, in trust to some friend, sir, who can tell?" (II. ii. 123–126). Truewit's quip reflects the actual law. Throughout the seventeenth century, a woman's efforts to convey her property to trustees before marriage were judged to be fraud against the marital rights of the future husband.[2] But Truewit's comparison is also meant to be clever, as his name implies. Virginity cannot be conveyed in a legal sense; a court cannot order it returned to the injured party. No property is literally transferred. Yet the comparison to a fraudulent conveyance is apt. It is not just Ben Jonson's knowledge of the law that we admire in this passage, but his literary conceit.

Even though Ben Jonson's play was first performed in 1609, the strain of the comparison recalls the moral anxiety about fraudulent conveyances typical of the literature that developed during the legal crisis of 1571 to 1601. But if the ethical dilemmas raised by the problem of fraudulent conveyancing did not cease completely in 1601, when Twyne's Case was settled, they did not begin in 1571, with the passage of 13 Eliz., c. 5. The concept of fraudulent conveyance occurred in Roman law.[3] It arose in canon law, where the pauper status of clerics complicated the collection of debts.[4] It had a noble history in England, where complex legal mechanisms were constantly devised to frustrate judicial processes that sought to take property for the benefit of creditors. From the time of the Magna Carta, the Parliament of England regularly protected royal interests against fraudulent conveyances. A series of statutes provided remedies against mortmain, subinfeudation,[5] conveyances to defeat a lord of his wardship,[6] fraudulent deeds used by those accused of treason to protect family property, as well as other devices, some still being invented in Shakespeare's day.[7] There were laws, indirectly related but drawing on a similar vocabulary, against dilapidations, conveying sheep into Scotland, and carrying away heiresses.[8]

Taking sanctuary was another part of the time-honored method of seeking to escape financial liabilities. The early Roman comedies of Plautus typically feature a slave or prostitute seeking protection in the temple of a god. During the middle ages, canon law and the Church in England provided havens for harried debtors. King

Edward I tried to counter this practice by passing a law to limit the use of sanctuaries for fraudulent debtors.[9] A century later, Edward III added to the law against conveying bodies to safety a measure designed to stop conveyances of property. His new bill, passed by Parliament in 1379, targeted those who avoided payment of debts by giving their tenements and chattels to friends. These friends or relatives in turn would kick-back profits and income, while the debtors found some safe haven.[10] But the bill had limits. As William Roberts explains, the statute extended only to those who put their property in trust before flying to sanctuary, but as long as they were exposed to execution, "such sale or assignment was not fraudulent within that act."[11] This limitation follows the general rule that fraudulent conveyances are valid transactions and cannot be undone unless a creditor raises a complaint.

In the case of those who sought sanctuary, conveyance has a double sense. First the debtor conveys himself to a safe place. At the same time, he might transfer his property to a friend or accomplice. These two senses of the word are related insofar as the transfer is secret or done to deceive. Spenser and others most often use the word "convey" in the sense of transferring something in secret. Duessa claims that her promised husband died and his body was "convaid / And fro me hid" (*Faerie Queene* I. ii. 24). It is likely that when Richard II says that Bolingbroke and his henchmen are all "conveyors," he is commenting on the odd combination of secrecy, moral ambiguity, and self-interest that prompts their conspiracy to remove him from the throne.

Despite a long history of statutes against fraudulent conveyances, a new law was passed in 1571. The language of the statute – still present in the law of many US states that include the key phrase "delay, hinder, or defraud creditors" – forbids

> fraudulent feoffments, Giftes Grantes, Alienations, Conveyances, Bondes, Suites, Judgments and Executions as well of Landes and Tenements as of goods and Cattells [i.e., chattels] ... devised and contrived of malice, fraud, covin, collusion or guile, to the end, purpose and intent, *to delay, hinder or defraud, creditors and others* of their just and lawfull Actions.
>
> (13 Eliz., c. 5; my emphasis)

Later lawyers found 13 Eliz., c. 5 the most significant of all the fraudulent conveyance statutes. Sir Edward Coke, the queen's attorney general, gave the statute two readings, in Packman's Case (6 Co. Rep. 18b [1585]) and Twyne's Case (3 Co. Rep. 80b [1601]), clarifying certain phrases and making the statute an essential feature of future legal thinking. The legal historian Garrard Glenn argued that Coke twisted the purpose of the statute, which was not to protect creditors, but to protect the interest of the Crown in land, especially the land of Catholic recusants. Despite Glenn's misgivings, I will show there was a commercial purpose to the statute; in fact, whatever the hidden motives the government had for shepherding 13 Eliz., c. 5 through Parliament, the legal cases that followed in the next generation invariably cited it in commercial contexts.

Partly political, partly commercial, the law of fraudulent conveyance provides an interesting insight into the ethical workings of Renaissance England. Although laws against fraudulent transfers of assets occur in every society that recognizes the obligation to pay debts, it is also true that civil societies have a certain tolerance for people who devise means to avoid the clutches of creditors. Anyone who appears unfairly oppressed by circumstances or misfortune will arouse sympathy. Creditors must be paid, or no one can do business. But what looks fraudulent from the creditor's perspective may, from the debtor's angle, seem to be a legitimate way to protect property – a family inheritance, for example – or defend against a powerful enemy, such as the state. Depending on the circumstances, we will sympathize with either the debtor or the creditor, love or hate Shylock, laugh at or despise Falstaff. Our changing reactions to such literary figures help us recognize certain ethical questions that society confronts.

The initial focus of the New Historicism involved the interrelationship of the court, theatrics, and the projection of royal power. If there was a single quote that summed up the queen's concerns, it might be her admission, on the eve of the Essex conspiracy, that "I am Richard II, know ye not that?" Richard II had been deposed in 1399, just as the earl of Essex wished to depose Elizabeth two centuries later. A look back at the source of the queen's remark will help us remember that there was more to England than the court and that commerce did not begin with the Industrial Revolution. The rise of mass production during the nineteenth century created the opposed camps of Capital, in the form of management, and Labor, often represented by unions.[12] These terms, particularly as they developed in Marxist thought, came to dominate our thinking in the twentieth century, but the roots of commerce and the problems of finance, although on a smaller scale, nonetheless stretch back through English history. The queen's famous comment comparing herself to a previous monarch actually occurred during an interview she held with William Lambarde, the aging author of the *Perambulations of Kent*, a book that set the pace for the study of English geography and customs. Lambarde also wrote a book titled *Eirenarcha* (1581), on the duties of justices of the peace. During their conversation, the queen complained about her political difficulties. But she also showed an interest in finance, at one point asking Lambarde the meaning of *praestita*. He told her it was money lent by her progenitors to subjects on bond for repayment. She then asked if *redisseisins* were unlawful and forcible, when they threw men out of their lawful possessions. Lambarde answered yes, and that there were rolls of fines levied on such evil doers. The queen then commented that "In those days force and arms did prevail; but now the wit of the fox is everywhere on foot as hardly a faithful and virtuous man may be found."[13] Falstaff could not have said it better.

The queen's interest in finance reflects the movement of England away from subsistence farming into a more vital economy. Lenders were necessary in the absence of banks.[14] Commerce was growing. Thomas Gresham bought ground for his Exchange in 1565, finished a building there in 1567, and hosted the queen for dinner in 1571, in the same season in which Parliament passed 13 Eliz., c. 5.[15] As always, politics and commerce were combined in the queen's affairs. In a typical set of instructions sent by Elizabeth to Henry Sidney, Lord Deputy of Ireland, she asked him to try to "compound" with merchants to whom she owed money because "a greater number of merchants of that realm do usually compound with the captains and other our creditors of that realm for divers sums of money much less than the principal debts are." The queen, it seems, was either an astute business woman or a methodical welcher.[16]

If there was no bright line between politics and commerce, it was because politics reflected the concerns not just of the nobility but of the gentry. The gentry opposed any laws that inhibited their freedom to make family settlements or secret conveyances of their property. Lawyers obliged by finding ways around anything that interfered with their profits. Fraudulent conveyancing laws, like all the changes in land law in sixteenth-century England, reflect the character of society.[17]

If, as Richard Weisberg claims, "literature provides unique insights into the underpinnings of the law" and if the main literary texts treated in this book provide such insight into the practice of fraudulent conveyance, nonetheless Richard Posner rightly warns us about a fundamental incompatibility of the outward structures of the law and works of fiction.[18] This incompatibility requires us to make three critical assumptions that separate literature from the law. First, we presume organic unity in a work of art – that the various actions that comprise the plot express a single theme – in contrast to a series of separable issues that compose legal thinking. Second, we regard works of fictions not as legal briefs about fraudulent conveyance but as dramatic presentations of what lawyers today call the "public policy" to which laws eventually conform. Third, we recognize that in a work like Shakespeare's *Merry Wives,* bourgeois characters use mercantile and legal language even when the matter is not mercantile and legal, so sometimes they talk literally and other times metaphorically. In that play, such characters serve as foils to Falstaff, who seems sometimes out of touch with, but sometimes perceptive about, certain matters of fraud.

We tend to take for granted that the language of debtor and creditor provides an appropriate metaphor for the relationships of lovers. One of themes of this book, however, is that the metaphor was fresh in Shakespeare's day. As society struggled with the limits of fraud, poets and playwrights found a set of metaphors to hand in finance. The following example from Shakespeare's *Two Gentlemen of Verona* suggests, moreover, how the problem of the literary representation of fraudulent conveyancing was solved: Proteus owes his heart to Julia, but while visiting Milan he falls in love with Sylvia. He forgets Julia and tells Sylvia he has given her his heart. Can Julia void his gift? In other words, can Julia claim the equivalent of a fraudulent conveyance and seize back the heart of Proteus from Sylvia? One may find a form of this reversal in Julia's refusal – during a complication of the plot in which she disguises herself as a pageboy – to give to Sylvia a ring that Julia herself had earlier given to Proteus as a pledge of her love. Julia cuts off Proteus's attempted conveyance, for it was fraudulent Proteus who urged her to deliver the ring to Sylvia, whom he prefers to Julia. Elsewhere, too, in Shakespeare's plays the giving or accepting of rings shadows in a curious way the possibilities of conveyances, deceptions, and fraud.

Although Julia is the only one who would have a cause of action were the plot of the play recast in terms of a transfer of property and a real court case, *The Two Gentlemen of Verona* is a play about frustrated conveyances, and its plot allusively suggests an awareness of the law. Not only does Proteus return to Julia, but earlier he himself exposes Valentine's plan to elope with Sylvia – it is a type of conveyance. Sylvia's father, the Duke, moreover, uses the appropriate language when he signals his awareness of the lovers' plot. He pointedly asks Valentine to help him understand how to he can "best convey" a ladder to reach a woman he claims to love (III. i.128). In another instance, Proteus, who wants Valentine out of the way, offers to "convey" him through the city gate (III. i. 253). Finally, Speed's puns on ships and sheep carry distant echoes of the laws against fraudulently conveying sheep out of England (I. i.

72 ff.). Even Launce's dog Crab gets into the act by lifting his leg under the Duke's table, frustrating Proteus's heartless attempt to give him as a gift to Sylvia. Shakespeare's *Two Gentlemen of Verona* illustrates how literature reflects and can add to our understanding of society's attitudes. On the one hand we have a lighthearted comedy. On the other, the plot (where a man named Valentine becomes an outlaw) and the language of the characters, with names like Proteus, coincide with questions about how changes in law influence society, why people disobey a law, and how they reconcile the difference between what they believe and what they do.

Fraudulent conveyances are always contested issues, even today, because to determine intent a court must usually rely on secondary circumstances, some of which will offer conflicting evidence. Such conflicts form the basis for Shakespeare's veritable fantasia on the theme of fraudulent conveyancing, *The Merry Wives of Windsor*, a play that was first written before Twyne's Case and then rewritten afterwards, perhaps more than once. Not only do physical conveyances contribute to the plot, but – as Patricia Parker has shown, in an article that was much on my mind when I first came across fraudulent conveyancing in a legal context – metaphorical conveyances, including the very concept of metaphor, construct the complex verbal world of the play.[19] This comedy provides more convincing references to fraudulent conveyances than any other work, yet the metaphors remind us that here, as in the other works, the literary use of the law is suggestive rather than precise.[20] *The Merry Wives of Windsor* is about fraud and deception and ethics in a general sense, but it also refers with some precision to the narrower legal topic of fraudulent conveyances. Mistress Page's legal language suggests that she is an astute woman who recognizes the delightful way Falstaff's carriage in a buck-basket parodies the practice of fraudulent conveyancing. Mr. Ford conjures a form of "constructive" fraudulent conveyance when he compares making love to someone else's wife with building on another man's land. The Host of the Garter Inn takes over Bardoloph's employment to help Falstaff manage his affairs. Compared to these characters, Falstaff appears curiously retrograde in his awareness of legal matters: the end of the Folio version holds up the possibility that Falstaff, said to owe Ford £20, has missed an opportunity to fraudulently convey his horses. In each case the play draws on a common issue in the legal thinking of sixteenth-century England.

The second chapter of this book looks back at the history of the law with which Shakespeare shows himself so familiar. It argues that this social practice, as well as the commercial purpose of 13 Eliz., c. 5, was at least as important as political motives when the bill was passed in 1571. It would seem as if the new law responded to a series of land appropriations that followed the Northern Rebellion of 1569, but a close look at some of the figures involved fails to prove that the statute was part of a new wave of persecutions against Catholic conveyors.

Chapter 3, while sketching in the historical and cultural background just before and after the passage of 13 Eliz., c. 5, finds evidence of a laissez-faire attitude toward fraudulent conveyancing in the works of Philip Sidney, as well as in the life of his father, Henry Sidney, who served for years in Ireland, where fraudulent conveyancing had an eventful history. Both men were typical of the period in that they regarded a man's conveyancing as his own business and were unable or unwilling to resolve the moral dilemma it raised. Sidney's openness to conveyancing finds expression in the plot of his *Arcadia*, where his heroes carry away a pair of eligible princesses. Sidney's plot innovation probably lies behind other literary elopements, since his work was read by both Spenser and Shakespeare. In *The Merry Wives of Windsor*, Anne Page elopes with Fenton, while in *The Merchant of Venice*, a play that also shadows some of the problems of fraudulent conveyancing, Shylock's daughter elopes with Lorenzo and Bassanio wins an heiress by contracting a debt.

Edmund Spenser, the subject of Chapter 4, shows a far sterner attitude toward fraudulent conveyances than that of the Sidneys. As a state functionary, Spenser exemplified the connection between the tax power of the state and creditors' rights, and he was obsessed by fraudulent conveyances. His *View of the Present State of Ireland* raises an outcry about the need to prevent them. Spenser attended the Irish parliaments that passed bills of attainder in 1585 and 1586, which included fraudulent conveyance provisions, and his own estates were founded on lands that had escheated to the queen, mainly after the attainder of the earl of Desmond. Possibly his final written words warned Queen Elizabeth that many Irish lords had entered into lease arrangements to protect their property before confederating in the rebellion that drove Spenser from his home in Cork in 1598. Therefore he asks "That provision may be made for the avoyding of such fraudulent conveyances made onlie to defeat her Maiestie of the benefit of their attainder."[21]

Spenser's experience in Ireland produced not only some political prose, whose authorship is somewhat in dispute, but poetry that expresses a surprising awareness of the difficulties of creating working rules of law. The problem of attainder surfaces in *The Faerie Queene*, in the episode of the baby with bloody hands (*FQ* II. ii), where Spenser gives expression to another area that Glenn considered tangential to the true history of his topic. That is the development of the law against fraudulent conveyances to defeat purchasers.[22] As it turns out, two of Prince Arthur's odder interventions as a character in *The Faerie Queene* reward our paying attention to this aspect of the broader topic of fraudulent conveyance and illustrate how the fiery passions that attached to both sides of the legal debate found literary expression.

The inadequacies of the law on fraudulent conveyances were in large measure resolved by Twyne's Case in 1601, which side-stepped the problem of proving intentionality directly by listing what it called badges of fraud – secondary indicators, in effect circumstantial evidence, from which the fraudulent intent of a conveyance could be soundly inferred.[23] At the same time, as I show in Chapter 5, the opinion written by Sir Edward Coke contains a number of narrative storylines. One story is political, to explain why the phrase "and others" in the original statute of 1571 (which voided fraudulent conveyances made to defeat "creditors and others"), applied to forfeitures to the Crown. Another story makes the point that the phrase "good consideration" should be read to mean "valuable consideration," a topic that also occurs in *The Faerie Queene*. The issue of equity that usually arises in discussions of *The Merchant of Venice* might be reframed along the lines of a third narrative Coke creates, one that reminds judges that a statute on fraud should be broadly construed.

England was not alone in wrestling with fraudulent conveyances, or telling stories about them. Two hundred years before Elizabeth I, the Italian city-state of Florence grappled with similar problems of politics and the need to protect creditors in order to encourage commerce. The source story of Shakespeare's *Merchant of Venice* derives from this period of Florentine history. Shakespeare started with the story of the debtor's bond, but he added the elopement of Shylock's daughter as well as Shylock's punishment by Portia, which follows her charging him with attempted murder.

In an era when contract law was still developing and the famous Statute of Frauds (which set out rules for when a contract had to be in writing) was a generation in the future, Shakespeare's audience might have understood Shylock's intentions, the justice of Portia's Alien Statute, or the problem of how to portray Shylock's pathos at Lorenzo's conveyance of his daughter Jessica against the paradigm of fraudulent conveyancing law. In Chapter 6, I argue that a grasp of the legal development of one form of fraud might extend our understanding of a play that is too often limited by discussions of anti-Semitism or the royal power to forgive. Portia's problematic evidence that Shylock attempted to murder Antonio, I argue, lies not in the formation of the bond or Shylock's waving a knife at Antonio, but on how Shylock construes the bond in court. The statute of Venice which Portia uses to punish Shylock mirrors the unworkable penalty provision of 13 Eliz., c. 5.

The developing law and the works of fiction it influenced are the subject, then, of the following chapters. The three main literary figures in the story of fraudulent conveyances are Philip Sidney, Edmund Spenser, and William Shakespeare – the three crowns of Elizabethan literature. The chapters devoted to them use the law to understand literature. The remaining two chapters treat the fraudulent conveyance statute and Coke's report in Twyne's Case. These chapters use literary and historical methods to analyze the law.

Notes

1   See the article on fraudulent conveyancing in *Corpus Juris Secundum: A Complete Restatement of the Entire American Law as Developed by All Reported Cases* (St. Paul, Minn.: West, 1936–), vol. 37, p. 853, citing *Planters' and Merchants' Bank v Walker*, 7 Ala. 926.
2   Susan Staves, *Married Women's Separate Property in England, 1660–1833* (Cambridge: Harvard University Press, 1990), pp. 49–55.
3   See Garrard Glenn, *Fraudulent Conveyances and Preferences*, 2nd ed., 2 vols. (New York: Baker, Voorhis, 1940), p. 82, and Max Radin, "Fraudulent Conveyances at Roman Law," *Virginia Law Review* 18 (1931): 109–130.
4   See R. H. Helmholz, *Canon Law and English Common Law: Selden Society Lecture Delivered in the Old Hall of Lincoln's Inn, July 5th, 1982* (London: Selden Society, 1983), pp. 8, 12; Lauro Martines, *Lawyers and Statecraft in Renaissance Florence* (Princeton: Princeton University Press, 1968), p. 176, 251–259; A. W. B. Simpson, *An Introduction to the History of Land Law* (1961; 2nd ed., Oxford: Clarendon Press, 1986), p. 174, who compares the medieval use to modern tax evasion, as when the Franciscan Friars, to maintain poverty, "found it convenient that property should be held by others to their use."
5   9 Hen. III, c. 35 (1236) was a statute against mortmain and subinfeudations (conveyance of lands to a religious house in order "to take the same land again to hold of the same house"). Frederick G. Kempin, Jr., *Historical Introduction to Anglo-American Law*, Nutshell Series, 3rd ed. (St. Paul, Minn.: West, 1990), p. 146, explains that a "tenant might convey land to a church with the understanding that the church would subinfeudate him for lesser services. The result was that the superior lord now had the church for a tenant, with the resulting loss of feudal dues, but the erstwhile tenant still had the benefit of the land with his obligations considerably reduced."

6   52 Hen. III, c. 6. Wardship was an artifact of feudalism, the system whereby one incurred certain obligations to the overlord whose land one held. It lasted until the Restoration. The parliament of 1585 passed a bill designed to counter devices that would defraud the queen of revenue from wardship, even though such a law interfered with the free alienation of property. "Wardship was a burden of a social as well as financial character.... It was antiquated, irrational; a greater benefit to officials and speculators than to the Crown; an anxiety to parents, a breeding-ground of corruption. Since the possession of any portion of land, no matter how small, held by knight service of the Crown, subjected its owner and the whole of his estate to wardship, this form of tenure became an encumbrance, interfering with a ready sale.... Consequently, owners of land thus encumbered hit on the device of disposing of it by way of a long lease, which left the purchaser unaffected.... The Lords cannot have been enthusiastic about the bill. True, they were more or less all irredeemably subject to wardship, and in so far were less affected than many of the Commons. But as potential sellers of land their interests were the same. As a House, however, they were evidently incapable of resisting the pressure of the Crown and its spokesman, Burghley." J. E. Neale, *Elizabeth I and Her Parliaments, 1584–1601* (New York: St. Martin's Press, 1958), p. 91.

7   A series of statutes under Richard II (11 Rich. II, c. 1–6) were aimed at five specific peers of the realm, accused of high treason, to void the "fraudulent conveyances of their goods to deceive the King." One bill under Henry VIII forced a single man, Sir John Shelton, to repeal fraudulent deeds and conveyances made to defeat the king and others of wardship, primer seisin, and relief and to make clear that he, condemned to die, did so while seised of those lands, which the king could then reach (33 Hen. VIII, c. 26). Later laws were aimed at recusants who sought by "covenous conveyance" "to defraud any interest, right, or title, that may or ought to grow to the Queen" or anyone else (23 Eliz., c. 2 and 29 Eliz., c. 6). Another statute (27 Eliz., c. 4, passed in 1585 and made perpetual in 1597 by 39 Eliz., c. 18) prohibited fraudulent conveyances to defeat purchasers (in other words, it gave statutory form to the obvious notion that you should not sell the same thing to two people at the same time).

8   Over the centuries the English Parliament passed laws against conveying sheep (8 Eliz., c. 3); shipping of horses out of England (1 Edw. VI, c. 5); and carrying away women (13 Edw. I, c. 34; 31 Hen. VI, c. 9; 3 Hen. VII, c. 2; 4 & 5 Ph. & M., c. 8).

9   John Bellamy, *Crime and Public Order in the Later Middle Ages* (London: Routledge, 1973), p. 107.

10 50 Edw. III, c. 6 was aimed at those who, to avoid creditors, gave their tenements and chattels to friends, who agreed to pass on the profits, and then sought sanctuary in the "Franchise of Westminster, of S. Martin le graund of London, or other such privileged places." The Parliament of Henry VII repeated the injunction of 50 Edw. III, c. 6 against deeds of gift made to defraud creditors by those who seek "sanctuary, or other places privileged" (3 Hen. VII, c. 4).

11 William Roberts, *A Treatise on the Construction of the Statutes of 13 Eliz. c. 5 and 27 Eliz. c. 4, Relating to Voluntary and Fraudulent Conveyances* (1800; 3rd American ed., Burlington, Vt.: Chauncey Goodrich, 1845), p. 13.

12 See, to take just one example, the discussion of Capital and Labor by David Ray Papke in *The Pullman Case: The Clash of Labor and Capital in Industrial America* (Lawrence: University Press of Kansas, 1999).

13 The New Historicism often finds its inspiration in older historians, and my reference to Lambarde is no exception. See A. L. Rowse, *The England of Elizabeth: The Structure of Society* (London: Macmillan, 1951), p. 38.

14 Ibid., p. 111.

15 Ibid., pp.122–123. He says the year was 1570, but that would be Old Style.

16 August 2, 1575. See *Calendar of the Carew Manuscripts, 1575–1588*, ed. J. S. Brewer and William Bullen (1868; Kraus Rpt.), p. 17.
17 See Rowse's chapter, "Law in the Society," *The England of Elizabeth*, pp. 360–385.
18 Richard Weisberg, *Poethics: and Other Strategies of Law and Literature* (New York: Columbia University Press, 1992), p. 3; Richard Posner, *Law and Literature: A Misunderstood Relation* (Cambridge, Mass.: Harvard University Press, 1988), p. 17: "In truth, the problems of literary and of legal interpretation have little in common except the word 'interpretation.'"
19 I am indebted to Patricia Parker's *Literary Fat Ladies: Rhetoric, Gender, Property* (London and New York: Methuen, 1987) for my original inspiration on the whole topic of fraudulent conveyances. Her article *"The Merry Wives of Windsor* and Shakespearean Translation," *MLQ* 52 (1991): 225–262, appeared while I was first working out my own ideas. Professor Parker then incorporated my work in her discussion of conveying in *Shakespeare from the Margins: Language, Culture, Context* (Chicago: University of Chicago Press, 1996), pp. 318, n. 32, 335–336, nn. 60–62.
20 I tend to agree with Richard Posner, *Law and Literature: A Misunderstood Relation*, p. 15, that the link between law and literature is rarely literal. On the other hand, Richard Weisberg, in *The Failure of the Word: The Protagonist as Lawyer in Modern Fiction* (New Haven: Yale University Press, 1984), p. 179, is also correct when he declares that the relationship "of interpretive theory to historical context is nowhere better approached than through literature's use of the law." The debate among theorists of law and literature has been extensive in recent years. A good survey of the law and literature debate can be found in Ian Ward's *Law and Literature: Possibilities and Perspectives* (Cambridge: Cambridge University Press, 1995), pp. 3–27, which reviews the work of Brook Thomas, Richard Posner, Richard Weisberg, Richard Rorty, Paul Ricoeur, Stanley Fish, James Boyd White, Robin West, Owen Fiss, Mark Tushnet, Ronald Dworkin, and the Critical Legal Studies movement. Many theorists relate law and literature because they emerge from the same culture and form a common root in language; I hope I can be a little more precise in this book, since each of the authors was actually involved with fraudulent conveyances in some way. For a somewhat similar approach, see M. Lindsay Kaplan, *The Culture of Slander in Early Modern England* (Cambridge: Cambridge University Press, 1997).
21 "A Brief Note of Ireland," in *Spenser's Prose Works*, ed. Rudolf Gottfried, vol. 9 of *The Works of Edmund Spenser: A Variorum Edition*, ed. Edwin Greenlaw *et al.* (Baltimore: Johns Hopkins Press, 1949), p. 245. Here and elsewhere, except for quotations from poetry, I lightly modernize spelling and punctuation.
22 27 Eliz., c. 4 (1585). "In the old days," Glenn admits, "every discussion of fraudulent conveyance included the rights of purchasers as well as creditors. There was, indeed, another Elizabethan enactment which was called the Statute of Conveyances in Fraud of Purchasers." Since Glenn dealt only with the rights of creditors, he mentions this statute "only for purposes of elimination" (*Fraudulent Conveyances and Preferences*, p. 103).
23 *Twyne's Case*, Mich. 44 Eliz., 3 Co. Rep. 80b. *English Reports*, 76: 809–823. The original version in legal French can be found in *Le Tierce Part des Reportes del Edward Coke* (London: E. Flesher, 1671), pp. 80–83. For a succinct account of how the court defined "badges of fraud" in Twyne's Case, see David G. Epstein, *Debtor–Creditor Law*, Nutshell Series (St. Paul, Minn.: West, 1990), pp. 65–67.

Chapter 1

Falstaff's Conveyances

> This doth the comedy handle ... and not only to know
> what effects are to be expected, but to know who be such,
> by the signifying badge given them by the comedian.
> Philip Sidney, 'Defence of Poetry'

The Merry Wives of Windsor, Shakespeare's only play that pictures contemporary, middle-class English life, weaves several references to fraudulent conveyancing through a plot that involves many legal themes: Justice Shallow's suit against Falstaff for poaching his deer, Falstaff's attempts to escape debts, the moral response of the wives of Windsor to Falstaff's sexual advances, the rules of the duel, the theft of horses. There is even a hint of the issue of same sex marriage at the end of the play when the two bumbling suitors, Abraham Slender and Dr. Caius, find they have carried away boys instead of Anne Page, who has managed to elope with her courtly lover Fenton. Each situation features some kind of ethical dilemma not dissimilar to the underlying issue raised by fraudulent conveyancing, which pits the plight of the powerless against society at large and the instrument of society, the law.

Besides its ethical concerns and its plot, Shakespeare's play suits the theme of fraudulent conveyancing because the difference between what is said and what is not said affects both the play's text and its textual history. The dumping of Falstaff in the Thames and the conveyance of Anne Page arise in what Patricia Parker has revealed as a "discursive network" that "links the transporting or translating of words with the transfer, conveying, or stealing of property".[1] Just as the play is at once both open and reticent about sex, it also finds a discursive mode for such unspoken practices as the ongoing trade in lands that once belonged to the Church and the ever-present practice of tax evasion. Shakespeare himself had no qualms about investing £440 in a lease that derived from a former church tithe, and he was twice cited, in 1597 and 1598, for failure to pay his share of the general subsidy that was the only real reason an English monarch allowed Parliament to meet.[2] Once called, Parliament could debate any topic, including, to a remarkable extent throughout the 1570s and 1580s, the problems of fraudulent conveyancing. It is, therefore, perhaps not remarkable that when Shakespeare revised *The Merry Wives of Windsor* during the period in which Twyne's Case (1601) was settled, he recognized, if he did not directly name, the local practices his plot reflects. Not that he was unaware of the terms of the law. The play has long been recognized for the legal language that distinguishes the later Folio from the earlier Quarto text.[3] Characters use words and phrases such as Star Chamber, quorum, Justice of the Peace, custa-lorum, "bill, warrant, quittance, or obligation,"[4] "the register" (of follies), "fee'd every slight occasion," "exhibit a bill in the parliament,"[5] cheaters,[6] exchequers, egress and regress, suits and oyes.[7] An earlier generation of critics used this language to argue that Shakespeare was a trained lawyer. More sober reflection has shown that these words and phrases were readily available and rarely employed with technical exactness.[8] Nowhere do we find a "conveyance" in the narrow sense of a transfer of title by deed. Yet Mistress Page ("fee simple with fine and recovery" and "waste") and Mr. Ford (building on "another man's ground") refer to practices that fraudulent conveyancing laws sought to keep in check, while Falstaff may or may not be involved in the mysterious disappearance of horses at the end of the play.

Conveying (the larger form of conveyancing) plays a metaphoric role in *The Merry Wives*, introducing not merely signs of the law (the legalisms pursued by earlier scholars) but subversive practices that inspired the law. The metaphors, parodies, and parallels for conveyancing illustrate a relationship between law and literature more productive than the illusion of legal substance, the representation of the adversarial process, or the use of legal terminology. The possibility and discourse, if not the legal technicality, of the law of fraudulent conveyance characterize this comedy.

The Education of Margaret Page

The plot of *The Merry Wives of Windsor* finds Falstaff financially embarrassed and involved in a number of carryings on to obtain money. Early in the play he plans to seduce two wives of Windsor, Mistress Page and Mistress Ford, not for love but to gain access to the moneybags of their rich burgher husbands. Much of the drama's humor derives from Falstaff's failure to dissimulate his intentions effectively. The wives learn his plot when he sends each of them an identical love letter. Falstaff's men, Pistol and Nym, then reveal his game to the wives' husbands. The result is a series of humiliations: most famously, Falstaff is "conveyed" in a buck-basket of dirty laundry to the Thames for a dunking, after Ford interrupts the knight's tryst with his wife. The conveyance saves Falstaff from the wrath of a jealous husband while punishing him at the same time.

Falstaff is a creature of the court, a companion of Prince Hal in Shakespeare's history plays. In *2 Henry IV* Falstaff's time as a law student at Clement's Inn is recalled (III. ii. 308), but in this play he is outwitted by a bourgeois woman, in part because he embodies the contradictions of a society where fraud is endemic and conveyancing is a matter of course. It turns out that Mistress Page (Anne's mother) knows a thing or two about transfers of assets.

Although Margaret Page would not have attended the Inns of Court (for men only), in several instances she sounds more like a lawyer than Falstaff. The plot of the Folio version suggests a reason for her knowledge. Her daughter Anne has a legacy, which her grandfather left her on his deathbed, of "seven hundred pounds of moneys, and gold, and silver" (I. i. 50). Hugh Evans, the Welsh parson, mentions her legacy during a conversation at the beginning of the play when the characters are showing off their knowledge of legal terms. This endowment makes Anne attractive to the bumbling Abraham Slender, whose cause is promoted by his lawyer uncle, Justice Robert Shallow. Doctor Caius, a French physician, and a gentleman of court named Fenton also woo her. The play does not specify which of Anne's grandfathers bequeathed her money, but a paternal patrimony would have probably descended to her father and not be subject to a separate bequest. Therefore the more likely benefactor is the father of

Margaret Page. This possibility is supported by the mild manner of her husband George Page, who gives the impression of a middle-class man who has married money. His even temperament contrasts to the bluff and bluster of his neighbor Francis Ford.

Whether or not George Page negotiated a substantial settlement with his father-in-law, it seems likely his wife's father withheld a part of his legacy and bequeathed it separately to his granddaughter. A woman's property went to her husband, of course, unless she managed to convey it away, but there was nothing fraudulent in this disposition unless George Page had married Margaret Page under the expectation that the money would be his (the situation Truewit conjures in Ben Jonson's *Epicene*). Nonetheless, if the grandfather who bequeathed Anne her legacy was in fact the father of Margaret Page, then that grandfather arranged for his wealth to skip a generation. He not only short-changed George Page, but – presuming she could control her husband's spending – he also deprived his daughter of a certain amount of income, perhaps creating some bitterness and giving Mistress Page reason to think hard about the transfer of wealth.

Perhaps for this reason, Margaret Page knows the language of the law. But she is also a member of an ethically aware, churchgoing society. Traditionally the first act of fraud – in the limited sense of theft by legal manipulations – was Jacob's deception of Isaac to win Esau's birthright.[9] Mistress Page, who seems to divine that Falstaff is after money as much as sex, cites it when she compares her letter from Falstaff to Mistress Ford's: "here's the twin-brother of thy letter; but let thine inherit first, for I protest mine never shall" (II. i. 72). It may be that Mistress Page compares her letter to herself as one who also did not inherit. Falstaff and her father are, in a way, two of a kind.

Mistress Page produces the densest legalism in the play after Falstaff makes his second attempt on Mistress Ford's virtue. His first attempt ends in his conveyance in a buck-basket of laundry. His third attempt finds him disguised as Herne the Hunter and tormented by fairies. On the second occasion he only escapes the wrath of Master Ford, who surprises Falstaff and his wife at home, by disguising himself as Mrs. Ford's maid's aunt of Brainford. Ford calls the woman a witch an "old cozening quean" (IV. ii. 172), then cudgels the disguised Falstaff and drives him away. Delighted to see Falstaff punished for his impudence, Mrs. Page comments that "The spirit of wantonness is sure scar'd out of him." She then adds two legal metaphors: "If the devil have him not in fee-simple, with fine and recovery, he will never, I think, in the way of waste, attempt us again" (IV. ii. 210). The first part of her sentence compares Falstaff's beating to an exorcism of the devil, who has surely been driven out unless he has undisputed possession of Falstaff ("fee-simple"), a property right (or "fee") often obtained, in the late sixteenth century, by the legal maneuver of "fine and recovery."[10] The second part refers to the legal action of waste. Both require explanation.

What is important about a "fine and recovery" is not the exact process of its execution but the way in which the history of property law had woven fraud into the very fabric of English society. A "fine and recovery" was a fraudulent form of conveyance that the courts sanctioned because no other way was possible to avoid the complexities of English land law. In theory the law of property in England went back to William the Conqueror, who asserted his right to every acre of England because, he claimed, he won the land by force. In practice he allowed Englishmen who recognized him as king to redeem their estates by some sort of payment. Thereafter all land was held of the king, either directly or indirectly. Those who held indirectly did so as tenants *in desmene*. Since tenants owed debts to the lord, usually some service defined by nature of the feudal tenure, anything the tenant did to avoid paying was a form of fraud. From the time of the Magna Carta, the English Parliament regularly passed laws to protect Crown interests and landowners against various forms of fraudulent conveyance.

Finding new forms of conveyance quickly became a favorite means to avoid payments. For example, to derive income from lands without losing seisin, tenants introduced the practice of subinfeudation, granting smaller and smaller estates out of those which they held. The tenant of a lord could convey or enfeoff his land to a new tenant in exchange for money. Although the tenant would retain ownership and owe feudal dues to his lord, the value of his estate would be nearly worthless, since the tenant's subtenant now held most of the value.

Clever tenants then figured out a way to put themselves in the position of the subtenant, to retain both title and the value of land without having to pay feudal obligations to overlord. As Frederick G. Kempin, Jr. explains, "A tenant might convey land to a church with the understanding that the church would subinfeudate him for lesser services. The result was that the superior lord now had the church for a tenant, with the resulting loss of feudal dues, but the erstwhile tenant still had the benefit of the land with his obligations considerably reduced."[11] Land held by the Church no longer generated income for an overlord or circulated in the property market and was said to be under a dead hand (mortmain). The resulting opportunity for fraud is made clear by the laws designed to prevent it. In 1236 the English Parliament passed a statute against mortmain and subinfeudation (9 Hen. III, c. 5). In 1267 the Statute of Marlborough curtailed fraudulent enfeoffments. Eventually, as the king and other overlords found their feudal profits shrinking, they passed the statute *Quia emptores* in 1290, which required a purchaser to substitute for the vendor in the feudal hierarchy and provide the same services for the overlord that had been required of the vendor. But new ways were soon found to avoid the new law. *Quia emptores* only applied to estates conveyed in fee simple. A tenant could still subinfeudate by granting less than a fee, such as life estate or an estate in tail. An estate in "tail" is one that is minced or pared from a full estate (from *tailler*, to cut), so that the owner does not have free power to dispose of it. The Statute of Westminster II known as *De donis conditionalibus* recognized the already ongoing practice and regularized it, creating a permanent opportunity for a form of fraudulent conveyance for the well-heeled.

The estate in tail may be regarded as an institutionalized hindrance to creditors, but there could be no legal question that it represented actual intent to defraud, since the owner did not create the estate from which he or she benefited. Yet there was an element of what Kempin calls a "pious fraud," when eventually lawyers found a way to convert the estate in tail to a fee simple. The means for making property alienable is the common recovery, which shows up in a number of references in Shakespeare's plays and other poetry.

> The common recovery was a completely fictitious suit – a pious fraud. The device went through many stages, but the simplest example is the single voucher. Suppose, for instance, that A was in possession as a tenant in fee tail and desired to convey a fee to B. B would sue him for the land, alleging that A had no legal title to it and that it really was owned by B.

A would enter an appearance and call upon X (from whom, he alleged quite fictitiously, he had purchased the land) to defend the title in accordance with the warranty given by X to A. This process was called vouching to warrant. X was called the common vouchee, because he usually was the court crier and frequently acted in this capacity. X would appear but would subsequently default, whereupon judgment would be given to the plaintiff, B, against A, and the court would give another judgment to A against X, presumably for lands of equal value, because of X's breach of warranty in defaulting. X, of course, was in fact not expected to give A anything. The suit resulted in the conveyance of a fee estate to B.[12]

Mistress Page refers to the element of fraud in the fine and recovery when she names the devil as the party who seeks Falstaff's fee simple. Implicit in her metaphor is a comparison of the trouble Falstaff has brought on himself by his sexual intrigues with the knotty problem of alienating property to a willing buyer. In one case the constraints are moral; in the other, legal. But by comparing aggressive male sexuality to the "pious" frauds necessary to alienate property, the virtuous Mistress Page expresses an ethical unease toward practices that society had otherwise countenanced. (Her attitude toward women's virtue is not dissimilar.) In this way the play reflects some of the social pressure that helped solidify the laws of fraudulent conveyancing in the Elizabethan era.

The second part of Mistress Page's sentence compares Falstaff's attempts on the ladies' virtue to the kind of fraud that arose in disputes over rights to exploit real estate. Paul S. Clarkson and Clyde T. Warren gloss "waste" as the "unauthorized use of land," "the spoil or destruction done, or permitted, to houses, lands, trees, or other corporeal hereditaments by the tenant in possession to the prejudice of the reversioner or remainderman in fee simple or fee tail."[13] But this account misses the point that such waste was a recognized form of fraudulent conveyance.[14] In 1601 Elizabeth's Parliament passed a statute that reflects the wider association of fraud and waste. 43 Eliz., c. 8, "an act against fraudulent administration of Intestates goods," targeted estate administrators who managed to give away goods before creditors could be paid because the creditors "for lack of knowledge of the place of habitation of the administrator cannot arrest him," or if they find him and sue him, learn he is unable to pay "the value of that he hath *conveyed away* of the Intestates' goods, or released of his debts, *by way of wasting*" (emphasis added). Mistress Page identifies *herself* as one with the potential to waste and understands that waste is a form of fraud. Again, the purpose of her comparison is to suggest that Falstaff's behavior may be acceptable according to some people's standards, but not her own.

Besides showing off her legal knowledge by making a pun on waste and waist, Mistress Page also directs various actions at fat Falstaff that have a hint of legality about them. As an active plotter – and the success of her intrigues makes her arguably the most intelligent character in the play – she vows revenge when she receives Falstaff's letter; she enlists Mistress Quickly to assist her; she instigates Mistress Ford to convey Falstaff in a buck-basket when Ford, like a judgment creditor, demands that his wife hand over Falstaff; she suggests disguising Falstaff as a woman when he will not enter the basket a second time; and she invents Falstaff's third humiliation, the Herne the Hunter scenario.

Mistress Page also associates legal language with the plans she conceives. The Folio assigns Mistress Page first use of the word "convey" in the play, one of several legalisms by which Shakespeare's revisions find legal language to catch up with and recognize the nature and complexity of the plot. In the Quarto Falstaff first uses the word "convey" in reference to his concealed transport in Mistress Ford's buck-basket ("convey me hence" [III. iii]), but his usage seems to be accounted for by the presence of the word in *Tarlton's News out of Purgatorie*, a probable source.[15] By contrast, when Mistress Page says "convey" in the Folio, one first feels the word signals a character's awareness of its legal and ethical associations: "If you have a friend here, convey, convey him out," she tells Mistress Ford. "Bethink you of some conveyance .... Looke, here is a basket."

The humor of the conveyance lies in its double sense as both the means of transferring title and the property itself. Where real property is at issue, a "conveyance" is always metaphorical (even when livery of seisin is confirmed by dropping a clod of earth), since no one can carry an acre of land.[16] A deed may be "conveyed," but it or another document has value only through what it represents. A marriage debt is similarly metaphorical, even though it may entail physical activity. Falstaff expects the wives to betray their husbands, to whom they owe their loyalty. Mistress Ford and Mistress Page, however, protect their reputations and chastity by secretly conveying Falstaff out of Ford's house. The buck-basket parody works because it inverts the literal and metaphorical aspects of a fraudulent conveyance. The "conveyancing" of Falstaff actually takes place, and Falstaff becomes, literally, the conveyance.

Another Man's Ground

Mr. Ford is another character aware of fraud. Having learned Falstaff intends to seduce his wife, Ford disguises himself as a stranger named Brooke (Broome in the Folio). He meets Falstaff at the Garter Inn, claiming he loves Mistress Ford and offering to pay Falstaff to seduce her on the theory that, having once fallen, she will then favorably receive his entreaties. Amazed at Brooke's profession of love and confession of failure that drives him to this extreme, Falstaff asks him, "Of what quality was your love then?" Ford responds with a legal metaphor, comparing his love of Mistress Ford to "a fair house built on another man's ground, so that I have lost my edifice by mistaking the place where I erected it" (II. ii. 215). Clarkson and Warren echo earlier legal scrutinists: "It was certainly true at common law that if a man by mistake erect a house upon another man's land it became a part of the land and the property of the landowner."[17] The rule is that whatever is affixed to the soil belongs to the soil.[18] The idea occurs in Shakespeare's sonnet 146: "Why so large cost, having so short a lease, / Dost thou upon thy fading mansion spend?"[19] The rule was a commonplace of the law.

But the rule also provided an opportunity for mischief. Consider a tenant who seeks a 20-year lease knowing that he wants to construct a building. The tenant will naturally bargain to have the price of his lease discounted to reflect the future value of the building that will belong to the landlord once the lease expires. Yet if the landlord can manage to accelerate the lease – perhaps by demanding payment when the tenant blunders into insolvency, or even by driving the tenant into financial trouble – the landlord will effect a conveyance to himself. Such a situation occurs when a landlord terminates a lease, leaving the lessee/debtor with no income to pay his creditors, thereby causing the tenant to forfeit his building or premises. Later lawyers would call this a "constructive" fraudulent conveyance, which occurs when there is no intent to deceive but a creditor is nonetheless compromised. When Ford refers to building on another man's land, his words touch an ethical sore point where the law was not yet clear.

Exactly this sort of situation affected Shakespeare's circle in 1597 when the 20-year lease that James Burbage had taken from Giles Allen for land on which to build the Theatre expired. Allen had the law on his side.[20] He owned the land, and when the lease was up he owned the building. Burbage knew his lease would expire and spent £600 on the Blackfriars, but a neighborhood petition drove him out. Shakespeare's company played at the Rose and the Swan for an interim year, then made plans to build the Globe: it was to finance this project that the Burbages allowed Shakespeare and five or so others to invest and thereby become part owners.

Although Allen had a legal right to his land and the buildings on it, to the Burbages and their resident theater company, including Shakespeare, it doubtless seemed that Allen was morally, if not contractually, obligated to renew the lease.[21] By putting the padlock, so to speak, on the acting company's source of income, Allen constructively hindered payment to the Burbage's creditors, who could have included anyone to whom they owed money, including the actors. Shakespeare's company reacted in kind to what they doubtless believed Allen had done. They literally disassembled the theater from Allen's property on December 28, 1598 and then ferried the timbers across the Thames to construct the new Globe Theatre.

The conveyance of an entire theater, like the buck-basket that carries Falstaff, suggests that Shakespeare's company was alert to gestures that could allusively mimic a fraudulent conveyance. As Richard Posner writes, law functions best in literature not as "a complex of rules and institutions" but as a "practice" that can be "imitated" in the Aristotelian sense.[22] The practice at which the statutes aimed was amazingly widespread. A. W. B. Simpson has called the late sixteenth and early seventeenth centuries "the age of fantastic conveyances," as lawyers manipulated legal estates to outwit the Statute of Uses and the Statute of Enrollments passed under Henry VIII.

> The chaotic state of the land law on points such as these was all the more lamentable during a period of social upheaval marked by an increase in the prosperity and social status of the lesser landowners, which, in its turn, brought an accompanying desire to "found families" and ensure that the family estate should not be alienated out of the family in the future.[23]

This common topic was readily available to Shakespeare and his circle in popular and indexed epitomes such as those published by Brook, Rastell, Pulton, West, Plowden, and the prolific Tottell.

We do not know that Shakespeare read these works, but we do know his friends (if not he himself) practiced the deceptions these books describe. For not only did Shakespeare's acquaintances take a dim view of the termination of the Burbages' lease, but, in a related gesture, they themselves readily conveyed property to avoid creditors. For example, before he died, John Brayne, the brother-in-law of James Burbage, had been Burbage's partner in constructing the Theatre. On the last day of September in 1591, an attorney named Henry Bett of Lincoln's Inn, who would have been well aware of the current state of fraudulent conveyancing law, mentioned in a deposition that Brayne, who spent his fortune improving the Theatre, habitually prepared deeds of gift whenever he anticipated being imprisoned for debt: "it was a Comon thing, with the said John Braine [sic], to make deeds of gift of his goods and Chattelles. The reason was ... to prevent his Creditors aswell before building of the Theatre, as since, for he being redie to be imprisoned for debt, he would prepare sutch safetie for his goods, as he could / by those deeds."[24] Bett uses the word "safety" with professional ease, as if admiring Brayne's prudent asset management, but the fact that Brayne was practically insolvent implies that he acted to defraud creditors.

Such conveyancing was not uncommon, at least among the businessmen associated with Shakespeare, and it is hard to say whether they were being prudent or malicious. In 1596, just before he died, James Burbage protected his estate "by making a deed of gift to Cuthbert of all his personal property, and another deed of gift of the Blackfriars to his second son, Richard" (Shakespeare's acting partner).[25] James died. As a result of this gift, Robert Miles (the executor and sole legatee of the Brayne estate) filed suit in 1597 against Cuthbert, Richard, and Ellen Burbage. Miles charged that James Burbage conveyed his estate to defeat Miles and other creditors of their due. Perhaps because the law was still unsettled, perhaps because he had no case, or perhaps because the Burbages were well connected at court, Miles lost his legal action both in Chancery and at common law, as did Giles Allen, who raised the same issue in 1599 when he sued the Burbages for the value of his lost building.

The prevalence and uncertainty of the practice of fraudulent conveyancing gives layers of meaning to Ford's speech to Falstaff. First, Ford suspects someone has made "shrewd construction" on his wife's "enlarged mirth." In this case the "building" is not vain desire but a sexual erection. Mistress Quickly unknowingly blunders onto the truth several scenes later, committing a malapropism when she defends, to Falstaff, the mistaken *direction* of the servants who tossed Falstaff in the Thames:

> *Quickly*: Alas the day! good heart, that was not her fault. She does so take on with her men; they mistook their erection.
> *Falstaff*: So did I mine, to build upon a foolish woman's promise.
>
> (III. v. 35–41)

Falstaff catches her meaning, but he is remarkably unaware of the risk he takes of being defrauded by "Brooke." We have seen that an unscrupulous landlord might let someone who was ignorant of his title build on his land. Ford, disguised as Brooke, similarly encourages Falstaff to "build" on his "ground" (that is, make love to his wife). By encouraging Falstaff to seduce his own wife, Ford may be compared to a ruthless landlord who encourages a man to build on his land and then manages to accelerate a lease or otherwise assert his rights to a building that the tenant has paid for. A creditor could not really argue that he intended to deceive him, but the attachment of a building to land would have the effect of a fraudulent conveyance. Ford's fraud is similarly constructive.

Even though Falstaff's response to Mistress Quickly suggests that he is aware of the dangers of building on uncertain ground, he misses the fraudulent conveyancing aspects of Ford's plot that Shakespeare himself was alert to. Instead, Falstaff's mind seems to conjure a law that arises from the works of nature (nature to which his mind compares woman), when he says that he has mistakenly built upon a "woman's promise" (III. v. 41). Fresh from a dunking in the Thames, Falstaff rather quaintly thinks in terms of riparian rights. Land is stable, but a riverbank can shift in flood, and the changing course of a stream may eliminate one's property interest.[26] A "woman's promise," Falstaff suggests, shifts like a shoreline, and one's possessions may be washed away.

Thinking like a Lawyer

Like Mistress Page and Ford – and in contrast to Falstaff's somewhat retrograde activity – the Host also thinks like a contemporary lawyer. He is eager to use the legal terminology of "egress and regress" ('said I well?" [II. i]),[27] and he worries that "Brooke" has a "shute [suit] against my knight." He somewhat suspiciously keeps a room for Falstaff even when the Garter has been taken over by Germans ("They have had my [house] a week at command. I have turn'd away my other guests" [IV. iii. 8]). English bankruptcy laws, like those of Rome, generally created some form of sanctuary, a place where a debtor could be free from arrest while he reorganized. Usually a church or abbey lands served as a sanctuary, but as Bacon recognized in his *Learned Reading on the Statute of Uses*, debtors desired a retreat to live in after conveying their assets to a friend.[28] They could then negotiate with their creditors, who would be willing to settle their claims at a discount because they would otherwise be unable to reach property held in trust for the debtors. The Garter Inn operates symbolically in this way – rather like a homestead in modern US bankruptcy law, a place creditors cannot touch – for Falstaff lives there uninterruptedly, giving him time to effect the transfer of Bardolph's employment to the Host of the Garter and to send love letters to Mistress Ford and Mistress Page, wooing them for their money.

Besides living in a kind of sanctuary, Falstaff also seems to have a precocious sense of what in later contract law will be called "mutual mistake" when he assigns Caius and Evans to different locations for their duel, effectively preventing their encounter. (A contract is void when a broker makes a sale by describing a different article to each party.)[29] The result is good comedy, based on legal principles.

As I just suggested, Falstaff has the cooperation of the Host as he connives with regard to the employment of Bardolph. The dismissal of a servant to evade debt is a very old legal trick. Justinian mentions fraudulent manumission and gives an example: "A grant of freedom amounts to fraud on creditors when the grantor is already insolvent at the time of the manumission or will become so by freeing the slaves."[30] Bardolph is not a Roman slave, of course, but in *2 Henry IV*, Falstaff says he "bought" him at St. Paul's (I. ii. 51). When Falstaff follows his announcement that he needs to "turn away" some of his followers by saying "I sit at ten pounds a week" (I. iii. 8), the Host of the Garter is not slow to realize that he receives most of that expense. (The tavern bill found on Falstaff in *1 Henry IV*, II. iv. 535–539, suggests that Falstaff spends 13 shillings a day for food and drink, which with half a crown or so for rent, comes to about £10 a week.) Mine Host picks up Bardolph's hire because he values a good customer. He is the beneficiary of Falstaff's transfer of Bardolph, and the transfer verges on fraud because of a trust relationship between Falstaff and the Host to the detriment of other creditors (although it was otherwise legal to *prefer* one creditor to another). As a tapster, Bardolph will spend much of his time doing what he would do anyway, fetching sack for Falstaff. Falstaff retains his service the way Pierce retained the sheep he conveyed to Twyne.

Falstaff's show of concern to find new employment for Bardolph conceals the transfer of assets that takes place. Openly, Falstaff defends letting Bardolph go by claiming he has lost his skill in filching. Pistol – who has just heard Falstaff rationalize his dismissal of Bardolph by claiming that he "kept not time" (I. iii. 26) – perhaps puts a right name to what has happened. Shakespeare's characters usually base their puns and word play on something someone else has just said or done. Pistol has heard Nym use the word "steal" a moment before, but he may have come up with the word "convey" in response to the way Falstaff engineers Bardolph's new occupation when he offers a synonym for theft: "'Convey', the wise it call. 'Steal'? foh: a *fico* for the phrase!"

Falstaff has told his followers he needs to practice deceit – "to shuffle, to hedge, and to lurch" – thus coloring even his inadvertent actions with a degree of intentionality. Pistol's suspicion of Falstaff's secret dealings helps account for his and then Nym's refusal to carry Falstaff's love letters. The distaste for pimping that they express seems like a sudden attack of virtue, but their possible suspicion is borne out when Falstaff seizes on their refusal and cashiers them for it. Whatever his true motive, and whether or not the Host connives with him (as Twyne may or may not have done with Pierce), Falstaff gets a kind of fresh start by releasing his men. He reduces his expenses, and he may also make money if Bardolph, Pistol and Nym are receiving a military salary that Falstaff can pocket. We remain uncertain as to whether Falstaff makes a sly reference to the deceptive practice of fraudulent conveyance when he refers to Bardolph's new occupation as a "good trade," but others, especially the perspicacious Host, seem well aware of what is happening.

Ford, Mistress Page, and the Host constitute a pattern of legal thinking that reflects the increasingly mercantile world of turn-of-the-century England. Their values contrast with those of the knightly class to which Falstaff belongs. England's gentry and aristocracy embraced a romantic ideology of exploration and commercial adventure that colors Falstaff's language.[31] As an apologist for empire, or like an old aristocrat, the knight believes that wooing women for their wealth makes fortunes.[32] Falstaff is certain the wives of Windsor will yield riches: he declares that Mistress Ford and Mistress Page are lands of "gold and bounty. I will be cheaters to them both, and they shall be exchequers to me. They shall be my East and West Indies, and I will trade to them both" (I. iii. 69–72). He means, "I will deceive them; they will be my source of wealth. I will take money first from one, then the other." But Falstaff's language undercuts him by echoing a commercial world to which he seems a stranger. In real life, "cheaters" were tax collectors, and they were capable of fraud that amounted to theft. The situation at Cadiz in 1596 shows such a corrupt representative of the Exchequer at work, as J. E. Neale tells the story:

> Both Howard and Essex were under promise and orders to save the plunder of the voyage for the Queen: they gave it with a bountiful hand to their men. An official had been attached to them to see the order carried out: he plundered with the rest.[33]

Whether or not Shakespeare knew about Cadiz, the problem of repossessing property that such embezzlers bought with the king or queen's money is typical of the precedents cited in Mannocke's Case.[34] This close connection between "escheators" for the Crown and fraud suggests the limited range of Falstaff's ideas on trading and cheating: he maintains an epic attitude of bravado and lying in a world where economic activity was increasingly seen as a technically sophisticated adventure.

Forgiveness or Arrest?

The problem of Falstaff's legal knowledge surfaces most acutely in the final act when Ford announces that Falstaff owes "Brooke" (the name that Ford assumes in disguise) the sum of £20, money that Falstaff has accepted in exchange for his promise to Brooke to seduce Mistress Ford. In the Quarto version of the play Ford mentions "a further matter" to Falstaff: "There's 20 pound you borrowed of M. Brooke Sir John, / And it must be paid to M. Ford Sir John" (V. v. 117 [1602]). Mistress Ford tells her husband to forgive his debtor, thereby effecting a reconciliation appropriate to the comedy's conclusion: "Nay husband let that go to make amends, / Forgive that sum, and so weele all be friends." She prefers to be generous rather than test Falstaff's integrity.

In the Folio, however, Mistress Ford says nothing about forgiving Falstaff. Instead, Ford announces that Falstaff's "horses are arrested" (V. v. 114) to ensure repayment of the debt. Lewis Theobald retained the Quarto reading, noting, in a quasi-judicial manner, that "Sir John Falstaff is sufficiently punished, in being disappointed and exposed. The expectation of his being prosecuted for the twenty pounds gives the conclusion too tragical a turn. Besides it is *poetical justice* that Ford should sustain his loss, as a fine for his unreasonable jealousy."[35] But Theobald overreacts. For one thing, Ford's legal move may have been merely practical: in *1 Henry IV* when Prince Hal hides Falstaff's horse before the Gadshill robbery, he knows that the fat knight is not likely to move far unmounted. Furthermore, if Ford has not taken Falstaff's horses as a joke, then the term "arrest" may be a legalism. Falstaff may have been compelled to give horses to the sheriff as pledges that he will appear in court. His horses would have been "arrested" by a writ.[36] But nothing indicates Falstaff knows what has happened. The more likely explanation is that Ford moved to seize Falstaff's assets before the knight could hide them or convey them to a friend.[37] Again, however, Falstaff seems unperturbed by the news, and it may be that Ford sent the bailiff too late. I am not the first to think that those horses of the Host stolen by the "Germans" may well have been Falstaff's: doubtless on their way to a place beyond the reach of creditors. Perhaps old Falstaff does know a thing or two about conveyances.

Falstaff's conveyance of his horses would be fraudulent if he had no other assets with which to repay his debt. He has clothes, and his room at the Garter counts as an asset if he has paid for it in advance. He may have an income either from an inheritance or as a military captain. But, more to the point for one seeking a quick sale, Falstaff also has an uncertain number of horses – say four, one each for himself and his men – whose value we may estimate at about £5 apiece, suggesting that "Brooke" knew his man if he purposely limited his lending to £20.[38] It is tempting to suggest that Ford is merely blustering when he claims to have arrested Falstaff's horses. The garbled state of the text allows two opposed but related interpretations: either Ford arrested Falstaff's horses to prevent a fraudulent conveyance, or Falstaff fraudulently conveyed them to prevent their seizure for debt.

As a figure in the shifting ethics of conveyancing, Falstaff operates both openly and secretly, intentionally and perhaps instinctively. In Shakespeare's history plays, Falstaff's illegal behavior threatens to mislead Prince Hal and derange society.[39] Shakespeare's comedy, however, absorbs Falstaff's deceptive stratagems because the mores of the society represented in the play show the same ambiguity that characterizes Falstaff.

Either Falstaff's debt is forgiven or not. Either his horses were stolen or Falstaff hired the thieves. The comic form of *The Merry Wives of Windsor* remains intact, despite what Theobald thought, if we follow the text and assume Ford did manage to arrest Falstaff's horses. Falstaff has traditionally been regarded as a *miles gloriosus* figure, the alazon or braggart of Roman comedy, or as a derivative of vice in the old morality plays. Recent critics, seeking to interpret the final pageant of *The Merry Wives*, see him as a carnival figure, a victim of folk-ritual, or a scapegoat who bears the vices of misplaced sexuality and deception "shared by the very citizens who taunt him."[40] I believe he is an effigy of fraud as well – a great literary figure, like Dante's Geryon, "quella sozza imagine di froda" (*Inferno*, xvii, 5). The original Twelve Tables of Rome allowed creditors to divide the body of a debtor among them.[41] Falstaff echoes the old Roman law when, reveling with the wives at Herne the Hunter's oak tree, he offers to divide himself up for their benefit, a haunch to each. Falstaff's symbolic role as a figure of fraud helps explain why Falstaff invites Brooke to Herne's oak to watch him give himself to Mistress Ford and also why Falstaff is ultimately forgiven his trespasses by the townspeople who mock him.

Although there have been recent defenses of Falstaff's role in this comedy, he has generally been taken to be a lesser wit than the knight of the history plays.[42] A. C. Bradley deplored Falstaff's degradation in *The Merry Wives*.[43] Samuel Johnson, thinking of Falstaff's influence on Prince Hal in *1, 2 Henry IV*, moralized that the danger of Falstaff's vice is its attractiveness to others.[44] I believe Bradley's view is misguided and that Johnson's observation applies to *The Merry Wives* as well as the history plays. Falstaff reflects a society in which fraud is endemic and social rules, including legal forms of conveyance, are in flux.

Fraudulent conveyances operate in a shifting moral sphere, where power blurs the line between right and wrong. Anyone who appears unfairly oppressed by circumstances or misfortune will arouse sympathy, including Falstaff, whose simultaneous punishment and escape reflects this ethical ambivalence. His role illustrates the observation of the Roman jurist Justinian that fraud may be admirable. That quality, says Justinian, explains the seeming redundancy of the phrase "false fraud": "The old lawyers described even malice or fraud as good and held this expression to stand for ingenuity, especially where something was devised against an enemy or robber," and so they "added the word 'evil.'"[45] Fraudulent conveyances, too, could be good or bad, depending on one's point of view.

Notes

1 See Patricia Parker, "*The Merry Wives of Windsor* and Shakespearean Translation," *MLQ* 52 (1991): 225–262, 236.

2   For these facts of Shakespeare's life, see Samuel Schoenbaum, *William Shakespeare: A Compact Documentary Life* (New York: Oxford University Press, 1977), pp. 221–222, 246–247.
3   The Folio, sometimes dated to a garter feast of 1597, seems to be a later version of the play than the Quarto, according to Grace Ioppolo, *Revising Shakespeare* (Cambridge: Harvard University Press, 1991), p. 120, who argues it was probably revised several times "to celebrate several Garter feasts": those of 1597, 1603, and possibly 1604. Elizabeth Shafer, "The Date of *The Merry Wives of Windsor*," *Notes & Queries* 236 (1991): 57–60, notes the paucity of evidence for a 1597 Garter production and concludes that all we can say with certainty about the date is that the Quarto version was written sometime before its publication in 1602. Whether the Folio version, which uses more legal terms, was composed before or after the Quarto does not really matter for my argument. Leah S. Marcus, "Levelling Shakespeare: Local Customs and Local Texts," *Shakespeare Quarterly* 42 (1991): 168–178, 173, finds key differences between the two texts: the play "exists in a Quarto of 1602 with an urban setting strongly suggesting London or some provincial city, and the standard copytext, the 1623 Folio version, which sets the play in and around the town of Windsor and includes numerous topographical references to the area, its palace, park, and surrounding villages."
4   These first terms, most of which are not in the Quarto, occur in the opening conversation of Justice Shallow and Slender, whose legal knowledge finds its image, a little later, in his apparent preference for Richard Tottel's *Songs and Sonnets* instead of Tottel's legal tomes. Unless noted, quotations are taken from *The Riverside Shakespeare*, ed. G. Blakemore Evans (Boston: Houghton Mifflin, 1974), but I have tried to be alert to the differences between the Quarto and the Folio, for which see William Shakespeare, *The Merry Wives of Windsor* (1602), Shakespeare Quarto Facsimiles, No. 3 (Oxford: Clarendon Press, 1963), cited by act and scene, and *The Norton Facsimile: The First Folio of Shakespeare*, ed. Charlton Hinman (New York: Norton, 1968), cited by through-line number.
5   The three previous examples are cited by H. J. Oliver, ed., *The Merry Wives of Windsor* (1971; London: Routledge-Arden, 1993), p. lxxviii, who declares the significance of the legalisms hard to detect.
6   According to Dunbar Plunket Barton, *Shakespeare and the Law* (1929; rpt. New York: Blom, 1971), p. 154, "Shakespeare used the word '*cheater*', either in its original sense of escheator or officer who enforced escheats or forfeitures to the Crown, or in its derivative sense of a 'swindler' or 'cheat.'"
7   "[T]he commencement of the mock trial of Falstaff at Herne the Hunter's Oak in Windsor Park at midnight ... is shortly followed by a parody of ordeal by fire," according to O. Hood Phillips, *Shakespeare and the Lawyers* (London: Methuen, 1972), p. 89. Barton, *Shakespeare and the Law*, p. 84, adds that Shakespeare "compares the starting of a fairy revel to the opening of a Court of Assize. The fairy Hobgoblin figures as Crier of the Court; and is ordered to open the revels as if it were an Assize: 'Crier Hobgoblin make the fairy o-yes.'"
8   See Barton, *Shakespeare and the Law*, pp. 7, 159; Arthur Underhill, "Law," in *Shakespeare's England* (1916; Oxford: Clarendon Press, 1950), 1: 381; and George W. Keeton, *Shakespeare's Legal and Political Background* (New York: Barnes & Noble, 1968), p. 301.
9   Patricia Parker, *Literary Fat Ladies: Rhetoric, Gender, Property* (London and New York: Methuen, 1987), p. 74.
10 According to Alan Harding, *A Social History of English Law* (1966; Gloucester, Mass.: Peter Smith, 1973), p. 91, "The conveyancers quickly developed ways of breaking entails, for the benefit of tenants-in-tail who wanted to alienate the land that came to them. The

conveyancers' cleverest invention was the common recovery. It was known that a tenant for life or a term of years sometimes fraudulently conveyed away the fee simple of the land he occupied by means of a collusive action: the purchaser claimed the land in court, and the tenant made only a gesture of defense, so that the purchaser 'recovered' the land by a legal judgment." For the more complex "fine and recovery," see Paul S. Clarkson and Clyde T. Warren, *The Law of Property in Shakespeare and the Elizabethan Drama* (Baltimore: Johns Hopkins Press, 1942), p. 127–128; Underhill, "Law," 1: 405; and Frederick G. Kempin, Jr., *Historical Introduction to Anglo-American Law*, Nutshell Series, 3rd ed. (St. Paul, Minn.: West, 1990), p. 157.

11   Kempin, *Historical Introduction to Anglo-American Law*, p. 146.
12   Kempin, *Historical Introduction to Anglo-American Law*, p. 158.
13   Clarkson and Warren, *The Law of Property in Shakespeare*, p. 166. The authors wittily point out that from a legal standpoint, Falstaff is a stranger, not a tenant: "Damage done or permitted by a *tenant* in possession (having an estate less than fee tail) would be waste, but damage done by a stranger would be trespass. Falstaff certainly was no tenant (metaphorically, of course)" (p. 167).
14   William Rastell, "To the Gentle Reader," in *A Collection in English, of the Statutes now in force, continued from the beginning of Magna Charta* (London, 1598), p. 522, lists the rule that one who sustains damage can have a "writ of waste out of the Chancery against the escheator for his act."
15   See Geoffrey Bullough, ed., "Tarltons Newes out of Purgatorie," in *Narrative and Dramatic Sources of Shakespeare*, vol. 2: *The Comedies, 1597–1603* (London: Routledge, 1958), p. 31: "and then was *Lionello* [Falstaff's equivalent] conveighed away."
16   Seisin is not the possession of land but the legal right to it. It is a famously murky concept in English law. But if the operation of it is arcane, the social policy behind it is clear. Seisin helped keep transfers open and public. "The notion that seisin was a 'thing' was so strong that a present freehold estate could be transferred only by feoffment, a highly ceremonial transaction which took place on the land and in which 'livery of seisin' was symbolized by handing over a twig or a clod in the presence of witness." Where the public was involved, opportunities for private fraud were diminished. See John E. Cribbet and Crowin W. Johnson, *Cases and Materials on Property*, 5th ed. (Mineola, NY: Foundation Press, 1984), p. 243, citing Percy Bordwell, "Seisin and Disseisin," *Harvard Law Review* 34 (1921): 592–624.
17   Clarkson and Warren, *The Law of Property in Shakespeare*, p. 164.
18   "*Quicquid plantatur solo solo cedit*"; "*aedificium solo cedit*": see Barton, *Shakespeare and the Law*, p. 122. William Rushton, *Shakespeare's Legal Maxims* (1907; New York: AMS, 1973), pp. 23–25, traces the maxim to Justinian and gives a variation in George Chapman's *May Day*. Clarkson and Warren, *The Law of Property in Shakespeare*, p. 166, cite Thomas Dekker's *The Shoemaker's Holiday* for a similar sexual metaphor: "hee / that sowes in another mans ground forfeits / his harvest."
19   Noted by Barton, *Shakespeare and the Law*, p. 114.
20   The first critic to connect Allen's attempt to take possession of the Theatre to Ford's metaphor was Roy F. Montgomery, "A Fair House Built on Another Man's Ground," *Shakespeare Quarterly* 5 (1954): 207–208. See also Andrew Gurr, *The Shakespearean Stage, 1574–1642*, 2nd ed. (Cambridge: Cambridge University Press, 1980), p. 130; Schoenbaum, *William Shakespeare*, pp. 207–208; Joseph Quincy Adams, *Shakespearean Playhouses* (1917; Gloucester, Mass.: Peter Smith, 1960), pp. 28–74; and their source, Charles William Wallace, *The First London Theatre: Materials for a History* (1913; rpt. New York: Benjamin Blom, 1969).
21   Cuthbert Burbage had the right to bear away the timbers for the Theatre for 21 years after

his father first signed the lease, but Allen seems to have attempted to make him miss that deadline by giving false promises that he would renew it. It fell due in September 1598, and learning that Allen himself intended to dispose of the materials, Cuthbert took action. See Adams, *Shakespearean Playhouses*, p. 62.

22 Richard Posner, *Law and Literature: A Misunderstood Relation* (Cambridge, Mass.: Harvard University Press, 1988), p. 79.
23 A. W. B. Simpson, *An Introduction to the History of Land Law* (1961; 2nd ed., Oxford: Clarendon Press, 1986), p. 186.
24 Wallace, *The First London Theatre,* p. 86. At the time he wrote Bett was an ally of the Burbages in defending their interests against Brayne's widow, who acted at the instigation of Robert Miles. Later Bett witnessed the assignment of the lease of the Theatre to Cuthbert Burbage.
25 Wallace, *The First London Theatre*, pp. 23–24.
26 Spenser draws on a similar law of the sea in the tale of the two sons of Milesio, owners of eroding islands, when Artegall convinces them that they must be content with what the sea delivers them and what it takes away (*The Faerie Queene*, V. iv. 4–20).
27 The terms "egress and regress" might occur, for example, in a lease where a tenant would leave the land but claim a right of return to harvest a crop; see Clarkson and Warren, *The Law of Property in Shakespeare*, p. 69.
28 Francis Bacon, *The Works of Francis Bacon*, ed. James Spedding, Robert Leslie Ellis, and Douglas Denon Heath, vol. 7: *Literary and Professional Works* (London: Longman, 1861), p. 412. See also I. D. Thornely, "The Destruction of Sanctuary," *Tudor Studies Presented ... to Albert Frederick Pollard*, ed. R. W. Seton-Watson (London, 1924), pp. 182–207, 183–186; Leah Marcus, *Puzzling Shakespeare: Local Reading and Its Discontents* (Berkeley: University of California Press, 1988), pp. 165–166; Garrard Glenn, *Fraudulent Conveyances and Preferences*, 2 vols. (New York: Baker, Voorhis, 1940), p. 84, and 32 Hen. VIII, c. 12 ("places of priviledge and tuition for terme" included Welles in Somerset, Westminster, Manchester, Northampton, Norwich, York, and Derby).
29 See Francis B. Tiffany, *Handbook of the Law of Sales* (St. Paul, Minn.: West, 1908), p. 53.
30 See *Justinian's Institutes*, trans. Peter Birks and Grant McLeod (Ithaca: Cornell University Press, 1987), p. 41 (1.6.3).
31 David Quint, *Epic and Empire: Politics and Generic Form from Virgil to Milton* (Princeton: Princeton University Press, 1993), p. 259, notes that although plunder is "the normal means for an epic hero to acquire portable property," there was a tradition of debased heroes who ventured among the merchants (ancient critics called Ulysses a hoarding merchant, and Juvenal referred to Jason as "mercator Jason"). The old categories were breaking down by 1600 when Elizabeth gave a charter to the East India company to trade wool cloth in the Indian Sea. Compare G. M. Trevelyan, *Illustrated History of England* (1926; London: Longmans, 1956), pp. 346–347: "Commerce was the motive of exploration as well as warfare, and all three were combined in some of the greatest deeds of that generation. Romance and money-making, desperate daring and dividends, were closely associated in the minds and hearts of men."
32 Falstaff represents what Immanuel Wallerstein, *The Modern World System: Capitalist Agriculture and the Origin of the European World-Economy in the Sixteenth Century* (New York: Academic Press, 1976), p. 18, calls the old view of the world of trade as a trade in luxuries (food and handicraft production), not "bulk" goods.
33 J. E. Neale, *Queen Elizabeth I* (1934; Harmondsworth: Penguin, 1973), p. 346.
34 Mannocke's Case (3 Dyer 295a [1571]) cites a cluster of cases based on debt, sanctuary, and fraudulent conveyance, including a case about a man who purchased land with the money of the king: "Walter de Chyrton customer al Roy esteant graunde dettor a luy, purchase terre ove la money le Roy, et prist lestate del terre a ses amies a defrauder le Roy,

mes il mesne prist les profitz, ceux terres fuerant extend al Roy in *Scaccario.*" The court of Exchequer voided the conveyances and gave the land to the king. The terms "direct" and "indirect" are the same as those in the Alien Statute in *The Merchant of Venice.* That play and 13 Eliz., c. 5 draw on a common language.

35 Lewis L. Theobald, ed., *The Works of William Shakespeare,* vol. 5 (London, 1803), p. 216. Geoffrey Bullough, *Narrative and Dramatic Sources,* 2: 11, condemns the horse stealing episode: "As it stands in both Q and F this is surely the worst-handled episode in all Shakespeare's plays." W. W. Greg, *The Shakespeare First Folio* (Oxford: Clarendon Press, 1955), p. 336, calls it "curiously fragmentary"; Robert S. Miola, "The Merry Wives of Windsor: Classical and Italian Intertexts," *Comparative Drama* 27 (1993): 364–376, says it is "badly garbled."

36 Normally the creditor would enlist a bailiff to execute the debt "upon the body" of the debtor: this is the language used in 1582, for example, in reference to the bailiff of the Manor and Liberties of Stebneth, who executed a debt of £100 against John Brayne. See Wallace, *The First London Theatre,* p. 91.

37 John Cowell's *Interpretor* (1601) offers another possible gloss in the writ of *arrestandis bonis ne dissipentur,* "which lyeth for him, whose catell or goods are taken by another, that, during the controversie, doth, or is like to make them away, and will be hardly able to make satisfaction for them afterward." Yet this writ fits the facts of the case imperfectly, since Falstaff did not take horses from Ford. Dr. Cowell was Reader in Civil Law at the University of Cambridge; he published *The Interpretor* in 1601. Ralegh believed he was a lackey to King James I, since he supported his view that the monarch was outside the law. See Keeton, *Shakespeare's Legal and Political Background,* p. 342. Notice that Ford arrests not Falstaff's horses but Falstaff. Keeton, *Shakespeare's Legal and Political Background,* p. 114, observes that Antipholus threatens Angelo with a suit for wrong arrest in *The Comedy of Errors.* Other methods of distraint would be available *after* a judgment in court, which we may presume Ford has not yet sought. At that point a judgment creditor in the king's court could send a sheriff to levy on the debtor's animals by a writ of *fieri faciat,* employing a legal process that went back at least to 3 Edw. I, c. 18; *elegit* (a transfer of the debtor's personal property to his creditor at an appraised price); and *capias ad satisfaciendum* (where a local sheriff arrests the judgment debtor, who stayed in prison until he paid his fine). See David G. Epstein, *Debtor-Creditor Law,* Nutshell Series, 4th ed. (St. Paul, Minn.: West, 1991), p. 66.

38 Indictments involving the theft of horses often included the value of the animal. J. S. Cockburn, *Essex Indictments: Elizabeth I. Calendar of Assize Records* (London: HMSO, 1978), lists prices in 1600: £6 each for a black and a sorrel gelding (#2973); 50 shillings for a gray mare (#2975); £3 for a gray gelding; £5 for bright-bay horse; £3 for a sorrel horse (#3011); £5 for a gray gelding, but 26 shillings for a white gelding (#3011). I owe this information on prices to Shawn Smith.

39 Daniel Kornstein, *Kill All the Lawyers? Shakespeare's Legal Appeal* (Princeton: Princeton University Press, 1994), pp. 134–142.

40 See Jan Lawson Hinely, "Comic Scapegoats and the Falstaff of *The Merry Wives of Windsor,*" *Shakespeare Studies* 15 (1982): 37–54, 43. See also Stephen Foley, "Falstaff in Love and Other Stories from Tudor England," *Exemplaria* 1 (1989): 227–246; and Anne Parten, "Falstaff's Horns: Masculine Inadequacy and Feminine Mirth in *The Merry Wives of Windsor,*" *Studies in Philology* 82 (1985): 184–199.

41 See Thomas Collett Sandars, ed. *The Institutes of Justinian* (London: Longmans, 1952), p. xv; Posner, *Law and Literature,* p. 93.

42 H. J. Oliver, *The Merry Wives of Windsor,* p. lxvii, denies that there is a "gap" between the Falstaff who "loses the battle of wits after the Gadshill robbery and is not allowed to forget it" and the one who can so easily be made to look foolish by the kind of honest

women of whom he has little experience, or between the Falstaff who is frightened of being found by a jealous husband and the one who ran away at Gadshill." Like others, he observes that Falstaff's defeat is necessary to the comic drama. Anne Barton, "Introduction to *The Merry Wives of Windsor*," in *The Riverside Shakespeare*, pp. 286–289, concludes that Falstaff is a "lesser creature" because his character is "no end in itself" but an expression of the play's comic plot (287), a point made also by E. K. Chambers, cited by G. R. Hibbard, "Introduction," in *The Merry Wives of Windsor*, ed. G. R. Hibbard (1973; Harmondsworth: Penguin, 1981), p. 55.

43 A. C. Bradley, "The Rejection of Falstaff," *Oxford Lectures on Poetry* (London: Macmillan, 1909), pp. 247–275.

44 See the last note to *2 Henry IV*, in Samuel Johnson, ed., *The Plays of William Shakespeare*, 7 vols. (1765; New York: AMS, 1968), 4: 356: "The moral to be drawn from this representation is, that no man is more dangerous than he that with a will to corrupt, hath the power to please; and that neither wit nor honesty ought to think themselves safe with such a companion when they see *Henry* seduced by Falstaff."

45 Justinian, *The Digest of Justinian*, ed. Theodor Mommsen, Paul Kreuger, and Alan Watson (Philadelphia: University of Pennsylvania Press, 1985), 1: 119: "Non fuit autem contentus praetor dolum dicere, sec adiecit malum, quoniam veteres dolum etiam bonum dicebant" (the praetor was not content to say fraud, but added the word false, since the ancients used to speak of good fraud too).

Chapter 2

"Creditors and Others": The Purpose of 13 Eliz., c. 5 (1571)

"Anima legis est executio."
Nicholas Bacon

In order to understand the main form of the law designed to prevent a practice of which Shakespeare and the characters in *The Merry Wives of Windsor* seem so cognizant, we need to assess the circumstances in which Parliament crafted it. Literature tends to exploit the ethical problems and cultural impact of the law, not the minutiae of statutes and case law. Nonetheless, as every jurist knows, laws are the result of history as much as logic. Whose interests was Parliament protecting in 1571 when it proposed a law protecting "creditors and others" against fraudulent conveyancing? Those of the government? Of sharp operators like Giles Allen? Or normal creditors who might have been ruined by the unethical behavior of Shakespeare's partners, the Burbages? It might be argued that Falstaff, that inimitable repository of every vice, incorporates also the unfair power of the court to control the lives of ordinary citizens. But power and corruption were not found only at the tables of the great – the usual argument of New Historicists. Fraudulent conveyancing laws came in several forms and served more than one audience. If *The Merry Wives of Windsor* reveals a society ready to defraud creditors and others, contemporaneous thinkers also faced the problem of how to craft a law able to accommodate competing interests.

The Royal Interests

In what has been the definitive chapter on the history of 13 Eliz., c. 5 (1571), Garrard Glenn characterized the law's origins as political and punitive, designed not only to protect the interests of the Crown in land, but to punish those who did not conform to the Elizabethan settlement.[1] Glenn was troubled, as many modern readers are, by the attitude of Reformation England toward Catholics. The fact is, said Glenn, that "a substantial part of the Crown's revenue had always flowed from convictions of treason and felony, with the resulting attainder and forfeiture of property to the Crown" (p. 89). It followed that "a canny conspirator would anticipate indictment or bill of attainder by transferring his assets to a friend, to be held in trust for the grantor's family" (p. 90). Although Ireland had a statute passed in 1310 that annulled conveyances made with intent to commit felony or rebellion, England had only the Statute of Uses, which could void a conveyance of land made by an attainted person, but did not apply to personal property. The new law corrected this deficiency. But its true purpose, Glenn believed, was to prevent Catholics from protecting their property against the ruinous fines that the Act of Uniformity (passed in 1559) imposed on recusants – those who refused to worship in public in an Anglican church (p. 91). Government bureaucrats designed the fraudulent conveyance statute to protect "creditors and others," where "others" was a code for the interests of the Crown.

The suspicion of a hidden agenda finds evidence in a troubling feature of 13 Eliz., c. 5, the inclusion of a penal provision, which seems out of place in a statute designed for commercial purposes. The law provided that everyone involved in a fraudulent conveyance "shall incur the penalty and forfeiture of one year's value" of whatever real estate is involved. They shall also forfeit "the whole value of the goods and chattels," one half to queen and the other half to any party bringing suit. The American states that based their fraudulent conveyance statutes on English law realized the absurdity of the provision – why should a creditor share with the government? – and, with one exception, omitted it. The English statute additionally provided imprisonment for up to half a year for guilty persons.

But it was not only the odd penal provision that made Glenn attribute passage of the statute to politics. He was also troubled that Parliament failed to relate the law to a bankruptcy bill passed the same year. One bill raised money for the government, the other only provided for creditors.

> Hence one was a government measure, and the other was not... This disparity excites amazement in view of the standardized lauds that constantly pour forth with regard to the Elizabethan Age. Those were the days of Gresham, of the awakening of modern trade, of the birth of insurance law and practice – so we are told – and yet a bankruptcy law is viewed as "of no great moment", and a statute of fraudulent conveyances is enacted as a revenue measure solely! (p. 94)

Whatever political origins the law had, by the early seventeenth century the statute had been redefined in commercial terms, as Glenn recognized in the remainder of his chapter. Courts tended to ignore the penal clause. Eventually the wording of the statute was incorporated into bankruptcy law. In 1603, by the statute 1 Jac. I, c. 15, a fraudulent conveyance became itself an act of bankruptcy, and in 1623, legislators copied the language of Elizabeth's statute into the Bankruptcy Act (21 Jac. I, c. 19).

Glenn's argument for the political origins of the law is convincing in part, but also overstated. To tell an accurate story we need to reconsider the weight of some of Glenn's evidence about the origins of 13 Eliz., c. 5; to consider how the Northern Rebellion might have prompted the government to beef up its fraudulent conveyance laws; and to reconnect 13 Eliz., c. 5 to related laws. For example, Glenn does not consider a similar law, the Statute of Conveyances in Fraud of Purchasers (27 Eliz., c. 4 [1585]), he deals "solely with the rights of creditors; and so this statute, that relates only to purchasers, is mentioned only for purposes of elimination" (p. 103). He therefore misses not only a strong cultural connection, but from the evidence of the parliamentary debates in 1572, a direct legislative link.[2]

There are several other indications that Glenn too zealously politicizes 13 Eliz., c. 5. First, Edward Coke is at pains in his reading of the statute in Twyne's Case to rule that "and others," in the phrase "creditors and others," refers to forfeitures to the Crown. If it was the original intent of the law to benefit the Crown, why did it take 30 years to make the point? Second, if we credit Spenser's complaints in *The View*, then whether or not the statute was politically designed, it did not work, at least in Ireland, where fraudulent conveyances by Catholics and traitors were epidemic. That deficiency may explain why Coke needed to provide a broad reading of the phrase "and others." Third, the penal provisions are contradictory. If the Crown were to benefit from forfeitures, why did the law include language giving half the value of a debt to aggrieved parties? Why not take it all? These three issues – Spenser's complaints about fraudulent conveyances, Coke's reading of the phrase "creditors and others," and the problem of penal laws, which shows up in *The Merchant of Venice* – will be considered in ensuing chapters.

Another point is that Glenn seems to be just wrong about the relationship between the statutes of fraudulent conveyance and bankruptcy. He argues that the separation of the statute on fraudulent conveyances from a bankruptcy law, 13 Eliz., c. 7, passed at the same time, proves its political intent. But the bankruptcy statute applied only to certain merchants and traders. To have combined it with 13 Eliz., c. 5 would have unnecessarily limited the application of fraudulent conveyance law. Finally, there is good evidence that despite Glenn's thesis, 13 Eliz., c. 5 was not part of an emergency measure, despite the after-effects of the Northern Rebellion in 1569. A version of it had been previously introduced to Elizabeth's second parliament, which met in 1566. We happen to have the list of proposed legislation that William Cecil drafted, including the name of the legal counsel responsible for each bill. As one historian has pointed out, Justice James Dyer drew up a bill touching fraudulent gifts intended to defeat the creditors of bankrupts. It did not pass the Commons that year, but did in 1571, when its substance was divided into two separate bills, one on bankruptcy (13 Eliz., c. 7), which was limited to tradesmen, and one of fraudulent conveyances (13 Eliz., c. 5).[3] That the law was passed separately is no argument, in itself, that it was not aimed at creditors.

Glenn's argument is not all one-sided. He admitted that 13 Eliz., c. 5 was an improvement over previous laws designed to protect creditors, because it covered not just lands, but goods. And he pointed out that it covered cases where no sanctuary was involved. Both points suggest that the purpose of the law was to update statutory language to protect creditors. For example, the statute of Elizabeth was broader than the bankruptcy laws already on the books, and legal writers regularly annotated the statute with references to 50 Edw. III, c. 6 (1376); 2 Rich. II, St. 2, c. 3 (1379); and 3 Hen. VII, c. 4 (1486). The most glaring loophole of these statutes is that they only covered fraudulent conveyances where the debtor actually entered a legally defined safe haven. Parliament corrected the problem by passing 13 Eliz., c. 5.

The text of 13 Eliz., c. 5 suggests that it was designed to meet many issues that arose or might arise in court. Whenever a wordy list of parallel terms occurs in a statute, there is a good chance that the statute is taking into account the clever actions of lawyers who have defeated similar measures in the past. 13 Eliz., c. 5 does just that. Henry VII's fraudulent conveyance statute voided only "deeds of gifts and goods and chattels," whereas 13 Eliz, c. 5 presents a grander list of "feoffments, gifts, grants, alienations, conveyances, bonds, suits, judgments, and executions." No doubt lawyers had successfully argued in the intervening years that 3 Hen. VII, c. 4 did not fit the facts of a particular client's case because the client conveyed a bond, or a suit, or an execution, whereas the statute referred only to goods and chattels. The source of debts would also have offered fertile ground for uncovering exceptions to the statute.

Henry VII's law covered only "duties" owed to "creditors." Now, instead of "creditors" the statute reads "creditors and others," while the debts owed are not just "duties," but "lawful actions, suites, debts, accounts, damages, penalties, forfeitures, heriots, mortuaries, and releases." Political or not, 13 Eliz., c. 5 seems to have been passed in order to keep statutory law up to date.

The Northern Rebellion

Whether 13 Eliz., c. 5 originated as a creditor bill drafted by Dyer to close key loopholes in previous similar legislation, or was designed by Burghley to foil the queen's political enemies, it seems to have failed to meet its first challenge, the Northern Rebellion of 1569. Many cases of fraudulent conveyancing arose among the conspirators. All seem to have been dealt with by common law provisions and a later statute.

In 1569, Thomas Howard, the fourth duke of Norfolk (and son of the famous poet, the earl of Surrey) arranged his affairs as men did at the time when they loved their children, owed money, sought to preserve their estates, and knew they might die. The queen had constantly outwitted him. He hated her advisors Robert Dudley and William Cecil. The loss of three wives seems to have unhinged him. He responded by plotting to marry Mary, Queen of Scots. To fulfill his designs he conspired with Catholic dissidents and disaffected elements in the north of England. Given the danger of his enterprise, he prudently conveyed away his property. He "executed a deed to ensure the succession of the Norfolk liberty to his eldest son Philip and his heirs male. He created trustees" to receive a lawful estate "to the use of the duke during his life."[4] The law of the time allowed him to retain the power to revoke the trust he had created – something that would later be regarded as a badge of fraud:

> The purpose of this "marvel of conveyancing" was to keep the Howard inheritance intact. A man holding land in trust enjoyed very considerable benefits. Because the legal estate was vested in feoffees he was secure from forfeiture, he could evade his creditors and, most important, he was quit of feudal incidents – the dues in the Court of Wards and Liveries which had cost Howard so much.[5]

Despite his careful financial preparations – not legally fraudulent, but then, the wealthy duke had the best lawyers – the strain of his political game cost the duke his nerve. He retreated to his sickbed in Norfolk, where he was easily sent for and then arrested in 1569. Without Norfolk's participation, the Northern Rebellion quickly failed. In its aftermath the other leaders – Charles Neville, earl of Westmorland, and Thomas Percy, earl of Northumberland – were ruined, their lands and goods confiscated.

The story of these ensuing confiscations reveals the practical difficulties that certain statutes passed a little later by Parliament seem designed, to some extent at least, to alleviate. At the time of the rebellion the Lord Lieutenant of the North was Thomas Fitzwater, the earl of Sussex, who regularly kept a court of oyer and terminer (the name means hear and determine).[6] On November 15 the rebels entered Durham in armor, tore a Bible in pieces, and declared their intention to make religion their cause. The legally proficient Sussex then issued a proclamation against the earls, saying that they had done "unlawful offenses" with Christopher Neville, Richard

Norton, Thomas Markenfeld, John Swynburn, Robert Tempest, Francis Norton, and others. He accused them of abusing the queen's name and proceeding in "rebellious enterprises."[7] The proclamation, Sussex said in a letter to the queen, was "sufficiently penned upon the statute of rebellion." The effect was to put in jeopardy the property of every participant, but an offer of pardon by a certain date softened the threat. With the advance of Lord Hunsdon, Lord Clinton, and the earl of Warwick (Ambrose Dudley) to reinforce Sussex, the rebel earls retreated. According to Holinshed's *Chronicles*, "They shrank quite away, and fled into Scotland, without bidding their company farewell. The earl of Warwick and his power marched on to Durham. But the earl of Sussex pursuing those other rebels that had not means to flee out of the realm apprehended no small number of them at his pleasure, without finding any resistance among them at all."[8] By December 22, the rebellion was over. Sussex reported that his men, locals whom he had threatened with financial ruin and then trained as soldiers, served willingly and there was no spoiling of the country.

But Sussex was wrong; there *was* spoiling. Thomas Cecil, the Lord Treasurer's son, served privately with 362 light horsemen. He wrote his father on December 21 that the horsemen did nothing but "spoil and rob" everywhere they went. "Diverse gentlemen mean, at the end of their chargeable journey, to crave in recompense some of the goods and livings by this rebellion forfeited to her majesty." He himself asked only to be let have charge of a garrison of continuance in the north. On December 23 he told his father that he would ask Sussex to let him have the guard of Richard Norton's house and demesne, until the queen disposed of his lands. Meanwhile Hunsdon was petitioning Cecil for the same sort of thing:

> If this rebellion be well used, it will be beneficial to her [the Queen], but it must be well foreseen, for lands and goods forfeited to the bishopric are the bishop's and not the Queen's. Most of the Earl of Northumberland's men are out of Richmondshire, which he has by being steward of Middleton and thereby steward of Richmondshire. If Her Majesty bestow the stewardship upon me, her own tenants should not serve against her. I wrote to my wife to ask it.

No wonder that Sussex warned the queen that in such times, she would have many "cravers" and that she should not make grants suddenly until informed by himself and Sadler to give "meet rewards to such as have deserved." On December 25 he wrote that the queen now had an opportunity to "frame good government" in the northern counties. The lands that will fall from the bishopric were too great for any one subject. The queen should compound with the bishop for her royalties. Sussex knew, from his Irish service, how the Queen liked to operate.

On December 28 Sussex wrote to Cecil that he meant to go to Durham for some days to execute, by martial law, "constables and other officers, that have seduced the people (under color of the Queen's Majesty's service) to rebel."[9] He intended to execute the worst in every town that sent troops to the rebels and expected the number to be not under six or seven hundred. He asked Cecil to let him fulfill his office without "abridgement" and to fine other offenders "and thereby to raise a commodity to the Queen's Majesty." He said he knew the law, and therefore would not execute anyone "that had inheritance or great wealth."[10] At the same time Sussex announced that he had rewarded some of his men with goods of some persons. He mentions about forty names.[11] Of the list of gentlemen in jail in Durham, only two were executed. At least one was spared because his father offered a ransom of £500, "which, if he be executed, she [the Queen] should have nothing."

The law, indeed, as Spenser mentions in the *View* and Coke in his *Institutes*, was that those "which are hanged by Martial Law, *in furore belli*, forfeit no Lands." Forfeiture occurred only by a legal judgment for a felony, which a summary execution would prevent. Otherwise, the judgment could happen in three ways: when the defendant was sentenced to hang, when he fled the realm, or when he was proclaimed an outlaw ("aut quia suspensus per collum, aut quia abjuravit regnum, aut quia utlagatus est").[12] Cecil knew the law too. On December 31 he told Sussex by letter to make executions in every market town where rebels gathered. He might use martial law on "rebels that had no freehold, no copyhold, nor substance of lands." Those with lands were to have a trial.

To sort out claims to property, Elizabeth appointed the York Commission, consisting of Sussex, Hunsdon, Sir Gilbert Gerrard (the Attorney General), and Sir Thomas Gargrave. Once the lawyers arrived to determine what lands would fall to the queen, issues related to fraudulent conveyancing surfaced. The commissioners wrote to Cecil on March 24, 1570:

> Sir, – Since our arrival here, [we have] proceeded by indictment against all such of the rebels as we be informed have landed, and be either out of the realm, or in prison, or have not appeared before us; and have also, for sundry respects, and specially *for that we know now what conveyance be made by the principal offenders of their lands, caused to be indicted some other persons that have no lands, and may, by such conveyance, defraud the Queen.*
>
> We mean not only to receive to composition all such persons as shall submit themselves to our orders, and have not above £5 land, according to our commission and instruction in that case; but also to stay execution of such other persons as have no lands, and shall be, for the Queen's benefit, attainted.
>
> There be condemned, eleven persons. Four are this day executed, as appointed for the first execution; and seven respited, under colour of a second execution, until her Majesty's pleasure be farther known.[13]

How far into society did the practice of conveyancing extend? In addition to prosecuting the "principal offenders," the commissioners detailed the names of some whose executions were delayed. One was John Markenfeld, a very young man, who was attainted "only to bring his title to his brother's lands (if he have any) to the [Queen]." Another was Henry Johnson. At his marriage he made over his lands to his wife, the daughter of Norton, "so as by his life the Queen shall have his lands, and by his death his wife shall presently have them, according to the estate." The same situation applied to Leonard Metcalf. He had made an estate to his wife, so the queen would lose by his death and win by his life. They also noted that he had very many children and was "a very honest and quiet man, and is generally lamented." Robert Claxton's situation was similar: many children, a quiet man, estate assured to his wife at his marriage.[14]

What the commissioners were finding was a set of conveyances that were not obviously fraudulent or prompted by the current crisis. Rather, the practice was deeply rooted – but perhaps with sound foresight – in local custom. As Barbara Hanawalt has observed, "in manorial courts one frequently reads that a husband and wife reverted their tenement to the lord and made a fine with him so that they could hold it again in joint tenancy. When the husband died, the wife would continue on the tenement for the rest of her life."[15] Custom determined the moral quality of these conveyances; social attitudes defined the limits of fraud. In responding to these cases, the queen, or Cecil for her, replied that Henry Johnson should be spared for his simplicity and John Markenfeld for his youth. As for Leonard Metcalf and some others: "We are nothing moved to spare them, for any respect of the profit that might come to us by their life; and yet knowing not of the manner and circumstance of their offence, how they have therein exceeded in any malice, we will not expressly command that they all shall suffer death." The draft of the letter that exists, with many corrections in Cecil's hand, leaves the decision to the discretion of the commission. There was more correspondence; ultimately they were spared.[16]

Law cases against other conspirators continued for years. About eight hundred people were executed after the victories in January and February. Sixty-six officials and priests were hanged in Durham. More were tracked through the countryside. Westmorland escaped and died abroad after 30 years of exile. Percy's younger brother Henry, who remained loyal, succeeded Percy by virtue of the remainder interest granted to him by a patent dating back to 1557.[17] Surveyors took stock of the earls' lands. Clergy lost their livings. Most of the confiscated estates went to men who accompanied Lord Hunsdon, Lord Clinton, and Sussex.

Despite the quick military solution and the rapid response of the lawyers, the problem of fraudulent conveyances did not go away. Early in the aftermath of the rebellion, on January 6, 1570, Sir Thomas Gargrave, sheriff of Yorkshire, asked Cecil for a bill of parliamentary attainder, "lest the friends of the rebels live still in hope of their pardon." These "friends" would have been those to whom conveyances had been made. When Parliament met, a bill of attainder was read in the upper house on April 1, and a second time on April 25. It was first read in the lower house on May 1, read a second time on May 5, and brought to the Lords with alterations on May 9. After a conference of the two houses on May 10, it was passed on May 15 as 13 Eliz., c. 26.

Probably because law suits arose in the following years between receivers of confiscated lands and those who claimed them as gifts, in 1576 Parliament passed another act directly inspired by the Northern Rebellion, this time "an act for the avoiding of frauds in certain conveyances and assurances made by the late Rebels in the North" (18 Eliz., c. 4). The new statute did not look back. It applied only to conveyances made in the period of two years following the declaration of rebellion on November 7, in the eleventh year of the queen's reign, 1569. The statute hardly raised the issue of fraudulent intent, and it excepted conveyances made for "good and true considerations."

The preamble to the 1576 statute made against the earls states the problem of fraudulent conveyance in typical language but also with candor. After the offenders "had intended and purposed to enter into that their ungodly and devilish practice of Rebellion," they

> did make *diverse secret and fraudulent estates and conveyances* of their lands, tenements, and hereditaments, to the intent thereby to defraud the Queen's Majesty of such forfeiture of their lands, tenements, and hereditaments, as her highness by reason of their several treasons should be entitled to have. (18 Eliz., c. 4; my emphasis)

The statute declares that many of these conveyances remain "secret, and not openly published." The result will be losses to the queen, either of the value of the land or the value of the income from the land. In the first case the queen's agents cannot sell the land because they do not know what land to claim. In the second, they cannot collect rent or the value of the use because they do not know the owners. The statute also implies that eventually this information will become known, but to speed things up and to avoid the expense of special commissions, the statute requires the enrollment of any conveyance made for a period of two years before the outbreak of the rebellion on November 7, 1569. Owners of any property so obtained from the attainted parties had one year to comply or the conveyances would be void. In effect, the statute protected the bona fide purchaser who was not in collusion with the rebels, but bought from someone who was. An original purchaser would be examined to determine if the conveyance was made by fraud and covin. He would also be open to an indictment on the charge and a trial by twelve men. If he were found guilty either way, the conveyance would be void. Finally, the statute fairly says that payment of good consideration would be proof that there was no fraud.

That the 1576 statute was necessary tells us that whatever the origin of 13 Eliz., c. 5, it was insufficient to meet the challenges that arose from the great crisis that preceded its passage. Certainly the 1571 statute was passed in highly charged circumstances. The earls of Westmorland and Northumberland had fled the country. The conquering armies had appropriated their property, sometimes to the detriment of the queen's interest. Pope Pius V issued a bull excommunicating Elizabeth. The duke of Norfolk, who had wavered from his plan to join the rebels and marry the queen of Scots, was under house arrest. Caught up in the Ridolphi plot, he would be executed the following year. Cecil was appointing commissions that put pressure on recusants to conform. Restricted by the oath of allegiance, no Catholics sat in Parliament. In his opening speech, the Lord Keeper Nicholas Bacon explicitly said that the purpose of the meeting was to provide means to pay the costs of the recent rebellion in the North.

Although the Northern Rebellion provides powerful circumstantial evidence that 13 Eliz., c. 5 should have been designed to void conveyances by the political enemies of the state, the passage of 13 Eliz., c. 26 and 18 Eliz., c. 4 undercuts any conviction that the earlier statute was framed to fit the aftermath of the rebellion. The problem, for one who sees the earlier statute as solely political, is that despite a wealth of parliamentary history and records of the forfeitures in the Calendar of State papers, there is very little to relate passage of the statute to the rising of the Catholic North. These missing links indicate the nature of the culture that wrote and considered this influential law. There was enormous resistance to passing a law against a practice in which so many were engaged.

The Parliament of 1571

For whatever reason Cecil – by this point, Lord Burghley – sent Parliament a bill on fraudulent conveyances in 1571, members of the House of Commons did not perceive it politically. This is not to say that anti-Catholic feeling did not run high. The parliament opened with Nicholas Bacon's attack on the "Romanish rebels" whose suppression had cost the queen so much money. Most of the debate recorded by an anonymous diarist in the Commons concerned aspects of the Church. The vocal Puritans were interested in Church organization, simony, the text of the Book of Common Prayer, and rules for attending divine service. But within the confines of debate between the Puritans and the supporters of the Anglican settlement, two additional preoccupations can be discerned.

In 1571, Parliament showed an inordinate interest, first, in the administration of laws, and second, in individual debt. Their first concern, the general problem of legal administration, takes some of the edge off the penalty clause that was Glenn's main argument for the political character of 13 Eliz., c. 5. Although there is no record of debate on this aspect of the bill, in a related issue some members argued against requiring bishops to punish non-attendance at church. Their debate reveals a distaste for assigning anyone to enforce penalty laws, "a device but of late brought in, in the time of King Henry the Eight, the first year of his Reign ... [which] showed the Evils and inconveniences that did grow by these men's doings; wherein no reformation was sought."[18] It was the sort of employment that would appeal to the worst sort of men, those out for "private gain," who would create a system prone to "evils and inconvenience."[19] Such was the attitude of the men who allowed the penalty provision to remain in 13 Eliz., c. 5, or tampered with it till it made little sense.

The second parliamentary concern during the 1571 debates was the problem of insolvent individuals. A Mr. Dalton, for example, wanted an exception made for those who could not attend divine service "for fear of debts."[20] He also demanded that the statute that became 13 Eliz., c. 5 be extended to include heriots (services required of a tenant by a landlord), a concern that in itself may explain the addition of the phrase "and others."[21]

Mr. Dalton's interest in heriots supports other evidence, supplied by the other statutes passed that year, that 13 Eliz., c. 5 actually represents an important stage in the separation of the interests of the state from those of creditors. The statutes passed in 1571 fall into two groups, one concerned with politics, the other group focusing on administration and commerce. The first three statutes are political. 13 Eliz., c. 1 defines certain acts, such as making war against the queen or proclaiming her a heretic, as high treason. It includes a provision, aimed at the queen of Scots, that specifically excludes from the succession any pretenders to the throne during the queen's lifetime. The second statute reacts to the Pope's excommunication of the queen by forbidding the publication of writings from Rome. Next, 13 Eliz., c. 3 establishes a presumption of fraud against uses created to provide income for overseas fugitives. The Parliament also passed acts of attainder against the earls of Northumberland and Westmorland and their followers.

It is hard to imagine why, if 13 Eliz., c. 5, was intended "solely," as Glenn put it, to protect the queen's interest, it did not declare itself openly. The first two statutes, on high treason and papal bulls, are not reluctant to speak the name of the queen or state her interests. The third statute, aimed at a specific form of fraudulent conveyance, the use, practiced by those who fled overseas, arose from the queen's power to control emigration.[22]

The second – and larger – group of bills passed in 1571, moreover, is about matters of administration and commerce, and 13 Eliz., c. 5 should probably be placed in this group, despite its similarity to the overseas fugitives bill. The fourth bill, for example, limited the time revenue collectors could sit on money owed to the Crown. The debate over 13 Eliz., c. 4 is instructive as background to the fraudulent conveyance bill that followed, since it offers a glimpse of the workings of those on whom the queen depended to collect revenue. Nicholas Bacon, the Lord Keeper, exhorted Parliament that the heart of the law is efficient administration (*"anima legis est executio"*).[23] John Popham – who represented Bristol and was probably the man who went on to become chief justice of the King's Bench – joined the debate on the problem of collecting subsidies by declaiming against the abuse of treasurers of the Crown. Many had "in their hands great masses of money, with the which either they themselves or some others their friends do purchase lands to their own use and after become bankrupts, and so cause or practise an enstallment of their debts, as of late some one hath stalled a debt of thirty thousand pounds, which occasioned the lack in the prince's coffers."[24] Mr. Sanpole, a member of Lincoln's Inn, added that people were unwilling to pay a subsidy when they saw the abuse of collectors, who keep the Crown's money for a whole year or "convert it to their own use, perhaps never to satisfy the same."[25] Government collectors and officials – who included military paymasters – used the queen's money to buy estates in their own names or those of their family or friends for their own "use, profit, or behoof." Despite the clamor, however, the practice remained common in England for several centuries.[26]

The sixth statute passed in 1571 affirmed the validity of letters patent and is no more political than a similar bill that had been passed under Queen Mary. The seventh was the statute of bankruptcy, and since it applied only to merchants, its commercial character is obvious. The same can be said for the following statute on usury, which limited interest to 10 per cent. Other subjects included sewers, navigation, church ministers, and leases of benefices; tillage; the traditional matter of bow staves, caps, and street repairs; and the transport of plate and grain within and without the realm. Finally, there was a continuance bill, the act of subsidy for which the Parliament was called in the first place, and a pardon from the queen for certain offenses. None of these bills was political.

Within the majority group of administrative and commercial bills it is possible to pair 13 Eliz., c. 5, "an act against fraudulent deeds, gifts, and alienations" with 13 Eliz., c. 10, "an act of frauds defeating remedies for dilapidations." The former is said to be for the benefit of creditors; the latter for the benefit of successors to ecclesiastical property, who could be defeated by "deeds of gift, colourable alienations, and other conveyances of like effect."[27] In fact, each of the 1571 statutes that contain provisions against fraudulent conveyances targets a different group – government collectors, overseas fugitives, ecclesiastical tenants. It follows that 13 Eliz., c. 5 may also be taken at face value, and that it is aimed at debtors, particularly commercial debtors.

Like most legislation, 13 Eliz., c. 5 originated in the Queen's Council, but what we read is a legislative compromise. Whether Cecil was seeking more revenue or another opportunity to persecute recusants is lost in the process. For there was both support for and opposition to laws against fraudulent conveyances. Everything – the issue of sanctuary, the wording of the statute, the 1566 version of the law that was reintroduced in 1571, the vagueness of the phrase "and others" when the Crown had no reason to hide its interest in forfeitures, the concern of the 1571 Parliament with administrative matters – points to the conclusion that the statute was only political insofar as the interest of the Crown coincided with that of creditors in general. Everything, that is, except the temper of the times, and on this score, Glenn may well point us in a fruitful direction, as we turn to Sidney, Spenser, and Shakespeare.

Although the interests of the queen and her ministers were not always coterminous with the welfare of her subjects, a telling moment in Holinshed's *Chronicles* for 1571 reveals what the queen was doing just before Parliament opened that year. It occurs just after Holinshed's long and brutal account of the Northern Rebellion and the English reprisals that extended afterwards into Scotland, followed by a series of disastrous floods in the autumn of 1570. On January 23, 1571, the queen went past the London Bourse and entered the establishment of Sir Thomas Gresham to dine. Gresham was a wealthy London financier, a man with a score of years experience serving the Crown, and the chief advisor on currency devaluations. His grasp of the latter area produced what we know as Gresham's law, which says that good money drives bad money out of circulation. On this occasion, his invitation to the queen was ceremonial. After dinner Elizabeth toured the center of London's financial activities. Then "by an herald and a trumpet" she renamed the building, which Gresham had constructed on the model of central markets in Europe, the Royal Exchange.[28] The change reflected the same growing needs that, arguably, also prompted the passage of 13 Eliz., c. 5, to protect creditors.

As a product of competing interests, the development of fraudulent conveyancing laws indicates not just the solution to a legal problem but the attitudes of society and its people. Shakespeare was 5 years old as armies moved north in a campaign against names – Westmorland, Northumberland – that would figure in the history plays he composed about the reigns of Richard II, Henry IV, and Henry V. Hunsdon, as Lord Chamberlain, would become his patron. Spenser was in his first year at Cambridge as the soldiers marched. Philip Sidney was at Oxford, occasionally writing obsequious letters to Cecil.[29] In the next chapter we will start with a bill of attainder that Sir Henry Sidney wrote in Ireland in 1569, one that failed to mention fraudulent conveyances, and then consider the implications of that absence to his famous son's literary work.

Notes

1. See "Origins and Present Status of the Law Against Fraudulent Conveyances," in Garrard Glenn, *Fraudulent Conveyances and Preferences*, 2nd ed., 2 vols. (New York: Baker, Voorhis, 1940), pp. 77–103.
2. "A bill for the enlarging of a statute made xiii Reginae Elizabethae that the same may also extend to such conveyance as be not of record" so that "privy covenants" do not defeat any sale after made bona fide. See T. E. Hartley, *Proceedings in the Parliaments of Elizabeth I*, 3 vols. (Leicester, 1981), 1: 343. It should be noted that the phrase "of no great moment" was applied by the diarists to many, many bills, not just the bankruptcy statute.
3. G. R. Elton, *The Parliament of England 1559–1581* (Cambridge: Cambridge University Press, 1986), p. 74. (Elton mistakenly refers to 13 Eliz., c. 5 as a bankruptcy statute.)
4. Neville Williams, *Thomas Howard Fourth Duke of Norfolk* (London: Barrie and Rockliff, 1964), p. 119.
5. Ibid., pp. 119–120.
6. According to R. R. Reid, "The Rebellion of the Earls, 1569," *Transactions of the Royal*

Historical Society 20 (1906): 171–203, Northumberland's discontent had grown from a lawsuit by the queen, in which she demanded mineral rights from his property. A year before the rebellion, Sussex wrote to William Cecil, the Lord Treasurer, that he meant to labor "to end the greatest causes by arbitrament, as proceeding of law breeds in these parts a grounded hatred between the parties." This quotation, and the account that follows in the text, is drawn mainly from letters summarized in the *Calendar of State Papers ... Elizabeth*, ed. Robert Lemon and Mary Anne Everett Green, 12 vols. (London, 1856–72), *1566-1579*. The suit is analyzed along Ramist lines by Abraham Fraunce in his *Lawyer's Logic* (1588).

7   Sir Cuthbert Sharp, *Memorials of the Rebellion of 1569* (London: Nichols, 1841), p. 51.
8   Holinshed, Ralph, *Holinshed's Chronicles of England, Scotland, and Ireland* (1588; New York: AMS Press, 1965), 4: 236–237.
9   Sharp, *Memorials of the Rebellion of 1569*, p. 121
10 Ibid., p. 122.
11 There are listed 113 names of minor note and then the "meaner sort," of yeomen, tradesmen, etc. See Sharp, *Memorials of the Rebellion of 1569*, p. 128.
12 Sir Edward Coke, *The First Part of the Institutes of the Laws of England* (London, 1670), p. 13.
13 Sharp, *Memorial of the Rebellion of 1569*, p. 225 (my emphasis). By January 6, Sussex had sent Cecil a list of the principal landowners and their worth: Westmorland's estates were valued at £534; Northumberland was worth only £39; Cuthbert Nevell, £3. Of the 20 names, most had fled. In Darlington Ward, 481 people had joined the rebellion. Out of a total of 794 names of all ranks, 194 were to be executed. There were other lists for other areas. From the payment schedule of the defenders of Barnard Castle, which lists many soldiers by rank and wage, we learn that George Bowes received 12s per diem; his lieutenant, 6s; 180 light horsemen were paid 16d per day each for 27 days. The cost of 100 soldiers for 16 days was £130. What strikes one is the disproportion between the small value of the property and the huge cost of the military operation, as Sussex requested thousands of pounds to pay soldiers. Taking property from rebels may have profited certain lords and soldiers, but not the queen, except indirectly as her followers were rewarded.
14 Sharp, *Memorials of the Rebellion of 1569*, pp. 226–227.
15 Barbara A. Hanawalt, *The Ties That Bound: Peasant Families in Medieval England* (New York: Oxford University Press, 1986), p. 221.
16 Sharp, *Memorials of the Rebellion of 1569*, p. 228.
17 Ibid., p. 358.
18 From Thomas Cromwell's journal, printed in Hartley, *Proceedings*, 1: 358.
19 See the summary of the Anonymous Journal in Sir Simonds D'Ewes, *A Compleat Journal of the Votes, Speeches and Debates, Both of the House of Lords and House of Commons Throughout the Whole Reign of Queen Elizabeth of Glorious Memory* (London, 1693; rpt. Wilmington, Del.: Scholarly Resources, 1974), p. 157; also in Hartley, *Proceedings*, 1: 201; and J. E. Neale, *Elizabeth I and Her Parliaments, 1559–1581* (New York: St. Martin's Press, 1958), p. 196.
20 Hartley, *Proceedings*, 1: 206.
21 His remarks can be found in D'Ewes, *A Compleat Journal*, p. 160.
22 According to the statute 13 Eliz., c. 3, departure from the realm with license from the queen is sufficient evidence for fugitives to lose those profits during their lives, as well as all their goods and chattels. The statute provides a penalty for the case where an offender "by fraud, collusion, and covin" makes secret provisions before leaving that his lands would be held to his use, thereby providing him with income. The statute further provides that commissioners and juries of 12 men investigate conveyances made up to two years

before a fugitive left the realm and report their results to the Exchequer. Those who hold the land to the use of a fugitive are liable to a fine of £20 and imprisonment. The statute does not apply to merchants. It ends with two provisions of mercy. First, in the case of someone who stays overseas beyond the term prescribed by his license, who never declares an "evil mind" toward the queen by word, writing, or open act, the Lord Chancellor or the Lord Keeper have authority to allot for the use of his "desolate wife and children" a "reasonable portion of the lands of such fugitive, not under the fourth part, nor above third part." Second, a fugitive who returns, submits to the queen, and receives Holy Communion "shall be restored to all his lands, and the profits thereof, which before was forfeited by virtue of this act." The provisions are very similar not to 13 Eliz., c. 5, but to 18 Eliz., c. 4, which, we have seen, specifically targeted the Northern rebels.

23   Hartley, *Proceedings*, 1: 199.
24   Ibid., 1: 202. His words entered the statute almost intact. He did not mention whom he had in mind, but it may have been Henry Sidney, then governor of Ireland.
25   Ibid., 1: 203.
26   The statute regularly pairs the terms "arrearages and debt," which may in part account for the phrase "creditors and others" in 13 Eliz., c. 5, where the "others" would be people owed money outside of a definite time frame, as occurs when taxes are collected somewhat irregularly. The solution the statute proposes is that any lands, tenements, or hereditaments so purchased or conveyed be seized and sold to cover the arrearage or debt. The bill was aimed at lands worth over £300 and not at goods and chattels. Sheriffs and escheators were excepted from its provisions. Bona fide purchases and conveyances made without intent to defraud were also excepted. The mechanism for enforcing the act was the commission, which would question defendants and make rulings. Where they determined that there was a "fraudulent conveyance," the defendant could "have his or their lawful traverse," that is, the right to appeal the decision and recover land "out of the prince's hands." For an example of this process, see Pimb's Case, cited in Chapter 4.
27   The bill allows suit against the receiver of the grant for the value of the property taken. It also limited long leases to 21 years.
28   Holinshed, *Chronicles*, 4: 258.
29   He signs his letter of July, 1569, "Tibi Obsequentissimus Philippus Sidneius." See *The Works of Sir Philip Sidney*, ed. Albert Feuillerat, 4 vols. (Cambridge: The University Press, 1962), 3: 76.

Chapter 3

Carried Away in Arcadia

> She hath allowed me to be one of that most noble Order of the Garter whereof I have been a Companion, and I am sure the poorest Companion that ever was, now full nineteen years.
>
> Sir Henry Sidney[1]

Following the Northern Rebellion of 1569, Parliament passed a bill of attainder against the earls of Westmorland and Northumberland and several dozen followers. It contained a savings clause and several rudimentary provisions against fraudulent conveyances. Northumberland's estate was preserved for his brother Henry Percy, who was assured of any properties that might pass to him by "any gift, grant or letters patent whatsoever heretofore made" (13 Eliz., c. 16). Since these grants included a patent of 1557 issued by Philip and Mary, Henry was duly rewarded for his loyalty. The other provisions worked somewhat negatively: The bill said that all conveyances made "before the said several treasons by the said several offenders" were valid for everyone except those people attainted. The statute presumed that a conveyance made to a conspirator was invalid, but one made to anyone else should stand. Five years later 18 Eliz., c. 4 specifically addressed "frauds in certain conveyances and assurances made by the late Rebels in the North." It enhanced the administration of the law by calling for registration within two years of any property conveyed from the rebels, thereby allowing the justice system to consider more deeply the possibility of fraud.

By contrast, Sir Henry Sidney drafted a bill of attainder against Shane O'Neill in Ireland in 1569 that did not include any provisions for fraudulent conveyances. The bill only referred, in a general way, to English tradition on the subject of high treason: "And the person or persons therein offending, and being attainted, shall suffer and sustain such pains of death, forfeitures of lands, and goods, as in cases of high treason by the laws of this realm hath been accustomed and used" (11 Eliz., c. 1 [Ireland]). [2]

The lack of provision against fraudulent conveyancing in Sidney's Irish statute gives us insight into the ambivalent attitudes of society towards the practice. This ambivalence reveals itself in the course of Sidney's several tenures as Lord Deputy of Ireland, in his family's relationship to the Crown, and in the artistic practice of his talented son Philip, particularly in his prose masterpiece, the *Arcadia*. Both the father and son were exemplars of a certain moral rectitude, or even fastidiousness, and both professed to be devoted servants of the queen, yet each in his own sphere recognized the moral dissembling of even virtuous people. For Henry Sidney there was a gap between his regal conception of himself as governor of Ireland and his actual performance on the ground. For Philip, whose tenuous financial position gives point to the images of debt found in his poetry, there is a certain dissonance between the complex conceptions his imagination was able to entertain and what many critics have seen as the inability of his fiction to accommodate his vision.

Henry Sidney as Draftsman

Like so many other newly important families in sixteenth-century England, the Sidneys benefited from royal favor, marriage, and Henry VIII's seizure of church properties. Henry Sidney's father William fought at Flodden Field in 1513. "On the dissolution of the monasteries he obtained large grants of land in Kent and Sussex, and, at Edward's birth, was appointed tutor, chamberlain and steward to the household of the Prince."[3] Sidney was born in 1529, eight years before King Edward VI, with whom he lived as a companion and from whom he received various estates. As Edward was only 10 when he became king in 1547, the country was governed by a council dominated by two regents, Edward's uncle Edward Seymour, soon to become duke of Somerset, and John Dudley, earl of Warwick, who would later be duke of Northumberland. In 1551 Henry Sidney married Northumberland's daughter, the Lady Mary Dudley. After vying with Somerset for several years, Northumberland fabricated charges and had him executed in 1552. It is obvious which side the Sidneys were on. Forfeitures followed Somerset's treason, and William Sidney was granted Penshurst, which had to belonged to Sir Ralph Fane, a Somerset supporter.

The cultural scene in which our fraudulent conveyancing laws developed was one of dizzying exchanges of property, where royal gifts were expected and fought for; nonetheless, an invisible line separated courtship from fraud. William died at Penshurst a few months before Edward VI's own death, on July 6, 1553, just over a year before Philip Sidney was born on the family's new estate. While the young king was ill, Northumberland forced him to compose a will that overlooked his sisters Mary and Elizabeth and passed his royal inheritance to Jane Grey, the wife of Northumberland's son Guildford Dudley. It might be too much to say that Northumberland's plot failed because the English people recognized that a testamentary provision produced by a dying man under duress was a form of fraud and the conveyance of property could be rescinded by a court. Northumberland had enemies, Mary had strength, and so the plot failed. But Northumberland had also crossed a line that separated acceptable from unacceptable conduct. No one supported him.

We are told that Queen Mary was not vindictive. Of 60 people involved in the plot, only seven went to trial and only Lady Jane Grey, Northumberland, Guildford Dudley, and two others were executed.[4] But it seems just as likely that Mary was able to accept a certain amount of reprehensible behavior because English society had a tolerance for it. Henry Sidney was a beneficiary of this ambivalence. He was the first to receive a pardon, although he had signed his name as a witness to "the illegal instrument by which Edward VI was made to set aside the Act of 1533 and transfer the succession from his father's daughters to the descendants of his father's sister."[5] The explanation given is that the queen had an affectionate memory of Henry's sisters Mabel and Elizabeth Sidney, who had died in her service.[6] His escape from a traitor's death at the age of 24 is the sort of experience that might explain his lack of support for fraudulent conveyancing laws. We must keep in mind Henry's personal attitudes as we review his political role as an enforcer of Crown policies in Ireland for the next 30 years. He knew what it meant to be at the mercy of the Crown and of creditors.

The aftermath of the failed Northumberland plot involved Sidney in yet another situation where only the practices of the culture could determine the line between asset management and fraud. The duke's wife had also been pardoned, although she had played a key role in trying to convince Queen Jane to nominate Guildford as King. But the attainders that followed Northumberland's execution meant that members of his family could not inherit property, since his treason had corrupted their blood. The duchess soon realized she needed to change her will to avoid leaving her children as her heirs in the event she died. "My three sons, and my brother Sir Andrew Dudley, standing presently attainted of High Treason," she wrote at the time, "my said will cannot take place according to my meaning in all things." She therefore had a new will drawn up, a form of conveyance that would protect her property by keeping it out of the reach of the royal treasury in the event of her death. She left everything to other heirs or in the hands of several executors, including Henry Sidney. Eventually her children fought under Pembroke at the siege of St. Quentin and, as a reward, had their blood restored. In the meantime the success of the conveyance depended on the trustworthiness of the new beneficiaries. It was prudent asset management by the duchess, buttressed by the loyalty of Henry Sidney, that saved the family patrimony.[7]

Despite his own pardon, within a few years Sidney felt that he was not "liked as I had been," and he sought service abroad. We learn his attitude, and so much else about his several tenures in Ireland, from a long letter that he wrote to Sir Francis Walsingham in 1583, when, desperate for money, he was negotiating his son's marriage to Walsingham's daughter. Ireland offered opportunities for advancement. Service abroad, moreover, was also a recognized way of defeating creditors, like taking sanctuary or being elected to Parliament. Sir Henry may not have been in debt yet, but he soon would be. Penshurst was expensive to maintain, and Sidney's involvement with government finances would give him other, more complicated opportunities to spend, if not reap.

Sidney was appointed vice-treasurer and receiver-general in April 1556, in the service of his brother-in-law Sir Thomas Radcliffe, Viscount Fitzwalter (named earl of Sussex in 1557), who was concurrently appointed Lord Deputy. Historians have regarded the viceroyalty of Sussex (the same man who later suppressed the Northern Rebellion) "as a turning-point in Anglo-Irish relations because of his association with the policy of plantation – highlighted in the parliamentary statutes." The sixth act of the Roll of Sussex's parliament (which ended March 10, 1558) affirmed the right of the king and queen to authorize the Lord Deputy to grant estates or lease to English and Irish subjects in certain counties where lands had been taken from dispossessed rebels driven out by Sussex, with exemptions for lands of the earl of Kildare and some ecclesiastics.[8] There were rumors about the idea of an English plantation in the northeast, and on Sussex's advice, royal approval was given for plans for an English settlement on the eastern shores of Lough Neagh. Sidney tried to build up an estate in the Lecale area (it was known as Lough Sidney for a while), but he did not succeed.[9] Although these arrangements seem similar to the later English policy of plantations, at least one historian believes that England's efforts, spearheaded by Sussex, are better seen as a part of an Anglo-Spanish alliance, based on Spain's colonial enterprises in the New World. In light of the association of fraudulent conveyance laws with English policies in Ireland, the subject of the following chapter on Spenser, it is interesting that English land policies and pressures were not at this time related to religion. They could not be, since England was Catholic. The main enemy in Ireland, from the English point of view, were the Scots.

After the death of Mary and the elevation of Elizabeth in November 1558, English and Spanish interests diverged. Sussex had been brought back to England in the crisis over the loss of Calais, while Sidney, at first the temporary head of government, was named Lord Justice of Ireland on December 13, 1558.[10] Once in office, Elizabeth restored Sussex as Lord Deputy on August 30, 1559. She sent instructions that he and Sidney peruse the laws passed by Parliament, confer with the Irish Council, "and upon determination which of them may seem meet, for that realm, either as they be or with other alteration."[11] The Irish Council was to consider a "variety of cases." The members included the earls of Kildare, Ormonde, Desmond, and Clanricard, as well as Sussex, Fitzwilliams, Stanley, and Sidney. As in England, membership on the Council was to a large extent determined by the same rationale that underlay the English jury system: it consisted of people who would already have knowledge about the affairs before it.

From the beginning the queen was concerned with the disposition of property, and she called for a new survey because "extraordinary leases have been made upon surmised and corrupt values."[12] She also faced, right away, the problem of Tanastry, the custom of Ireland by which land passed not to the oldest surviving male, but to any powerful, often pre-selected, member of a clan. The question was broached with regard to O'Neill, whose bill of attainder Sidney composed 10 years later, "Whether might not O'Neill, before the country was made an earldom, by a rebellion forfeit the country to the Prince?" An objection was offered that O'Neill could forfeit no more than the interest he had during his life. After his death, it was the right of the country to make a new O'Neill. The queen's advisers countered that "O'Neill's rebellion was not only the offense in his own person, but all his captains, gallowglass, and kerne aided him in the rebellion, and so it was a rebellion of all the people of the country; and so the rebellion of the whole made a forfeiture of the whole." From the English perspective, the whole system of Tanastry operated like some nightmare form of fraudulent conveyance to keep land from the grasp of the Crown. But the English forces were not in control on the ground and the issue remained unsettled, even as the queen pressed Sidney to attaint O'Neill. On June 11, 1567, she wrote to Sidney of her desire to hear of the extirpation of Shane O'Neill and her resolve to plant people in Ulster.[13] Two years later Sidney gave the queen what she wanted.

The purpose of a bill of attainder is to confirm the forfeiture of property that follows from treason and by the doctrine of corruption of the blood, to cut off future claims by would-be heirs. Today in the USA the Constitution prohibits bills of attainder (Article I, section 9 [3]), and even in cases of treason, no attainder "shall work Corruption of Blood, or Forfeiture except during the Life of the Person attainted" (Article III, section 3 [2]). Spenser complained that the Irish practiced fraudulent conveyance to cheat the queen of the benefit of their attainder. Sidney, however, faced a preliminary, or threshold issue. In England all land had been held from the Crown since the time of William the Conqueror, and on that basis, the queen had a right to forfeitures. But William had not conquered Ireland; therefore Sidney first had to establish the queen's right to forfeitures. His attempt to do so has notable literary features.

Sidney's bill begins with a series of rhetorical and historical accounts designed to assert England's dominion over Ireland. Starting with an ethical appeal, which included promotion of himself as an expert on the subject, Sidney conjures a vision of England's past glory in Ireland, when there were "populous, rich and well governed regions, welthy subjects, and beautifull cities and towns," before the "iniquitie of times" impaired them until they were "utterly lost" (p. 309).[14] He himself appears in the law, as "your Majestie's Deputy Sir Henry Sidney." He blames Ireland's destruction on "insurrections, rebellions & horrible treasons" and offers his services to prove that the queen has title to the "dominion and territories of Ulster as a foundation layd for your highness to plant and dispose the same" (p. 310).

Sidney's literary flair continues to characterize his law as he justifies the queen's rightful intervention as an attempt to save the land from "so great and cruell a tyrant," for O'Neill is a "vile, abhominable, and sedicious person" (p. 310) whose title is based on the murder of his predecessor and usurpation of his lands. His depredations were stopped only by "the diligent ministery, actuall war, and politique persecutions of your Majestie's painefull, prudent, and well disposed Deputie Sir Henry Sidney, knight of your honourable order, a man most fit for the reformation of this your realm" (p. 313). Having blackened O'Neill's character and promoted his own, Sidney then proves that the queen should have "prioritie of title to hold and possess anie part of the dominion or territories of Ulster" (p. 315).

A notable scholar, Sidney ransacked books in Latin, English, and Irish to establish various claims and ancient titles that justify English rule. On the theory that if it is written, it must be true, he starts with the notion that a former king of Britain made a grant of the land to the progenitors of the Irish, who were then living in "Biscan," the area around Bayonne in France.[15] Later, according to Geraldus Cambrensis, Henry II established dominion, first when he received Dermot MacMurrough, prince of Leinster, and again when the Irish kings submitted to him in 1162, after Henry landed in Ireland. Henry then gave the country to his youngest son John, who "came in person into Ireland, and held the same land" (p. 316). The conquest was confirmed by the clergy who gathered at Armagh and declared that English rule was "decreed and deemed" due to the "sin of the people of the land." Yet another title derived from Richard II, who landed in Dublin and other places and received the voluntary submissions of many Irish captains. Finally, the people themselves accepted English rule because they were "persuaded by the just and gracious dealing of your deputie here" (p. 317). That deputy, of course, was Sidney himself.

The Irish statute Sidney composed is not a little reminiscent of the pompous style parodied by Henry's son in the *Arcadia* when Philanax, also a royal deputy, prosecutes Musidorus and Pyrocles, the heroes of the story, charged with attempted rape and murder.[16] Both Philanax and the preamble are overly prolix. The preliminaries to the statute are far from finished when Sidney begins to list the various occasions under Henry VIII when, under the policy of surrender and regrant, the inhabitants of Ireland exchanged their customary tenures for English titles to property (p. 319). There is a little digression as Sidney praises himself for abolishing "coign and livery" (the practice of quartering men and beasts instead of paying regular rents). Then he hits the main theme of the statute, the forfeiture of the estates of O'Neill and his "adherents" to the queen that follows from his attainder for treason (pp. 321–322).

With its literary flare, Sidney's bill against O'Neill contrasts with an earlier, more workmanlike bill, 28 Henry VIII, c. 1 (Ireland), that attainted the earl of Kildare. That bill negatively exempted from Kildare's forfeitures "any sale, gift or payment without any fraud, deceit or collusion ... made to or by the said Earl" (p. 83). A long-arm provision in the same bill barred fraudulent conveyances of Irish property by anyone convicted of treason in England. It again used a negative formulation, exempting "any sale, gift, or payment without any fraud, deceit or collusion had not been made to or by them or any of them" (p. 86). The bill also voided trusts "conveyed from any of the said persons attaynted or to be attaynted in forme aforesaid, sithence or after the day of the offences" (p. 87). This earlier statute gave Sidney a precedent for including fraudulent conveyance language when he composed his own bill of attainder, but Sidney left it out. It is possible that Sidney relied on an earlier 1310 law against fraudulent conveyance in Ireland, but I do not think so.[17] He preferred to tell a story about an evil man and legitimate justice.

The story Sidney did not buy into was one about the evils of avoiding creditors. A few years later, in 1571, he sat as a Member of Parliament that passed 13 Eliz., c. 5, against fraudulent conveyances to defeat creditors and others, as well as the bill against fraudulent conveyances by fugitives and the bill against clergy who sought to avoid responsibility for repairing property. We have no record of his votes on these measures. But Sidney was very possibly the target of a bill aimed at debtors to the state. Sir John Popham, the member for Bristol, introduced the bill that became 13 Eliz., c. 4, an act to make people in his position "liable for the payment of their debts."[18] He is probably the same Popham who later decided Twyne's Case and who, moreover, three years before that heard Giles Allen's suit against Cuthbert Burbage for tearing down the Theatre.[19] According to the Anonymous Journal, Popham was assisted by Doctors Lewes and Yale, who were sent from the Lords with a bill to this effect, "that treasurors, receavers, collectors, *etc.* should not convert her Majestie's money to their own private use, nor wilfully to consume the same, which if they should do then that offence to be felony, provided that the debt must be above 300^{li}." There follows, as Lewes and Yale appeared in Parliament for the government like two attack dogs, the legal French that is the true sign of the English common lawyer: "*Enter auters le cause de ceo est le faite de le Sor Treasurer per 30000^{li} enstall et ceo fait discovert per Brinigam de Ireland per grand parte*" (among other reasons for the bill was the £30 000 due from the Treasurer of Ireland, as reported by Bingham) (p. 218). "The specific reference appears to be to Sir Henry Sidney," notes T. E. Hartley, the editor of the Parliamentary debates.[20] We have no record of a comment on this embarrassment, but Sidney would have blamed his enemies for it, not his own malfeasance.

Owing money to the government was not an untypical situation for government treasurers and collectors of subsidies at the time, or later. Officials were regularly able to spend government cash before accounting for it. It was not uncommon, therefore, for them to die in debt. J. E. Neale explains why:

> Holders of Crown moneys seem to have postponed accounting as long as possible, meanwhile employing the cash in their private transactions.... The Crown might be said to

have been acting, willy-nilly, as a benevolent, non-interest-charging, all-risks-bearing bank to supply its officials and others with capital. Some – perhaps most – of those cases of public servants dying heavily in debt to the Queen, which have drawn from posterity many tears and barbed criticism of royal ingratitude, derive from this type of fraud.[21]

Henry Sidney would seem to fit Neale's analysis, yet he would have justified his spending. In his 1583 letter to Walsingham, he complains that he has three sons and "if I dy tomorrow next I should leave them worse than my father left me by £20,000, and I am now fifty-four yeres of age, toothless and trembling, being five thousand pounds in debt, yea and £30,000 worse than I was at the death of my most deere king and master, King Edward the VIth."[22] Sidney regarded a regal presence, which cost money, as a way of asserting English power.

Like other office holders, Sidney believed he put to good use the funds he withheld from the queen. During his years in Ireland he led military expeditions and rode circuit in inclement weather: "and how pleasant a lief it is that tyme of the yere, with hunger, and after sore travaill to harbour long and cold nights in cabins made of boughs, and covered with grass, I leave to your indifferent judgement," he told Walsingham.[23] When he was not sleeping under a bush in the rain, Sidney preferred to travel in style, with a standard bearer, trumpeter, surgeon, horsemen, ordnance, and foot soldiers. He had a chair of state set in a regal tent that he used to receive homage from Irish lords. In 1566 he spent £13 000 in half a year. His phrasing in a letter to the queen indicates that he regarded his expenses as minimal, since he traveled with "mine own household, *but* fifty English spears, fifty English shot, and fifty gallowglass; these footmen I always kept about me in my journey as my guard."[24] However he handled the queen's money, Sidney regarded himself as an upright servant.

It is hard to say where Sidney drew the line in managing or manipulating his assets to avoid creditors. During years when the great lawyers of the realm like Popham, Egerton, and Coke were amassing fortunes in real estate, Sidney seems not to have increased his holdings in land. He ran an ironworks, but in 1572 he turned down an offer of a barony from the queen because he did not believe he had the resources to support the spending the position would require. His refusal is all the more notable, since an earl could not be sued for debt. In 1583 he assured Walsingham that he expected to find himself in debtors' prison and forced to sell lands. Yet the motive behind the letter, which by certain phrasings and the circumstances one suspects Philip had a hand in composing, is to excuse Henry from making a substantial settlement to benefit Walsingham's daughter, who was to marry his son.[25] Marriage was an honorable way for a gentleman to finance himself, and despite the appearance that Sidney engaged in the endemic accounting frauds of the times, there is more than a little truth to his reputation for honor and honesty.

Although Sidney's own ambivalent position, typical of the times – as a man who had been under the shadow of treason, and one whom the queen allowed to slide into debt – may account for his omission of a fraudulent conveyancing clause from the 1569 bill of attainder against Shane O'Neill, he may also have regarded the provision as superfluous, since it was only with difficulty that English law reached O'Neill's northern territories. A non-concept within the system of Tanastry, fraudulent conveyancing was viable only within the framework of English law. A law against the practice required English judges to enforce it, and the courts in Ireland were ill equipped for the task. Desmond's fraudulent conveyance in 1574 was the exception that proved the rule: he held his lands according to English custom and had cutting-edge legal advice. (He was also regarded as a friend of Sidney, who suffered at court because he did not like Desmond's main enemy, the earl of Ormonde.) Such circumstantial evidence again supports the view that Sidney regarded conveyancing as a sign of prudence, not fraud. Yet even he seems to have known the ways of the world.

We can see that Sidney was not ignorant of the need for laws against land fraud (which usually involved some form of fraudulent conveyancing) when, two years later, he praised the Queen's surveyor, Lancelot Alford, for his work on the escheated lands of Condon of Armoy, who had been attainted. Sidney claimed that "More has been done for the recovery of the Queen's decayed rents and embezzled lands than was ever done in the memory of man." In Munster, he said, two professors of law, James Dowdall and Nicholas Welshe, had done as much as "was to be looked for of men of their quality, wanting men of war and force to execute their orders, arrests, and decrees." On April 27, 1576, Sidney asked the Queen for 300 horse, 700 soldiers, and, he added, three lawyers to be Chief Justices of three principal and common benches and one more to be Attorney General. His request was turned down. On July 6, the month Philip came to visit, the Privy Council answered that "such opinion is conceived of the barbarism there, and so small are the gains and entertainment there, as at all times when any have been chosen to be sent thither, they do ever make some means to her Majesty whereby they may be stayed." [26] Jurisdiction, a good case for the Queen's prerogative, and force were more useful for recovering forfeitures than the courts.

It would be too much to say that Henry Sidney sympathized with Shane O'Neill. But he knew what it was to owe money. Always pressed, in 1578, he was embarrassed to be recalled from Ireland. His son Philip sent him advice on how to procrastinate, to give his friends, especially his wife, time to work. But Philip himself, it seems, had to carry his father's accounts to the queen.[27]

Philip Sidney's Debts

Whether Philip Sidney inherited his father's ideal of public service or his disinterest in accumulating wealth, his finances were never certain. He borrowed money during his grand tour (1572–1575), and Edward Wotton – who shared riding lessons with Sidney while they were at the emperor's court in Prague – witnessed the deed in which Sidney borrowed the life-savings of Hubert Languet.[28] In his letter to the queen advising her not to marry, Sidney makes the otherwise odd comment that papists are often rich "because the affairs of the state have not lain on them," presumably in contrast to the Sidneys.[29] Later in the letter he notes that a good prince should possess "virtue and justice," then "religion and equity," and then the same thing again but with an addition, "piety, justice, and *liberality*."[30] On August 2, 1580, Sidney pleads "the curse of my poverty" for staying away from court. In his "Defence of Poetry," he is poignantly sensitive to how comedy can sting, for if the form makes us laugh at the faults of others, "Nil habet infelix paupertas durius in se / Quam quod ridiculos homines fecit" (the worst of poverty is that it makes men look ridiculous).[31]

Not unaware, it seems, of Sidney's financial problems, nonetheless Thomas Moffett, in a letter written in 1593 to Philip's nephew William Herbert several years after Sidney's death, pointed out that debt did not diminish Sidney's honor, for it indicated a lack of greed: "Our Philip, indeed, judging that not all money is honourable or necessary to a man, a thousand times preferred that he should be ruined and lose his head than that he should increase his own gains by public losses or stain his conscience and his honour. ... For he saw how unbecoming to a man is such greediness." Philip had good credit, despite his expenses for embassies, Christmas festivities and jousting, clothes, and liberality to others, including learned visitors: "however much was wanting, citizens continued to lend as much to the borrower in his pecuniary need."[32] Moffett overstates his case, since Sidney was not immune to financial incentives, but he makes his point about Sidney's adherence to a code of honor.

What is revealing for an investigation of attitudes towards fraudulent conveyancing is that Sidney's financial misfortunes usually involve both moral awareness and circumstances that darken his conduct. After Sidney returned from his grand tour in 1575, he invested £25 in Martin Frobisher's first voyage, despite the warnings of his scholarly mentor Hubert Languet: "Do not let the cursed hunger after gold, which the Poet speaks of, creep over that spirit of yours, into which nothing has hitherto been admitted but love of goodness and desire of earning the good will of all men."[33] Thinking he had found gold, Frobisher sailed again in 1577; this time Sidney invested £50 for his stake. Frobisher's third voyage to Hudson Bay concluded what turned out to be a financial disaster. He brought home 200 tons of worthless rock. The receiver, Thomas Allen, charged Sidney and Dyer with unpaid debts for stock and levied on them on April 25th, 1579. That means Sidney had signed his name but not paid in. He must not have thought he was doing anything wrong, but circumstances worked against him.

After the Frobisher episode, Sidney became involved with Humphrey Gilbert in a scheme to colonize North America, from which he stood to control 3 000 000 acres of land. Where Frobisher brought back only worthless rock, not gold, Gilbert died during his expedition of 1583; otherwise Sidney might have made a fortune in America.

Sidney's involvement with Gilbert not only involved greed for gold. It directly involved him with laws against fraudulent conveyances. Gilbert had a grant from the queen for almost unlimited land yet to be discovered in North America. Walsingham, according to Roger Kuin's reconstruction, had a scheme for ridding England of Catholics by sending them out as colonists. The problem was that the law against fraudulent conveyances by overseas fugitives (13 Eliz., c. 3) would prevent the two principal Catholic backers of the scheme, Sir Thomas Gerrard and Sir George Peckham, from leaving the country. They had planned to make arrangements for others to run their estates at home and forward proceeds abroad – money that would be necessary to operate the new colonies. It was up to Sidney to convince the queen of the unfairness of the law in this instance, for which service, Kuin proposes, he received the grant from Gilbert on July 7, 1582.[34] Once again Sidney is on the side of the conveyor and debtor.

Part of the Sidney hagiography is that he lacked an "eye for the main chance."[35] His friend Fulke Greville portrays him as a courtier overlooked by the queen, who failed to give him the political appointment he believed he deserved as a statesman dedicated to the glory of God and a Protestant league. It is often said that the single most important event in his life was his death at Zutphen. In that Dutch town his thigh was shattered as he bravely led a charge against a Spanish supply train that emerged from the morning mist, revealing a line of soldiers far longer than his band of adventurers had expected. He died of gangrene after making generous provisions in his will and was given the largest funeral of the century in London. The other side of the picture is that Sidney knew exactly why his career was stalled. His definition of moral philosophy, as he said in a letter to his brother Robert, was the study of the effect of the passions on the virtues and vices. Its purpose, like that of poetry, was virtuous action, but action in a sense that contrasts with the doings of a more practical man like Humphrey Gilbert. In a proposal for a college in Ireland, Gilbert defined moral philosophy as the study of what is needed for conquest – military strategy and supply, for example.[36] Sidney differed. He was above all a student of people, and as an observant young man, he must have learned something about the real world from his involvement with Walsingham. Like many scholars, he never made money.

Sidney's acquaintance with Walsingham could only reinforce for him how blurred the line was between prudence and deceit, which was already a feature of his written but unpublished fiction. As Kuin points out, Walsingham hardly needed Philip Sidney to intercede with the queen to suspend the law against fraudulent conveyances by fugitives. He probably used Sidney's role as an excuse to extract the 3 000 000 acre-grant from Gilbert. But that was not all. A year later, in July, 1583, Sidney granted Peckham 10 per cent of the land in his grant in exchange for Peckham's furnishing a ship for the next expedition. The narrator of "Astrophel and Stella" bemoans the uselessness of "great expectations," and we usually think of Sidney's disappointment that, with the birth of a son to Leicester in 1581, he was no longer heir to his uncle's fortune. In the real world, however, Sidney continued to use expectations to meet the objections of the investors who were putting up real money. As Moffett said, Philip's credit was good, despite his debts.

Sidney's debts cut one way on his attitude toward creditors, but his dependence on royal favor cut the other. The contrast, so reminiscent of his father's, between his sympathies for the disinherited and for the needs of his own friends characterize a letter of recommendation he wrote to Christopher Hatton, urging him to arrange a grant of Powerscourt, the beautiful estate south of Dublin, to his friend Edward Denny. In urging the suit he could not overlook the fortune of the man who would be dispossessed: "As for him, that sues for it in the Court, he is indeed a good honest fellow, according to the brood of that nation; but being a bastard, he hath no law to recover it, & he is much too weak to keep it."[37] In a similar letter, often cited to demonstrate Sidney's sympathy for Catholics, he writes to assuage Lady Kitson about "a present intention of a general mitigation, to be used in respect of recusants."[38] He himself was reluctant to accept forfeited lands, in contrast to Walter Ralegh, or Sidney's friend Edward Dyer, who was involved in schemes to detect concealments, or Edmund Spenser, who was accumulating and trading estates in Ireland while Sidney was writing the *Arcadia* or attending at court.

A model courtier, Sidney regularly participated in entertainments and tournaments, including one with Ralegh in 1579, but 1581 was an especially busy year. He jousted in a tournament in January and on Accession Day that autumn, and his expenses mounted. His most elaborate, and costly, outing occurred on 16 April, when Sidney, Fulke Greville, and two others appeared at Whitehall as the "Foster Children of Desire." According to the published account, Sidney was dressed

> in very sumptuous manner, with armour part blue and the rest gilt and engraven, with four spare horses having caparisons and furniture very rich and costly, as some of cloth of gold embroidered with pearl and some embroidered with gold and silver feathers very richly and cunningly wrought. He had four pages that rode on his four spare horses who had cassock coats and Venetian hose all of cloth of silver, laid with gold lace and hats of the same with gold bands and white feathers, and each one a pair of white buskins. Then had he thirty gentlemen and yeomen and four trumpeters who were all in cassock coats and Venetian hose of yellow velvet laid with silver lace, yellow velvet caps with silver bands and white feathers, and every one a pair of white buskins.[39]

With such expenses, it is not surprising that a letter to his uncle Leicester on December 28, 1581 reveals that Sidney owed £3000. He was resorting to usurers and several times mentions that he is encumbered by debts.[40] He had asked Burghley for £100 a year in "impropriations" and apparently pressed the queen to accept his service. She seems to have responded by offering him recusants' lands. These lands were the subject, of course, of laws against fraudulent conveyances. Katherine Duncan-Jones captures Sidney's mood and moral dilemma in her biography of the poet: Sidney feels ashamed for being willing to profit from persecuted Catholics, but feels scorn for his own poverty:

> I know not truly what to say, since Her Majesty is pleased so to answer for as well may Her Majesty refuse the matter of the Papists and then I have both shame and scorn.... Truly I like not their persons and much worse their religions, but I think my fortune very hard that my reward must be built upon other men's punishments.[41]

Sidney's poetry reflects his personal convictions. In poem 18 of his poetry sequence *Astrophel and Stella*, he compares unbridled passion to financial mismanagement, two things to which he was susceptible. The poem has been praised for its strong verbs, action, movement, and the way it combines the parables of the talents and the prodigal son.[42] In this poem, his poetic persona has been devoted to reason and learning but wants only to lose "more" of what heaven "hath lent" to him:

> With what sharpe checkes I in my selfe am shent,
>   When into Reason's audit I do go:
>   And by just counts my selfe a banckrout know
> Of all those goods, which heav'n to me hath lent:
> Unable quite to pay even Nature's rent
>   Which unto it by birthright I do owe:
>   And which is worse, no good excuse can show,
> But that my wealth I have most idly spent.
>   My youth doth waste, my knowledge brings forth toyes,
> My wit doth strive those passions to defend,
>   Which for reward spoile it with vaine annoyes.
> I see my course to lose my self doth bend:

> I see and yet no greater sorrow take,
> Than that I lose no more for *Stella's* sake.[43]

This poem makes no sense if the narrator believes that misspending on Stella is not in some sense immoral but at the same time, prudent. We may add that it was a form of fraudulent conveyance for a bankrupt to continue payments to one creditor, thereby defrauding others. A similar trope occurs in sonnet 52, when the poet grants "*Stella's selfe*" to "Vertue" as long as "Vertue" will "graunt" her body "to us." The poem may offer a witty conceit for Stella's body, but the conceit is based on the seriousness and lack of qualm in the desire for it, resulting in a moral indeterminacy. The same witty use of profligacy underlies sonnet 62: "Deare, love me not, that you may love me more."

Sidney's poetry sequence was written after 1581, when he attended the third and last session of Elizabeth's Fourth Parliament. Even if he had never heard of the practice before, he would have learned something about fraudulent conveyancing at that session, since the issue was raised in several forms and on several occasions. The queen herself, in a surprising addition to protocol, mentioned the problem of debtors' evading creditors in her opening response to the House Speaker's disabling speech. A new Speaker traditionally offered to withdraw himself as unworthy of the queen. By disabling himself, the Speaker rhetorically allowed the queen to confirm his election by the House. The Speaker – in this case, Mr. John Popham, Solicitor General, of Bristol – also included "three petitions," for freedom from arrest for the members and their servants, for liberty of speech in the House, and for his own access to the queen. On this occasion the queen added a novel condition to her grant of freedom from arrest, when she said that she "would not have any purposely become of the House or retain servants indebted to defraud other creditors of the due debts." As Neale observes, she was probably thinking of Smalley's case from the previous session in 1576.[44] But it was not only the queen who was concerned about the parliamentary immunity from arrest for debt.

The case of Smalley is instructive because it illustrates the growing problem in those years. It happened that a man named Edward Smalley was sued for a battery. He had cut open another man's cheek and was ordered by a jury to pay £100 in damages. Smalley, however, had sureties whom he wanted to protect. His scheme was to have himself arrested for debt, then have his master, Arthur Hall, claim a parliamentary privilege from arrest. Due to a legal technicality, the plaintiff could not then get a second writ of execution. The plan went forward, and the House was therefore faced with the dilemma of defending its ancient privilege from arrest for debt. The members either had to hand Smalley over to the sheriff or countenance an obvious fraud. To the Speaker's dismay – and Popham was a lawyer who believed the law should not be interfered with – the House favored its privilege. It ignored the justice of the plaintiff's suit and voted to have Smalley released. It was this fraud of a creditor that bothered the queen, and her attitude toward the incident lends support to the thesis that 13 Eliz., c. 5 had not been solely inspired by politics.[45]

Whether Sidney thought Smalley should have been allowed to evade his creditors may be judged by his own behavior in 1584, when he sat in the first session of Elizabeth's Fifth Parliament. During this term, his own servant John Pepler was arrested for debt, and Sidney – like Smalley's employer Arthur Hall – used his parliamentary privilege to free him. On Monday, March 15, 1585, "It was ordered upon a motion this day by Mr Recorder of London that a Warrant for a Writ of Priviledge be awarded for setting at liberty of *John Pepler* now prisoner for debt in the Counter in *London*, servant unto Sir *Philip Sidney* a member of this House."[46] His privilege benefited Sidney in two ways: he showed himself a friend to his servant, and the debt could be delayed. Once again we find Sidney on the side of debtors and conveyors. Did he act with prudence, or was there a whiff of intent to defraud creditors?

If Sidney was at all attentive in Parliament – and we have little record of his activities there – he could not help but have been aware of the ethical debate that framed itself around conveyances by debtors and others. The central business began with a speech by Sir Walter Mildmay that would prompt a new recusancy bill, which naturally involved fraudulent conveyances. In his attack on recusants, Mildmay listed six proofs of what he called the Pope's "implacable malice": 1) the Northern Rebellion; 2) his maintenance of rebels and other fugitives; 3) the bull of 1570 that excommunicated the queen; 4) the invasion of Ireland by James Fitzmorrice; 5) Desmond's rebellion; and 6) the invasion of strangers and fortifying of Ireland, which referred to events at Smerwick, in Ireland. Mildmay observed that recently priests and Jesuits had been sent to England, whose principle errand was "by creeping into the Houses of men of behaviour and reputation, not only to corrupt the Realm with false doctrine, but also ... to stir up sedition." He called for laws to constrain obedience, a strong navy, and support for the army in Ireland, using native levies, not mercenaries, which he condemned, saying it was a sorrowful practice on the Continent. Sidney served on the committee assigned to devise an appropriate bill.[47]

Three features of the "due obedience" bill that finally passed concern our story. First, it contained a fraudulent conveyance clause. Second, it was this bill that created the pressure on Catholics to make fraudulent conveyances – pressure that Glenn believed existed 10 years earlier. Third, the bill that passed was milder than the one introduced. The first version of the bill that emerged from the committee on which Sidney sat was, Neale observes, a severer version of a 1571 bill that the queen had vetoed. She was willing to allow a penalty for failure to attend church, but refused to punish failure to receive Holy Communion. She did not believe consciences should be forced, and as Francis Bacon observed, did not seek a "window on men's hearts."[48] The measure that passed in 1581 followed the queen's policy. It was hope of this milder measure that Sidney apparently referred to in his letter of March 28, 1581, to Lady Kitson.

Parliament's recalcitrance is noteworthy, because by 1581, the nature of the Catholic threat had changed.[49] Exiles had founded a seminary at Douai, which by 1574 had begun sending missionaries into England. The Jesuits arrived in 1580, and Edmund Campion and Robert Parsons were hunted men. Sidney had known Campion at Oxford in 1569, and the two reunited in Prague in 1574. Campion considered Sidney a "poor wavering soul," and believed that Philip's conversion would "astonish his noble father, the Deputy of Ireland, his uncles the Dudleys, and all the young courtiers, and Cecil himself."[50] A few months after the end of Parliament, Campion was captured, examined personally by the queen, and finally executed for treason on December 1, 1581. Despite its anti-Catholic feeling, however, Parliament at least partly disfavored not only the financial pressures applied to Catholics but the use of conveyancing laws to enforce them.

The fraudulent conveyance clause the bill contained also indicates the unsettled state of the law. It refers back to 13 Eliz., c. 5, either because the clause in the bill is redundant or, more likely, the authors of the bill believed 13 Eliz., c. 5 was not sufficient of itself to stop fraudulent conveyances by recusants, and that this combination sufficiently broadened the earlier law:

> And be it likewise enacted and declared, that every graunt, conveyance, bond, judgement, and execution, had, or made, since the beginning of this Session of Parliament, or hereafter to be had, or made, of covenous purpose to defraud any interest, right or title, that may or ought to grow to the Queen, or to any other person by means of any conviction or judgment, by vertue of this statute, *or of the said statute of the sayd xiii. yere*, shall be, and be adjudged to be utterly void against the Queen, and against such as shall sue for any part of the said penalties in form aforesayd. (23 Eliz., c. 1; my emphasis)

Valuable as they are, the parliamentary records do not reveal all we might want to know. First, the journals give no other indications of Sidney's work. Second, despite many references to various fraudulent conveyance measures, the terms of the debates are hard to identify. A bill against "secret conveyances and deceitful sale of land" was read on March 7 and again on March 14, but it was dashed in the Lords and a new bill had to be proposed. It too never passed, but the debate probably indicates the controversy that preceded passage of 27 Eliz., c. 4 in the next parliament. Some of the other unclear references may have concerned a provision that was included in the "due obedience" bill. What is important is that Sidney was present as these various measures were introduced and read once, twice, or three times, according to parliamentary procedure. Proximity, if nothing else, connects the "bill for avoiding of encumbrances against purchasers," which was read for the second time on January 26; a bill for the speedy recovery of debts, which was read for the first time the next day; and a bill, never passed, also read on January 27 "against secret and stolen contracts of children without consent of parents." But there is more, since these measures cohere to form a picture of a cultural obsession with the problem of fraudulent conveyancing. The last bill, in particular, relates directly to Sidney's *Arcadia*, whose plot turns on stolen children.

The Ravishment Plot

It was Sidney's genius in the *Arcadia* to develop a plot that could represent the moral ambiguity of fraudulent conveyances. The problem was how to balance the interests of creditors, including the state, who sought to counter fraud with the desire of men in varied circumstances to retain control of their lives and property. Sidney's solution, which has often been misread as an artistic flaw, takes the form of the separate ravishments committed by the heroes of the story.

The plot of the *Arcadia* involves two princes, Musidorus and Pyrocles, who arrive in Arcadia and fall in love with the daughters of Basilius, the local duke or king, depending on the version. Basilius has ignobly retreated to the countryside because he fears an oracle that says his elder daughter Pamela will be "stolen," while the young daughter Philoclea will "embrace / An uncouth love."[51] To woo Pamela,

Musidorus secretly disguises himself as a shepherd. Similarly, to approach Philoclea, Pyrocles dresses as an Amazon. Both suitors have obstacles to overcome as well. Basilius has assigned a foolish shepherd named Dametas to keep a vigilant eye on Pamela, while Philoclea's parents keep an eye on their younger daughter themselves. Pyrocles suffers a further misfortune when Basilius falls in love with his Amazon disguise, while Gynecia, Basilius's wife, falls in love with the man hidden underneath the disguise. Eventually Musidorus deceives Dametas, the guardian shepherd, and leads Pamela on horseback toward a seaport to take ship, promising he will marry her. That very day Pyrocles finally solves his dilemma by devising a plot to deceive Philoclea's parents. He has his bed moved to a cave, allegedly to escape the heat of the country, then arranges separate assignations with Basilius and Gynecia. They each meet the other instead of the lover they hoped to find. Meanwhile Pyrocles creeps into their daughter's room, locks the door, and in the *Old Arcadia*, apparently makes love to Philoclea (*OA* 211 and 237, *NA* 395). Pyrocles thus ravishes Philoclea literally while his cousin Musidorus only ravishes Pamela in the broader sense of making off with her.

Both sets of lovers are caught. During a pause in their elopement, Musidorus holds an internal debate, typical of Sidney's style, in which his passion conquers his reason. Unable to control himself, Musidorus does his best to rape Pamela as she sleeps, but some unruly peasants interrupt him. Pyrocles, too, is discovered, and both princes go on trial for having violated the local law of Arcadia "which, without exception, did condemn all to death who were found ... in act of marriage without solemnity of marriage" (*OA* 251, *NA* 737). Their trial is held conjointly with the murder trial of Gynecia, who had brought a potion into the cave where she unexpectedly met her husband. Basilius seems to die after drinking it, and Gynecia is arrested.

Set in a legal context by these courtroom trials, Musidorus's flight with Pamela is referred to as a conveyance three times, twice by Philanax and once by Musidorus, and it is closely linked to Pyrochles' sexual intercourse with Philoclea. During his prosecution of the princes for various infractions – as "disguisers, falsifiers, adulterers, ravishers, murderers, and traitors" – the prolix Philanax accuses Musidorus of trying to have "conveyed away the undoubted inheritrix of this country" (*OA* 335) and then again of trying to "convey away the lady of us all" (*OA* 345, *NA* 830–831). Musidorus throws the term back in his face by belittling the idea that he "conveyed away the princess of this country" (*OA* 347, *NA* 833). How could he convey one who was a princess? His persuasion could not be treason, only error, since the final decision was hers. When Sidney revised his story, he extended the trope to the other pair of lovers.[52] In the *New Arcadia* Pyrocles no longer sleeps with Philoclea but instead asks her to run away with him to his kingdom of Macedon. She answers that she will do so "if you can *convey* me hence in such plight as you see me" (*NA* 688, my emphasis), and then she faints. Sidney's attention to language signals the close connection between ravishment and fraudulent conveyance, retaining, even in revision, the ambivalent attitude toward his heroes that duplicates the difficulty in devising fair laws that faced English jurisprudence.

Ravishment is the form of fraudulent conveyance appropriate to the pastoral form of the *Arcadia*, where problems of commerce would violate decorum. The princes in the story never worry about money. These creatures of Sidney's fantasy are wealthy young men who travel with a treasure chest that is always available when they need it. They dress in gorgeous jewels at their trial, where Musidorus adorns his dark hair with rubies and Pyrocles wears diamonds on his white velvet cloak and a single white ribbon binds his auburn locks (*OA* 325, *NA* 808).

If the princes are debtors, it is because they believe they owe all their love to the daughters of Basilius, a debt that Philoclea calls in when Pyrocles threatens to kill himself to save her honor after the pair are discovered *in flagrante*. During a long debate on suicide that follows, Pyrocles argues that he owes a debt to Philoclea because of the trouble he has caused her. His life is all he has to pay: "the infiniteness of your goodness being such as it cannot reach unto it, yet doing all I can and paying my life, which is all I have, though it be far (without measure) short of your desert, yet shall I not die in debt to mine own duty" (*OA* 256, *NA* 742). Philoclea counters that he is only acting out of passion. By dying he presumes to know what God wants, but God's purpose is inscrutable. She in effect accuses him of a fraudulent conveyance, since by throwing away his life, he is really retaining the use of it, and thereby avoiding the true debt he owes to her – his life. Philoclea is appalled that Pyrocles would give his life away rather than pay his debt of love to her. Pyrocles is impressed that this young girl reasons so well, but in a telling response, he ignores her logic and makes another attempt to kill himself. What looks like fraud to Philoclea is an act of honor to Pyrocles.

It may have been Sidney's own experience that connected the topics of ravishment and fraudulent conveyance in his imagination. They arose on the same day in Parliament in 1581. They were also deeply implicated by English law, which connected problems of debtors with various attempts to defraud the Crown of its revenues. As little kingdoms in themselves, families had similar protections against men who would *convey* or *carry away* their women. One term or the other occurs in a series of laws that begin with 13 Edw. I, c. 34 (1285), which made it a felony to "ravish a woman married, maid, or other, where she did not consent." Some women did consent, and so the statute added "And of women *carried away* with the goods of their husbands, the king shall have the suit for the goods so taken away." Others were coerced: 31 Hen. VI, c. 9 set out in its preamble the problem of men who took women "into their possession, *conveying* them" into places where they have most power, and forcing them to sign indentures of servitude. The act allowed a judicial inquiry, and upon examination of the parties, the obligation might be declared "void, and of no force nor effect." 3 Hen. VII, c. 2, restated the penalty for "*carrying* a Woman *away* against her will that hath lands or goods," affirming that the crime was a felony.[53] Finally, 4 & 5 Ph. & M., c. 8, set out in its preamble the problem of "maidens and women children of noblemen, gentlemen, and others," especially "heirs apparent of their ancestors," who by "flattery, trifling gifts, and fair promises" be "often times *taken and conveyed away*" to the "displeasure of Almighty God, disparagement of the said children, and extreme continual heaviness of all their friends." It established that it should not be lawful "*to take or convey away, or cause to be taken or conveyed away* any maid or woman child unmarried, being within the age of sixteen years" against the will of the father or such person as the father has appointed by his last will and testament. (The penalty was attainder, two years in prison or payment of such a fine as shall be assessed by the queen's council in Star Chamber.)

The laws against the ravishment of women are related to, and use the language of, fraudulent conveyance, because to ravish a woman, particularly an heiress, was tantamount to defrauding a family of its property interest in her. In Sidney's *Arcadia*, Euarchus bases the punishments he metes out to the princes on this principle, the defense of the family, not the violence of rape – in the sense either of kidnapping or having carnal knowledge – or the statutory law of Arcadia, under which the princes could be condemned to death for being "found in act of marriage without solemnity of marriage" (*OA* 251, *NA* 737). Therefore even though Euarchus finds Philoclea not guilty of the charge of intercourse and spares her life, he sentences her to a nunnery on the vague conclusion that she is "not altogether faultless" (*OA* 329, *NA* 812). Euarchus has read his Aristotle and points out that judgment cannot be applied "by a free discourse of reason and skill of philosophy, but must be tied to the laws of Greece and municipal statutes of this dukedom." Philosophy is too general and leaves "to every man a scope of his own interpretation," he says, but laws provide "assured bounds, which once broken, man's nature infinitely rangeth" (*OA* 350, *NA* 835). Nonetheless, he makes a decision based not on the law but his own morality. This ambiguity mirrors the ethical dilemma of fraudulent conveyancing laws, which must judge whether a free gift may outweigh another duty.

Implicitly recognizing a gap between strict morality and the law, Euarchus gropes with the problem of how to punish Pyrocles. Since he cannot find Pyrocles guilty of intercourse without staining the reputation of Philoclea, whom he has already found technically innocent, Euarchus must find some other penalty for the prince. He does so by ruling that Pyrocles "offered violence to the lady Philoclea, an act punished by all the Grecian laws with being thrown down from a high tower to the earth." But what violence? I do not think we are ever clear what exactly Eurarchus punishes. Is it what we today would call an assault – an act that puts a victim in fear of harm although no battery occurs – or does Euarchus react because it is an assault *on a princess*? The punishment of being tossed off a tower is meant to be suitable to the crime – a sort of *contrapasso* – but the imagery is more suggestive than enlightening. It may be that the guilty Pyrocles must fall because he aspired too high. It may be that he must be dashed into the *earth* because of the *physical* character of rape. Most likely, I think, his fall is meant to illustrate the "general ruin" (the Latin root of "ruin" means "to fall") that follows from rape, because rape does two things. It makes parentage uncertain, causing "confusion" and unsettling society. And it allows the delinquent's offspring to inherit whatever forms of property are available to the woman. Despite obvious affection for his hero, Sidney allows a sense of right to enter his story.

Although his story eventually sides with the princes, who must live for there to be a happy ending, Sidney does not mock Euarchus, whose name means "good leader." When Euarchus condemns Musidorus, he clarifies his belief that the princes' true crime, to his stern eyes at least, is that of interfering with a father's right to dispose of his daughter, his property:

> The other young man confesseth he persuaded the princess Pamela to fly her country, and accompanied her in it – without all question a ravishment no less than the other; for, although he ravished her not from herself, yet he ravished her from him that owed her, which was her father. That she was heiress to the state elevated the crime. This kind is chastised by the loss of the head, as a most execrable theft; for if they must die who steal from us our goods, how much more they who steal from us that for which we gather our goods. (*OA* 351, *NA* 836–837)

Unlike Pyrocles, Musidorus never admits he tried to use force. He is sentenced to lose his head, because he ravished the head of state. But his crime, if there is one, was against Pamela's father, not Pamela. Musidorus is the classic conveyor: we root for him, even though we know what he does is wrong.

The Intractable Ending

The ethical dilemmas raised by Sidney's work – for 200 years the most popular piece of original English prose fiction – have been the subject of vigorous debate over whether the plot collapses under their weight. This debate centers on the ending of the story. Critics have long noticed that the revival of Basilius, who takes over from Euarchus and pardons the princes, does not logically explain why he should condone their behavior, other than that Basilius is glad to be alive. According to William Ringler, the ending of the story "completely undercuts the heroic adherence of Euarchus to 'sacred Rightfulnes,' for the princes escape punishment, not by any revelation of a change in the nature of their offence, but by coming before a less impartial and less idealistic judge." Ringler believed that "Sidney himself apparently became aware of the ethical ambiguity of this scene," and he made two changes. First he eliminated "the heroes' attempts upon the chastity of the princesses." Second, Sidney changed his story to show that the princes were married *before* the trial took place, thereby eliminating the charge of abduction as well.[54] In the older version an oracle had warned the duke that

> Thy elder care shall from thy careful face
> By princely mean be stolen and yet not lost;
> Thy younger shall with nature's bliss embrace
> An uncouth love, which nature hateth most.
> (*OA* 5)

In the new version, the oracle adds a line, telling Basilius (who is now a king), that his daughters will already be married to the defendants when they are tried for his murder:

> Both they themselves unto such two shall wed,
> Who at thy bier, as at a bar, shall plead
> Why thee (a living man) they had made dead.
> (*NA* 395)

But as Roger Howell has pointed out, there was not a great moral fuss about "marriage by consummation on the basis of private betrothal" in Sidney's England.[55] Similarly, Michael McCanles has objected that "the elopement is just as surely predicted in the new *Arcadia* version as it is in the original version. In short, the two versions of the oracle predict the same conclusion, that given in old *Arcadia* Books 3–5."[56] The upshot is that the ending of the *New Arcadia*, in the text as we have it, must be doing the same work as that of the *Old Arcadia*. (Sidney died before his revisions reached this portion of the story.)

Most scholars believe Sidney finished composing the *Old Arcadia* in 1580, a year when he resided from March to August with his sister Mary, to whom the work is dedicated. In October he wrote to his brother Robert, on the Continent, that he hoped to send him a copy by February. Ringler believed the book was therefore at the scriveners, but according to Jean Robertson, "the evidence suggests that the first draft was more or less completed by the spring of 1581," which puts the completion *after* the meeting of Parliament that year, an interlude, along with the court entertainments that cost Sidney so much money, that may have delayed his completing the work.[57] But it hardly matters whether Sidney's attitude toward conveyancing preceded or followed from his time spent among the lawmakers; he was intimately part of the culture within which the conveyancing debate was taking place.

As a political thinker, Sidney was obsessed in both versions of the *Arcadia* by the implications of Basilius's foolish retirement in fear of the oracle. But the errors of the duke cannot justify political rebellion, nor can the revival of Basilius relieve the princes of responsibility for their behavior toward the princesses. Instead, Sidney's art "cultivates an ambivalent response," according to Ann Astell, and it is up to the reader to develop self-knowledge and humility by weighing moral precepts against the "circumstances and the necessity to act."[58] It follows that despite the objections of commentators who find the plot of the *Arcadia* too slender to support the weight of moral inquiry it has to carry – the question of how to respond to a retiring prince, and justifications for rebellion, lying, cross-dressing against class and gender lines, as well as ravishment – the elopements in the *Arcadia* illustrate a class of ethically ambiguous activities such as the law grappled with under the rubric of fraudulent conveyances.

The debates over fraudulent conveyances in Parliament condemned practices Sidney must have approved of – the way the Dudleys handled their property as they faced treason charges in 1553, the reluctance of men of his father's class (the higher nobility) to strengthen the government's ability to prevent even an O'Neill from taking steps to protect his estate, the slightly dishonest protection that service in Parliament afforded to servants in debt – and suggests that the morally elusive ending of the *Arcadia* aims at a more specific target than just the general malaise of a young gentleman whom the queen chose not to trust. While the English lawyers slowly refined their statutes and cases on conveyancing, Sidney's art made a case for the passions that drove conveyors and provided counterarguments to the reasons that would rein them in.

The ethical conflict between generosity and integrity – paying a debt before giving a gift – determines when a conveyance is fraudulent. It also determines what love is honorable. After Sidney's *Arcadia* appeared, this conflict commonly manifested itself in Renaissance literary works depicting young ladies who might be tempted to open their chaste treasures instead of honoring the debt they owed their families. The connection may seem strained, but George Puttenham's *Arte of English Poesie* specifically mentions the use of debt imagery in love poetry. Discussing the difference between a metaphor and a catachresis, Puttenham explains that a metaphor occurs when a word is wrested from its own signification and transported (carried over; *meta* + *phorein*) to "another not so natural but yet of some affinitie or conveniencie with it." An example he gives is "as the man of law said, *I feel you* not, for I understand not your case, because he had not his fee in his hand."[59] A catachresis, however, is a form of metaphor "without any just convenience." It is a "plain abuse," as in the verse "*I lent my love to losse, and gaged my life in vaine.*"

> Whereas this word *lent* is properly of many or some such other thing, as men do commonly borrow, for use to be repaid again, and being applied to love is utterly abused, and *yet very commendably spoken by virtue of this figure.* For he that loveth and is not beloved again, hath no less wrong, than he that lendeth and is never repayde.[60]

Puttenham's choice of debt as an example of catachresis is doubly interesting in light of his own behavior: he married the widowed Lady Windsor and defrauded her by conveying away her manor of Heriard: John Throckmorton, who was in trouble as a Catholic and previous supporter of Queen Mary, helped with the conveyance.[61] Like Henry and Philip Sidney, Puttenham sided with the conveyors.

A literary ravishment is an inexact metaphor for a fraudulent conveyance but not less effective for that. When Sidney wrote the *Arcadia*, it would probably have been felt as a catachresis; by the time the topic reached Spenser and Shakespeare, it was common enough to be a metaphor. Later authors were probably not aware of Sidney's attitudes or circumstances, yet they picked up the association he made in his fictional plot between elopements and conveyances – between passion, or necessity, and reason. If Sidney's plot creaks, he was nonetheless a model for poets as talented as Spenser and Shakespeare. *The Faerie Queene* continues the metaphoric connection between ravishment and fraudulent conveyances. In *The Merchant of Venice* Lorenzo ravishes Jessica even as she carries away her father's moneybags.

Sidney's own impecunious circumstances, his father's involvement with bills of attainder, and his attendance in Parliament where men spoke both for and against laws against fraudulent conveyances may be sufficient to explain the curious feature of his *Arcadia*, that its heroes Musidorus and Pyrocles engage in a form of fraudulent conveyancing, the ravishment of heiresses, and yet go unpunished. But it was Sidney's brother Robert, one of the earliest readers of the *Arcadia*, who first applied what might be learned from the story. What he did reminds us that the laws against the vigorous pursuit of heiresses went against the grain for many adventurous men who sought to wive it wealthily. Robert, whom Malcolm Wallace said "had an eye for the main chance which was foreign to" his brother, married the wealthy Barbara Gammage, age 22, after his return from touring Europe. Her father had died on September 8, 1584, and she was at once inundated with offers. The queen tried to keep her from the entanglements of marriage, but her royal mandate arrived too late. Robert had already married his heiress. "The ceremony was performed," on September 23, "two hours before the arrival of the Queen's messenger forbidding it."[62] The queen was thwarted, but the ceremony was lawful, and Robert, having carried away the bride, barely avoided a charge of defrauding the queen's interest.

In Contrast, Edward Dyer

Sidney's poetry associates extravagant spending with uncontrollable passion, and the same attitude informs his fiction, his theory of poetry, his father's politics, and his brother's marriage. Yet his friend Edward Dyer and his acquaintance

Edmund Spenser held very different views. Unlike Sidney, they aligned themselves with those government measures that other men felt obliged to circumvent.

The association of Spenser, Sidney, and Dyer is one of the most tantalizing in Elizabethan literary history. In October 1579, Spenser wrote to Gabriel Harvey that Philip Sidney and Edward Dyer "have me, I thank them, in some use of familiarity."[63] We usually speculate about whether Spenser really had the opportunity to sit with Sidney, his social superior, and discuss poetry. But we might also wonder if they discussed their careers, which in any aristocratic circle would have meant how to attain an income-producing estate. In that case the more interesting conversation might have been that between Spenser and Dyer.

We have seen that Sidney was too morally troubled to accept without reservations the forfeitures of poor men who had run afoul of the law. Yet his uncle Leicester, who would probably be more obviously shadowed in Spenser's *Faerie Queene* had he not died in 1588, seems to have helped Spenser do just that when he arranged for him to obtain a post with Lord Grey. A year later Spenser was in Ireland picking up escheated estates, something Sidney himself found distasteful. At the same time Sidney's boyhood friend and biographer Fulke Greville was in the navy off the coast of Munster, reporting on the spoils to be had there.[64] And Dyer was ruminating, not for the first time, on a plan to search for concealments. "Concealed lands," as A. L. Rowse explains, "meant lands, usually monastic or chantry, which should have come to the Crown by the Dissolution, but which had somehow been concealed and withheld."[65] Already in 1574 Dyer had a license for lands to the value of £100, and more was to come later.[66]

Edward Dyer's granduncle was Sir James Dyer, Lord Chief Justice of the Common Pleas. His father was a "gentleman steward" of the household of Henry VIII, who in February 1540 received property from the suppressed Glastonbury Abbey. Edward, born in 1543, went to Oxford in 1558 and to court, with Leicester, in 1567. In 1576, as a reward for his *Song in the Oak*, he received a license to control tanners, one of the first monopolies Elizabeth issued.[67] After the queen rejected Sidney's advice on her proposed marriage to Alençon, Sidney and Dyer retired from court in January 1580. While Sidney was writing his *Arcadia*, Dyer returned to court, where he participated in "commissions, legal appointments, financial responsibilities."[68] He also obtained a loan from the queen for £3000, for which he mortgaged his estates. The debt burdened him for life. In a letter to Walsingham, the Portuguese ambassador said Dyer was little better than a bankrupt. In 1586 the Exchequer threatened proceedings to collect.

Faced with ruin, Dyer once again positioned himself to search for concealments. In March 1588, he received a patent from the queen, good until 1593, to discover any property that either through confiscation or failure of heirs ought to have reverted the Crown.[69] He would investigate titles to land and buildings, and if he discovered any, he would declare them, make certain payments to the Crown, and keep the rest for himself. First, however, he had to pay £4000 to buy out Sir Edward Stafford, who had previously held the grant. One wonders what Sidney would have thought, had he been alive, of his friend's occupation. Even as corrupt a figure as the earl of Northampton (Norfolk's brother, who became a favorite of King James), decried a project for discovering concealed lands, noting to Robert Carr the evil of allowing one subject to fleece another in the name of the king.[70] In the event, landowners outwitted Dyer's agents, and Burghley refused to extend his patent. The Lord Treasurer started to seize Dyer's lands but died before the process was completed. Robert Cecil, who succeeded his father, granted Dyer an extension for the £3000 he had owed since 1580 and also extended his patent for concealments, but although Dyer's agent William Tipper made over £2000, Dyer never was out of debt. He died in 1607, owing the huge sum of £11 200.

Dyer's impecunious demise is both similar to and different from that of Sidney 20 years earlier. As gangrene lethally infected the thigh wound Sidney received in his heroic charge at Zutphen, the dying poet penned a will that left lavish bequests to friends, family, and doctors. Unfortunately Henry Sidney and his wife had died only a few months previously, and Sidney probably did not realize the poor condition of his estate. His father-in-law Francis Walsingham wrote that it "doth greatly afflict me, that a gentleman that hath lived so unspotted a reputation, and had so great a care to see all men satisfied, should be so exposed to the outcry of creditors. His goods will not suffice to answer a third part of his debts already known."[71] Although Sidney died in debt, he was honored for his generosity and for his integrity. He had not, like Dyer, sought out concealments, and unlike Spenser, he never railed against fraudulent conveyances.

Notes

1 "Sydney's Memoir of His Government in Ireland," a letter written in 1583 to Sir Francis Walsingham, as he and Sidney negotiated their children's marriage, printed in *The Ulster Journal of Archaeology* 8 (1860): 179–195, 192.
2 The statute can be found in *The Statutes of Ireland* (Dublin, 1621), pp. 309–324. The passage cited is from p. 321. A year later in the parliament of 1570, another bill of attainder was passed for Thomas Queverford, but again, there is no language to prevent fraudulent conveyancing.
3 Mona Wilson, *Sir Philip Sidney* (London: Duckworth, 1931), p. 18.
4 Conyers Read, *The Tudors: Personalities and Practical Politics in Sixteenth Century England* (New York: Henry Holt, 1936), p. 126.
5 Wilson, *Sir Philip Sidney*, p. 20.
6 Ibid., p. 21.
7 For further on this episode, see Margaret P. Hannay, *Philip's Phoenix: Mary Sidney, Countess of Pembroke* (New York: Oxford University Press, 1990), p. 9.
8 R. Dudley Edwards, *Ireland in the Age of the Tudors: The Destruction of Hiberno-Norman Civilization* (New York: Barnes & Noble, 1977), p. 85.
9 Ibid., p. 88. Edwards is the historian referred to in the next sentence.
10 Ibid., p. 89.
11 *Calendar of the Carew Manuscripts Preserved in the Archiepiscopal Library at Lambeth*, ed. J. S. Brewer and William Bullen (London, 1867–73), 3: 280.
12 *Calendar of the Carew Manuscripts*, 3: 281. Lists survive of people who petitioned for property. The queen authorized the use of more surrender and regrants "in tail male" (p. 293) and asked the Exchequer to prepare a "breviate" of debts owed to the Crown (p. 295).
13 David Beers Quinn, *The Voyages and Colonizing Enterprises of Sir Humphrey Gilbert*, 2 vols. (London: The Hakluyt Society, 1939–1940), 1: 118.
14 11 Eliz., c. 1, printed in *The Statutes of Ireland* (Dublin, 1621). Page numbers in the text.
15 The source is probably Geoffrey of Monmouth. See Edwards, *Ireland in the Age of the Tudors*, p. 122.

16 There have been several critical attempts to relate the style of Philanax's oration to Philip Sidney, but not usually to his father. Blair Worden, *The Sound of Virtue: Philip Sidney's Arcadia and Elizabethan Politics* (New Haven: Yale University Press, 1996), calls Philanax an "exceptional counsellor" (p. 146), "whose public spirit earns him the hostility of private-spirited men" (p. 147). Warden asks, "Has Philanax ever been in love? ... Had Philip's father Sir Henry? Could Sidney have shared the kind of wit that illuminates the *Arcadia* with any of these men?" (p. 329).

17 The statute itself is not well documented in contemporary sources; most scholars rely on the version published in 1621 in *The Statutes of Ireland*. Spenser does not seem to think there is any earlier, controlling law on fraudulent conveyances. If the law against fraudulent conveyances was honored in the breach, that is, known to exist in Ireland but ignored, there was all the more reason for Sidney to restate it.

18 It is possible that the Popham from Bristol was John's brother Edward; see J. E. Neale, *Elizabeth I and Her Parliaments: 1559-1581* (New York: St. Martin's Press, 1958), p. 219.

19 Charles William Wallace, *The First London Theatre* (1913; rpt. New York: Benjamin Blom, 1969), p. 164.

20 See T. E. Hartley, *Proceedings in the Parliaments of Elizabeth I*, 3 vols. (Leicester, 1981), 1: 219, n. 85, for April 22, 1571. "Two of Sir Henry Sidney's debts appear on sheriff John Smith's shrieval account for Kent for the year 1600–1."

21 Neale, *Elizabeth I and Her Parliaments: 1559–1581*, p. 219.

22 "Sydney's Memoir of His Government in Ireland," printed in *The Ulster Journal of Archaeology*, 8 (1860): 194.

23 *The Ulster Journal of Archaeology*, 3 (1855): 42.

24 *Calendar of the Carew Manuscripts*, 2: 46. My emphasis.

25 *The Ulster Journal of Archaeology*, 8 (1860): 194: "And now, deere Sir and brother, an end of this tragicall discourse, tedious for you to read, but more tedious it would have been *if it had come written with my own hand as first it was*: tragicall I may well tearme it, for that it began with the joyfull love and great lyking with likelihood of matrimoniall match between our most deere and swete children, whom God bless, and endeth with declaration of my unfortunate and hard estate." My emphasis.

26 *Calendar of the Carew Manuscripts*, 2: 53.

27 Sir Philip Sidney, *The Defence of Poesie, Political Discourses, Correspondence, Translations*, ed. Albert Feuillerat, vol. 3 of *The Works of Sir Philip Sidney* (Cambridge: At the University Press, 1962), p. 123: Sidney writes to his father, who is upset about his early removal from a term governing Ireland in 1578, that he is sent for to the queen, "being armed with good Accounts and perfitt Reasons for them, &c."

28 This occurred in January 1575. See James M. Osborn, *Young Philip Sidney: 1572–1577* (New Haven: Yale University Press, 1972), p. 278.

29 "A Letter Written by Sir Philip Sidney to the Queen Elizabeth, touching her marriage with Monsieur," in *Miscellaneous Prose of Sir Philip Sidney*, ed. Katherine Duncan-Jones and Jan van Dorsten (Oxford: At the Clarendon Press, 1973), p. 48.

30 Sidney, *Miscellaneous Prose*, pp. 54 and 56. My emphasis.

31 Ibid., p. 116.

32 Thomas Moffett, *Nobilis or A View of the Life and Death of a Sidney*, trans. Virgil B. Heltzel and Hoyt H. Hudson (San Marino: The Huntington Library, 1940), pp. 79 and 82.

33 *Sidney-Languet Letters*, trans. with an introduction by S. A. Pears (London: Pickering, 1845), p. 126. Languet refers to Virgil's *Aeneid*, III, 57: "auri sacra fames." The brother of Sidney's new friend Edward Dyer sailed with Frobisher in June, 1576.

34 Roger Kuin, "Querre-Huhau: Sir Philip Sidney and the New World," *Renaissance Quarterly* 51 (1998): 549–585.

35 Malcolm William Wallace, *The Life of Sir Philip Sidney* (1915; rpt. New York: Octagon

Books, 1967), p. 310. See also p. 323 ("The truth is that Sir Philip's judgment of men was by no means profound") and p. 402 ("he was constantly possessed by a double sense of the reality on the one hand, and on the other the unreality of all human striving").

36 See Beers Quinn, *The Voyages and Colonizing Enterprises of Sir Humphrey Gilbert*, 1: 28.
37 Feuillerat, *The Works of Sir Philip Sidney*, 3: 137.
38 Ibid., p. 134.
39 Roger Howell, *Sir Philip Sidney: The Shepherd Knight* (Boston: Little, Brown, 1968), pp. 86–87, citing Henry Goldwell, *A Brief Declaration of the Shewes* (London, 1581).
40 For the references to "usurers" and "combres," see the letter to Lord Burghley of October 10, 1581, in Feuillerat, *The Works of Sir Philip Sidney*, 3: 136.
41 Feuillerat, *The Works of Sir Philip Sidney*, 3: 139. See Feuillerat, *The Works of Sir Philip Sidney*, 3: 136–137, and the summary by Katherine Duncan-Jones, *Sir Philip Sidney: Courtier Poet* (New Haven: Yale University Press, 1991): "Painfully, [Sidney] was still appealing to Hatton for aid. Campion was dead, and the authorities were cynically accumulating more and more fines and goods from those who had the courage to continue to practice the old religion. Sidney could not afford to be too squeamish about this.... It seems that an earlier bid for office had collapsed. Perhaps the Queen had deliberately substituted for it the offer of forfeited goods, to force Sidney into the anti-Catholic camp.... Presumably this means 'shame' for his willingness to profit from the persecuted Catholics and 'scorn' for his continued poverty" (pp. 219–220). In an earlier letter to Christopher Hatton, December 18, 1581, Sidney had written, "some of my friends counsel me to stand upon Her Majesty's offer, touching the forfeiture of Papist's goods. Sir, I know not how to be more sure of Her Highness in that, than I thought myself in this. But though I were, in truth, it goeth against my heart, to prevent a prince's mercy: my necessity is great: I beseech you vouchsafe me your honorable care and good advice."
42 Richard McCoy summarizes new-critical readings of the poem in *Sir Philip Sidney: Rebellion in Arcadia* (New Brunswick, NJ: Rutgers University Press, 1979), p. 80.
43 *The Poems of Sir Philip Sidney*, ed. William A. Ringler, Jr. (Oxford: At the Clarendon Press, 1962), pp. 173–174.
44 The following summary is indebted to Neale, *Elizabeth I and Her Parliaments: 1559–1581*, pp. 333–345.
45 The problem was compounded by the argument that the sheriffs who arrested Smalley might become liable for his debt, as well as the difficulty of determining just which official should procure his release. Lack of precedent paralyzed the process. The crisis continued because Hall refused to compromise. He had a pamphlet published about the quarrel that was "shocking to the self-esteem of the Elizabethan House of Commons" (Neale, *Elizabeth I and Her Parliaments: 1559–1581*, p. 345). Neale says Hall wrote it, but it was obviously composed by a lawyer and is as good an example of a statement-of-facts from a legal brief as can be found in print. See Arthur Hall, *A Letter Sent by F.A. Touchyng a Quarell betwene A. Hall, and M. Mallerie* (London, 1576).
46 See Sir Simonds D'Ewes, *A Compleat Journal of the Votes, Speeches and Debates, Both of the House of Lords and House of Commons Throughout the Whole Reign of Queen Elizabeth of Glorious Memory* (London, 1693; rpt. Wilmington, Del.: Scholarly Resources, 1974), p. 368. Wallace, *The Life of Sir Philip Sidney*, p. 315, observes that the petition was granted to Sidney even though a similar favor was denied the servant of another member, because it appeared that the man had arranged to become a servant precisely in order to escape arrest. An earlier suit for debt resulted in a finding of contempt against Anthony Kirle, who ordered the arrest of a servant of Alban Sepneth, a member of the House (D'Ewes, *A Compleat Journal*, pp. 347–348). A later case, in 1589, involved a

subpoena brought in the matter of a contested election, not a debt, by a respected lawyer and former member of the House (D'Ewes, *A Compleat Journal*, p. 432).
47 D'Ewes, *A Compleat Journal*, p. 285; Neale, *Elizabeth I and Her Parliaments*, 1559–1581, pp. 382–385.
48 The remarks of Francis Bacon are cited by Neale, *Elizabeth I and Her Parliaments: 1559–1581*, p. 394.
49 See A. L. Rowse, *The England of Elizabeth: The Structure of Society* (London: Macmillan, 1951), p. 440: there was little persecution of Catholics during the first 10 years of Elizabeth's reign, but Pius V nonetheless approved the excommunication of the queen; Philip II and the emperor were dismayed. In 1570 scores of Catholic families sent their sons to study at Louvain and Douai, and they seeped back into the country as priests. The Society of Jesus took over in 1580. Rowse notes that Lady Egerton (the great lawyer's foster mother, for he was a bastard), was a recusant. The way around recusancy fines was for the head of the family to go to church occasionally, while the wife and children abstained. Recusant women were a difficult problem: they were more obstinate than men, according to Rowse, and had no property to get hold of. The obvious move for the men was a fraudulent conveyance: "members of the family got a lease where possible, to keep the lands in the same hands. Or Recusants made over their lands to other members of their family before they became liable to forfeiture. ... In Lancashire – and doubtless elsewhere – the practice grew up of J.P.'s and even ecclesiastical commissioners themselves taking grants of Recusants' lands and goods in collusion, while the recusant retained the use of them. All was fair in this kind of war; thus when Sir John Bridgewater, the author of *Concertatio Ecclesiae Anglicanae*, a well-beneficed man and a chaplain of Leicester, went abroad to become a Jesuit, he had the financial prescience to lease out his livings before going" (p. 451).
50 Campion's letter cited in Wallace, *The Life of Sir Philip Sidney*, p. 178.
51 For convenience I cite from Sir Philip Sidney, *The Old Arcadia*, ed. Katharine Duncan-Jones, Oxford World's Classics (Oxford: Oxford University Press, 1985), referred to in parentheses as *OA*, and from *The Countess of Pembroke's Arcadia*, ed. Maurice Evans (Harmondsworth: Penguin, 1977), referred to as *NA*, but I have checked for variants in the standard editions, the wrongly titled *Countess of Pembroke's Arcadia (Old Arcadia)*, ed. Jean Robertson (Oxford: Oxford University Press, 1973), and *The Countess of Pembroke's Arcadia (The New Arcadia)*, ed. Victor Skretkowicz (Oxford: Oxford University Press, 1987). Sidney's *Old Arcadia* was not published until the twentieth century. After he died, his friend Fulke Greville edited the 1590 edition, which went as far as his revisions extended in Book 3. In 1593, Sidney's sister Mary, the countess of Pembroke, printed the *New Arcadia* and added the remainder of the story from the *Old Arcadia*, beginning roughly where Sidney's revisions had stopped in Book 3. She made several editorial changes to minimize the disruption, such as updating the aliases of the heroes, which Sidney had changed. Dorothy Connell, *Sir Philip Sidney: The Maker's Mind* (Oxford: Clarendon Press, 1977), p. 128, n. 1, argues, rightly I think, that we should not use the title "The Countess of Pembroke's Arcadia," since Ringler showed that most of the changes in the text were authorial, that it was Philip, not his sister, who removed sexual material from the elopements of the princes with the princesses, and that the countess did not know about the revisions until Fulke Greville revealed them to her.
52 Ringler, *The Poems*, p. 376, argues convincingly that Sidney himself rewrote the Philoclea–Pyrocles seduction.
53 It was passed at the same time as 3 Hen. VII, c. 4, a fraudulent conveyance law that voided all deeds of gift made to defraud creditors, and 3 Hen. VII, c. 13, a statute on conspiracy to murder.
54 Ringler, *The Poems*, p. 379. For a further summary of views on the unsatisfactory ending,

see Robert E. Stillman, *Sidney's Poetic Justice:* The Old Arcadia*, Its Eclogues, and Renaissance Pastoral Traditions* (Lewisburg, Pa.: Bucknell University Press, 1986), p. 23; Edward Berry, *The Making of Sir Philip Sidney* (Toronto: University of Toronto Press, 1998), p. 70 (Berry finds unsatisfactory closure due to "an underlying lack of commitment to his 'idle work' itself" and his role as an author); and Blair Worden, *The Sound of Virtue*, p. 367, who suggests that "Sidney may not have wanted a rounded ending. Or he may judge it unfitting, or find it impossible, to give a capacity for depth of virtue to Basilius, on whose failings the public theme of the *Arcadia* has turned."

55 Howell, *Sir Philip Sidney: The Shepherd Knight*, p. 168.
56 Michael McCanles, *The Text of Sidney's Arcadian World* (Durham, NC: Duke University Press, 1989), p. 205.
57 See Jean Robertson's introduction to *The Countess of Pembroke's Arcadia (The Old Arcadia)*, p. xvii.
58 Ann Astell, "Sidney's Didactic Method in *The Old Arcadia*," *Studies in English Literature 1500–1900* 24 (1984): 39–51, 48–49. To explain the old *Arcadia*'s problematic ending, critics have either argued for a "harmonious synthesis of seeming opposites in the finale," usually by finding some kind of Platonic or Christian love to resolve the "paradoxes of the human condition," or they have argued that Sidney creates a debate that he leaves unanswered, showing "the irreducible complexities of the experienced life." Astell has resolved this debate by showing that Sidney's didactic theory of art, which leads not only to well-knowing but also to well-doing, goes beyond the mere plot and depends on a dialogue between the author and the reader.
59 George Puttenham, *The Arte of English Poesie*, (Cambridge: The University Press, 1936) pp. 178–180.
60 Ibid., p. 180. My emphasis.
61 A. L. Rowse, *Sir Walter Ralegh: His Family and Private Life* (New York: Harper, 1962), p. 74, supplies this information. He suggests that the conveyance perhaps accounts for the laudatory appearance of Sir John in this treatise, which is otherwise unexpected and corroborates Puttenham's claim to authorship. According to Gladys Doidge Willcock and Alice Walker, in their introduction to *The Arte of English Poesie*, p. xxii, Puttenham – a lawyer admitted to the Middle Temple in August, 1556, at the age of 27 – was consistently represented by his enemies as a forger of deeds, addicted to covenous practices, and an exploiter of legal graft.
62 Wallace, *The Life of Sir Philip Sidney*, p. 312.
63 See "Three Proper, and Wittie, Familiar Letters," dated 1580, in Edmund Spenser, *Poetical Works*, ed. J. C. Smith and Ernest de Selincourt (Oxford: Oxford University Press, 1912).
64 See Vincent Carey and Clare L. Carroll, "Factions and Fictions: Spenser's Reflections of and on Elizabethan Politics," in *Spenser's Life and the Subject of Biography*, ed. Judith H. Anderson, Donald Cheney, and David Richardson (Amherst: University of Massachusetts Press, 1996), p. 36.
65 A. L. Rowse, *Eminent Elizabethans* (Athens: University of Georgia Press, 1983), p. 192, n. 8.
66 C. J. Kitching, "The Quest for Concealed Lands in the Reign of Elizabeth I," *Transactions of the Royal Historical Society* 24 (1974): 63–78, believes that concealment was due to legal problems of identifying land from dissolved monasteries, not religious rebellion, but it is hardly unlikely that a good bit of self-justified fraud was involved.
67 Ralph M. Sargent, *The Life and Lyrics of Sir Edward Dyer* (Oxford: Clarendon Press, 1935), p. 35.
68 Ibid., p. 73
69 Ibid., p. 133.

70 According to Kitching, "The Quest for Concealed Lands," p. 70, finders typically kept half to a third. For Northampton's corruption, see Linda Levy Peck, *Northampton: Patronage and Policy at the Court of James I* (London: George Allen & Unwin, 1982). His comment may be found on page 169. For Northampton's character, see Rowse, *Sir Walter Ralegh*, p. 101: "Anyone who knows anything about Lord Henry Howard knows what a reptile he was. A clever man, learned, devious, secretive, the dead Norfolk's brother, he was as false but far more talented. A crypto-everything by nature, crypto-papist he was also a crypto-homosexual; that gave him a bond with James I, with whom he was in high favor and whose mind he sedulously poisoned, in Elizabeth's last years, against Ralegh."

71 Wallace, *The Life of Sir Philip Sidney*, p. 392.

Chapter 4

Purchase and Consideration in *Faerie Queene* IV and V

> "If they shall judge fraud herein, God judge them with
> more grace than they have judged of it, and me."
> Sir Walter Ralegh[1]

Sidney was born with a silver spoon but also knew disappointment, none greater perhaps than the three-year interval from 1581 to 1584, between the birth and early death of his uncle Leicester's young son, when it seemed his hopes of inheriting an earldom had been dashed. Despite this blow to his great expectations, Sidney's brilliance as a writer suggests that he knew the solace that talent brings as its own reward. Spenser was even more talented as a poet, but he had to earn his way in the world. Born in 1554, the same year as Sidney, he received a first-class education as a scholarship student at the Merchant Taylor's School, where Richard Mulcaster was the headmaster, and then at Pembroke Hall, Cambridge, where he spent seven years.[2] He may have traveled to Ireland in 1577 before becoming secretary to the Bishop of Rochester. On October 5, 1579, he wrote to his friend Gabriel Harvey that he was in the service of the earl of Leicester and in "some use of familiarity" with Sidney, to whom that year he dedicated his first major work, *The Shepheardes Calendar*. In 1580 he became private secretary to Arthur, Lord Grey of Wilton, and arrived with him in Ireland on August 12. Except for occasional visits to England, he stayed there until his death in 1599. During his stay he was favored with various escheated properties, including, in 1586, 3028 acres in Cork, a small part of the half-million acres of scattered parcels that the earl of Desmond forfeited to the Crown as a result of his rebellion. Schooled in the ways of the world, Spenser shows an understanding of the ways of fraud when he pictures a financial con man in *Prosopopoia*, or *Mother Hubberds Tale* (1591).

> for he was school'd by kinde in all the skill
> Of close conveyance, and each practise ill
> Of coosinage and cleanly knaverie.
> ...
> Now like a merchant, merchants to deceave,
> With whom his credite he did often leave
> In gage, for his gay masters hopelesse dett:
> Now like a lawyer, when he land would lett,
> Or sell fee-simples in his masters name,
> Which he had never, nor ought like the same:
> (lines 855–868)[3]

In contrast to Sidney's *Arcadia*, where a pair of princes convey a couple of heiresses and are pardoned, the deceitful conveyor of women in Spenser's *Faerie Queene* is a villainous enchanter named Busirane who is forced to give up his prize. Sidney and Spenser had different attitudes about fraudulent conveyancing, yet both were artists, and their great works do not limit themselves to propaganda on one side of the issue. Sidney has his princes arrested, and the charges against them metamorphose from murder conspiracy to false conveyance of another man's property – Basilius's daughters. Spenser condemns fraudulent conveyances in his political prose and minor poetry, but like Sidney, creates a more liberal or balanced view of this legal issue in his narrative poetry. *The Faerie Queene* is circumspect, as befits a poetics based on moral philosophy. Moreover, its romance form incorporates various aspects of life, including politics and commerce, as it presents a picture of deception, self-justification, and conveyances gone awry.

Reconsidering 13 Eliz., c. 5

The political intent, if there was one, of England's 1571 law against fraudulent conveyances to defeat "creditors and others" seems to have misfired badly. A generation after the Northern Rebellion prompted that year's parliament to action, the tract known as *The View of the Present State of Ireland* complains loudly that malefactors used fraudulent conveyances to hide property that rightly belonged to the queen. It may have been that opportunities for land transfers to minions of the state were more plentiful in Ireland than elsewhere in Britain during the 1580s and 1590s. But if *A View* accurately gauges the situation, the 1571 law did not live up to its authors' ostensible expectations.

In fact, the passage of the bill may have been more commercial than political. Parliament revisited the issue of fraudulent conveyances in 1572, and the debates, in a body that was almost fanatically anti-Catholic, reveal little interest in the use of fraudulent conveyance laws to increase Crown revenues or punish recalcitrant Catholics and other rebels. Other laws covered these political issues, most notably bills of attainder, which regularly included provisions against fraudulent conveyances made to defeat the interests of the state. Instead, Parliament debated and in 1585 finally passed a bill against fraudulent conveyances made to defeat purchasers (27 Eliz., c. 4). The new law protected those who gave valuable consideration in exchange for property against various forms of competing claims. By contrast, the 1571 law had been designed to protect not purchasers but "creditors and others," where the word "others" was not extended to cover forfeitures to the state until Twyne's Case in 1601. If Burghley, the queen, and their lawyers originally intended it to cover the powerful interests of the state, they were too embarrassed by their greed to say so loudly, or they simply failed of their purpose.

As a product of Parliament, not the policy of Burghley, the 1585 bill unambiguously concerned commerce. It is therefore surprising that when we trace the theme of secret conveyances in Spenser's *Faerie Queene*, we find it associated with references to purchasers rather than "creditors and others." Spenser's romantic epic is usually read as a dark mirror of England's colonial policy in Ireland, and Spenser himself benefited from the politics of land appropriation. His home at New

Abbey had been forfeited by Lord Baltinglas (whose own father had picked it up during the dissolution of the monasteries), and Spenser's later estate at Kilcolmen was part of the vast redistribution of lands that followed from the attainder of the earl of Desmond.

It is possible that both 13 Eliz., c. 5, the 1571 law, and Spenser's *Faerie Queene* consciously veiled their references to the political agenda behind the laws of fraudulent conveyancing. But it is also possible that both the law and Spenser's poem reflect an increasingly commercial world where people were less concerned with the morality of state policies than with the practical problems of competition and fraud. The disjunction between "creditors and others" and "purchasers" may provide evidence for those scholars who argue that the man who composed *The Faerie Queene* did not also pen the anti-Irish sentiments of the *View*.[4] Or it may be that Spenser distinguished the brazenness of a fraud to defeat purchasers from the more socially acceptable, if morally questionable, contrivances that debtors devised to escape the clutches of creditors and the power of the state. For fraudulent conveyance flourished not only in Ireland, but also everywhere men of property sought to control what they owned. However political was the original intent behind the 1571 law, however much the *View* rails against the fraudulent Irish, all landowners – even Burghley, who had experienced the Tower under Queen Mary – realized their fortunes could turn. Politics is not only the expression of power, but also the reaction against it. No wonder the law did not work for so long.

The State of Ireland

Spenser's attack on fraudulent conveyances occurs at the beginning of his *View of the Present State of Ireland* in the section that surveys half a dozen or so areas where the operation of English law creates special problems in Ireland. At this point the *View* is considering the mismatch between Irish society and certain English laws. Irenius, the dialogue speaker who has experienced Ireland directly, complains that Irish lords avoid forfeiting their estates (the normal penalty for felons and rebels) by giving away legal title to their property while retaining its benefits, or use, during their lifetimes. In particular he denounces the "close and colorable conveyances of the lands and goods of Traitors, Fellons, and fugitives" whereby the queen is "defrauded of the intent of the lawe." He then gives the example of the earl of Desmond, who "before his breaking forth into open rebellion ... had conveyed secretly all his lands to feoffs of trust, in hope to have cut off her majesty from the escheat of his lands."[5] His respondent Eudoxus seems sympathetic to the problem of fraudulent conveyances, but what he leaves unsaid is as important as his comments. Eudoxus never touches the problem of fraudulent conveyances by felons. He does not press Irenius for details on the bill of attainder against the earl of Desmond. Nor do he or Irenius seem aware that 13 Eliz., c. 5 might be available either as a law or as the model for a law against fraudulent conveyances by traitors.

The reaction of Eudoxus points to the legal uncertainty of the issue Irenius raises. When Irenius complains about people who flee overseas after having made colorable conveyances to their benefit and profit to support them while they are away, Eudoxus objects that this situation can be remedied, because there is a law against it in

England. He is thinking of 13 Eliz., c. 3, an act against overseas fugitives, which voided feoffments made up to two years before a fugitive's departure. Later, in the discussion of remedies, Eudoxus opines that although Ireland has not enacted a similar statute, "yet might her majesty by her only prerogative seize the fruits and profits of those fugitives' lands into her handes till they came over to testify their true allegiance" (p. 210). Eudoxus may have in mind the notion, later expressed in Twyne's Case, that 13 Eliz., c. 5 did not make new law, but only declared the law and custom of the land. The queen, by her prerogative, could seize fugitives' lands.

But Eudoxus never mentions the statute destined to have the greatest influence on the development of subsequent law. Passed in 1571 and numbered 13 Eliz., c. 5, referring to the year in which Elizabeth's Third Parliament sat and to the order of passage of the bill, the law nullified any otherwise legal transfer designed to "delay, hinder, or defraud . . . creditors and others." The statute contained a provision that it should lapse by the end of the first session of the next Parliament, but the following year, when the Fourth Parliament sat, the bill was extended (14 Eliz., c. 11). The Fifth Parliament extended it again in 1585, when it passed a related law against fraudulent conveyances to defeat purchasers (27 Eliz., c. 4), the product of a debate among Members of Parliament that had been going on since 1572.[6]

Despite these extensions, at the time Spenser wrote it would not have been clear how far either statute extended into Ireland. There had been no recent bill to adopt English statutes. English common law excluded the mere Irish, and special provisions, which Spenser condemns, such as living in the palatinates, kept English justice from reaching many of the Anglo-Irish. Ireland had its own fraudulent conveyance law that extended back to 1310 (at least according to the Irish statutes published in 1621).[7] It seems to have been honored in the breach, not the observance, like the provisions of the proto-racial laws of the Statute of Kilkenney that forbade intercourse among the Irish and English. Custom, as Spenser observed, weakened the grip of English laws of inheritance. The same enervating process of time seems to have antiquated the earliest fraudulent conveyance statute. As a result there was an ethical gap between the wishes of an administrator and land seeker like Spenser and the interests of those who already owned property and naturally opposed laws that threatened to strip away their wealth in times of trouble.

It seems likely that if Spenser knew about a statute voiding fraudulent conveyances by traitors he would not fail to have Eudoxus mention it. Neither interlocutor gives a hint that any law against fraudulent conveyances by traitors is on the books or available as a model for the Irish Parliament to imitate. Eudoxus should suggest, as he does with regard to overseas fugitives, the subject of 13 Eliz., c. 3, that a similar law exists against "creditors and others." But he does not mention the statute. The Variorum editor is probably right that no English statute existed to prevent fraudulent conveyances by rebels; otherwise provisions against fraudulent conveyancing would not have been included in the bills of attainder passed by the Irish Parliament in 1586.[8] The *View* does not support the thesis that the purpose of the passage of 13 Eliz., c. 5 was political, not commercial.

If 13 Eliz., c. 5 was not recognized as a weapon against Catholic conveyors in Ireland, nonetheless Irenius's political interests explain another oddity of Eudoxus's response, his failure to press the issue of conveyances by common criminals. Irenius perhaps mentions felons because the same law applied to felons and traitors regarding the crucial issue of when a transfer was fraudulent and when not. According to Sir William Staunford's *Les plees del corone* (1560), the forfeiture of land relates to the time of the treasonous or felonious act, but the forfeiture of goods and chattels relates to the moment of attainder following conviction.[9] That is, a gift of money by a murderer after his deed would be good, but the queen's escheators could void a gift of property. The silence of Eudoxus may indicate a problem not with the issue of timing, but with the nature of the forfeiture that followed a felony. Under English law, following a statute of 25 Edw. III that had been in effect since Queen Mary repealed her father's treason laws, traitors forfeited all their land directly to the Crown. Intermediary lords lost their rents and profits, following the feudal theory that they were to blame for the actions of their tenants. A felon, however, forfeited his property to his lord; the Crown only received a year's income along with the right to waste (that is, to exploit natural resources such as timber) for that period of time. The government had an interest in all forms of fraudulent conveyances, but the forfeiture of a felon could not be the basis of the kind of redistribution of Irish lands that motivates Irenius.

Not only does Eudoxus not comment on fraudulent conveyances by felons, he also offers the inadequate suggestion that bills of attainder might solve the problem of fraudulent conveyances by traitors. In response, Irenius reminds Eudoxus how difficult it is to move such a bill through the Irish Parliament.[10] Eudoxus does not ask for details, but we know them from a letter Sir Henry Wallop wrote to Elizabeth's councilor Lord Burghley. According to Wallop, the earl of Desmond had conveyed his estates "to the use of his son, with certain other remainders" (that is, people to whom the estate would pass should the son die) in a document bearing the date of September 10, 1574. Yet this document alone was not enough to produce a bill of attainder.

Parliament was not prepared to attaint a man only because he conveyed his land. The freeholders who made up the Irish Parliament were more than ready to accept that Desmond had cleverly protected his estate from forfeiture. As Wallop explained, Parliament at first refused to pass a bill of attainder without a special proviso recognizing the validity of Desmond's conveyance, which one of their own members guaranteed had been made in good faith:

> for the validity of the said feoffment for that one John Fitz Edmund Fitzgerald of Cloyne, then being of the Parliament House, and one of the foeffees (the other feoffees are the Lord of Dunboyne and the Lord Power), alleged the feoffment to have been made *bona fide*, and without collusion, which drew most of the House to have great regard thereof.[11]

The members changed their minds, however, when the government produced a document, dated July 18, 1574, that proved that only a few weeks before Desmond made the conveyance of his property to his son, he had entered into rebellion.[12] Wallop had found this document, which he called a "combination," when he entered Desmond's home at Askeaton in April 1580 while taking part in Sir William Pelham's brutal march through Munster in pursuit of the earl. So fortuitous was this finding that one almost suspects Wallop forged it, but the evidence points to its validity. We know that Wallop, the treasurer of Ireland, had been assigned to search for papers. And it was not just fictional characters like Shakespeare's Hotspur who foolishly sent out letters enlisting support and then found themselves incriminated by them.[13] Always expecting help from Spain, the rebels pressured other lords into their alliance with threats of the retribution they would face after an English defeat. Documents like the one Wallop found were drawn up to keep pressure on the participants not to back out when lured by offers of pardon that Elizabeth often and effectively extended. This letter of conspiracy seems almost too good to be true for the government, but it must have been legitimate because other participants were present in the Parliament House when it was produced and did not deny it.

What happened next testifies to the values of Dublin society, which could tolerate self-interest but not bold deception. The letter, or "combination," included not only Desmond's name, but the name of one of those who had claimed that Desmond's conveyance had been made in good faith, "the afore-named John Fitz Edmund," who promptly lost his credibility. As Wallop explained in his letter to Burghley,

> This combination (bearing date before the feoffment, and the feoffee that spake therein being one of the conspirators), being read in the House, and he not able to deny his hand to be it, presently caused the House to conceive very hardly of him, and also without further delay to pass the bill, which otherwise in respect of the feoffment aforesaid, I believe, verily, they would not have done until another Parliament.

Three factors convinced Parliament to accept a bill that would void Desmond's conveyance: timing, good faith, and collusion. Timing alone was not the key to the government's victory. Since Wallop's letter also admits that Desmond had been pardoned for that particular conspiracy, his attainder was actually based on the rebellion he began in 1579. There was also the issue of good faith. The circumstances under which Desmond's conveyance was composed could not support the claim that it was made bona fide, as John Fitz Edmund Fitzgerald of Cloyne had claimed. Twyne's Case would later point out that these words are unnecessary and actually raise more doubts than they settle. If his insistence on the good faith of the earl was suspicious, his claim that there was no collusion when the conveyance was made became patently untrue once Wallop produced what he called the "combination." Fitz Edmund himself was both a conspirator and a beneficiary of the conveyance.

As with the badges of fraud, no single factor is dispositive; rather, judgment depends on taking a number of factors into account. But why was John Fitz Edmund sitting in Parliament? Wallop is quick to testify in his letter to the man's good character – "The said feoffee hath a good pension from Her Majesty, and already hath a warrant for a good quantity of land, to be passed unto him from Her Highness." He had once been a rebel, but by 1581 a colonial administrator had described him to Burghley as "the only sound subject her Majesty hath in Cork."[14] The answer is that he was probably the recipient of a royal pardon.

The common law was slow to presume fraud from circumstances, but would do so when necessary. Wallop's letter suggests that the drama of seeing Fitz Edmund's lie exposed let the air out of the House's willingness to defend Desmond's conveyance. The sense of honor that motivated men in that age also accounts for the importance they placed on good faith, and the negative stigma of collusion. Collusion was evidence of a deceit, and all the fraudulent conveyance statutes mention it. Although it is hard to tell if the Irish Parliament quite refined its thought this way, Fitz Edmund's initial insistence that Desmond made his conveyance *without collusion* suggests that the implications of a conspiracy were well understood. Shocked by the timing of the conveyance, overwhelmed by the evidence of fraud, the Irish Parliament accepted a provision voiding all transfers made as far back as 12 years before the bill of attainder.

The Desmond episode illustrates the surprisingly complex understanding of the issues involved in crafting a law against fraudulent conveyances that Spenser probably witnessed in the Irish Parliament. Yet the *View* mentions none of these technical issues. The fictional Irenius does not propose language for a particular fraudulent conveyance statute, even when Eudoxus presses the issue. This reluctance fits the general pattern of Spenser's prose. The *View* specifies the laws that need to be changed to fit the Irish, not only fraudulent conveyance laws, but sumptuary laws, the laws of distraint, fees paid to clerks for copying complaints, and the over-endowment of power to towns and counties palatine. By contrast, the remedies Spenser proposes are typically vague. It seems to have been Spenser's view that the queen's prerogative sufficed to adjust overly powerful political units. Irenius complains that the laws concerning distraint needed to be more clearly written, and that juries interfered with inquiries into escheated or concealed lands. Irenius finally says that he will leave legal issues to the "grave Consideracions" (210) of those concerned to seize the fruits and profits of the fugitives' lands for the queen. It is impossible to discern precisely what Spenser identifies as the way to counteract fraudulent conveyances.

The vagueness of the *View* may have been tactical, however, for both words in the phrase "grave Consideracions" have double meanings. In addition to denoting thought, "consideration" is the legal term for value given. It is one of the factors, like timing, good faith, and collusion, as well as secrecy and whether or not a gift was revocable, that a court could use to determine whether a conveyance was legitimate or fraudulent. The word "grave" also has two senses. It means serious, but it is also Spenser's marker for Lord Burghley. The opening to Book IV of *The Faerie Queene* refers to his "grave foresight" and the dedicatory sonnet Spenser wrote for him refers to his charge of "grave affairs." Spenser may have guessed that Burghley, as the queen's chief councilor, had been the force behind all the fraudulent conveyance statutes since 1571. His double puns reveal but prudently veil his surmise.

Whatever the queen or her minister might do to solve Ireland's problems, the mere lack of consideration could not invalidate a conveyance. There was no law against giving free gifts, which could be valid even against those who claimed to have paid money for property. The issue of consideration lay dormant in 13 Eliz., c. 3, 13 Eliz., c. 5, and in the fraudulent conveyance clauses in bills of attainder (although one of the two key points of Twyne's Case is that the courts *did* need to attend to what these bills meant by "good consideration"). More obvious, during Spenser's lifetime, was the problem of a revocable gift, which raised doubts about the validity of a conveyance if a second party claimed to have paid valuable consideration for a property. Consideration therefore became a key issue in the related law against fraudulent conveyance made to defeat purchasers. The issue was, if a man sells the same property twice, which purchaser is the true owner?

Parliament proposed ways to sort out the competing claims of purchasers. Some members thought the first transfer should have precedence; that is, the statute should look backwards. Others thought the second should have precedence: as one member put it in 1572 – for debate on this bill began only a year after 13 Eliz., c. 5 was passed – "all assurances made to the intent to defraud any person shall be void against the second bargain."[15] Some believed the second conveyance should have precedence unless the first was properly enrolled before a clerk of the justice of the peace, or else at London before a judge or clerk appointed. On June 3, 1572, Mr. Loveless said that he had a number of clients who had come to him, greatly endangered and almost undone because they had purchased an estate and then found it encumbered. He assured Parliament that "the bill toucheth no estate made with consideration, nor any except it be fraudulent and covenous." Another member raised a troubling hypothetical: If a father transferred land to his son, and then renounced his son and transferred it to someone else, would the gift to the son be good or void? Mr. Loveless believed that "the considerations which are not to be allowed to be good cannot possibly be expressed." As the parliamentary debates show, the statute left open the value of love and family ties. It would be up to Star Chamber to define the meaning of "good consideration."

Purchasing Amoret

Spenser wrote the second installment of *The Faerie Queene* during the period of crisis when there was no general fraudulent conveyance law applicable to traitors. He himself was facing the problems that caused his complaints in the *View*. English courts had not yet clarified the law Parliament had passed to protect purchasers. In the first installment, Spenser associates various forms of the verb "convey" with secrecy and immoral or indecent activity.[16] The body of the false Duessa's husband, a demonic parody of Christ's disappearance from the tomb, is said to have been "convaid" in Book I of *The Faerie Queene*. The waste products of Alma's castle are "convaid" to Port Esquiline in Book II. In the second installment, the theme of conveyancing is far richer. It surfaces in the story of Scudamore and Amoret, in the episode of Aemylia, in the activities of Prince Arthur, and in Guyon's repossession of his horse. Each of Spenser's symbolic pageants highlights a particular badge of fraud – consideration, good faith, collusion, timing – although these factors are weighed to varying degrees in the stories, just as, according to Twyne's Case, they must be by a court of law.

By 1596 Spenser had developed a new awareness of the problems of fraudulent conveyancing. The original version of *The Faerie Queene* ends in Book III as Britomart finds Busirane using charms and magical writing to seduce Amoret, who is tied to a post with her heart in a pan (III. xii. 30–31). Meanwhile Amoret's husband Scudamore is helpless to penetrate the fires that protect the gates of Busirane's castle. The general meaning of the allegory is that adultery, which Busirane practices, can defeat a husband who lacks the magic of married love symbolized by Britomart. When Britomart at last delivers Amoret to Scudamore, the couple hug in a mythical embrace: "Had ye them seen, ye would have surely thought, / That they had been [a] fair *Hermaphrodite*" (III. xii. 46 [1590]). The hermaphrodite was an image of God, because universal generation was conceived as sexual. In revising, however, Spenser cancelled the image.[17] In the 1596 version, when Britomart returns to the gate with Amoret, Scudamore is gone.

The 1596 edition of *The Faerie Queene* added the language of fraud and conveyancing to images of magic when Spenser rewrote the story of Amoret and

Scudamore. Spenser's new stanzas say that the magic flames that had barred Scudamore from his wife had, in fact, been a fraud, the work of "th'enchauntor selfe, which all that fraud did frame" (III. xii. 43 [1596]). Book IV begins with a brief reminder that Busirane is a "vile enchanter" (IV. i. 3), the original conception of his character, but then continues to redevelop him as figure of fraud. Moreover, we learn that Scudamore had "bought" Amoret "in perilous fight" (IV. i. 2), and that despite Scudamore's precedence, Amoret was "conveyed quite away" when Busirane participated in a masque at her wedding. Separated from her husband by fraud, then rescued, Amoret travels through Book IV with Britomart until eventually she meets Scudamore, who, although he never recognizes her presence, explains how he won his wife at the Temple of Venus. This locus is described in a section of the poem that contains a series of stories warning against the perils of squires of low degree who overreach themselves by courting noble women like Belphoebe or Aemylia. Scudamore's activity contrasts with the moral of these other episodes.[18] The proper way to find a mate is to come from the right social class and wait for parents to negotiate a match. But Scudamore, it seems, is no heir. He does not win Amoret the old fashioned way: instead, he earns her.

Scudamore's language changes Amoret's story from a mystical conception of marriage to the problem of fraudulent conveyances used to defeat purchasers. As Scudamore tells the story, he won the Shield of Love at the Temple of Venus where he defeated 20 knights who maintained that "castels ancient rights" (IV. x. 7). By that means, he says, he "purchased" Amoret ("And purchased this peerlesse beauties spoile," IV. x. 3). In the language of the common law, a purchase is a legal right to possession gained by any means except inheritance. The word need not be strictly associated with conveyancing; Spenser uses the term in a similar line in his sonnet sequence, where he calls his beloved "the happy purchase of my glorious spoil" (*Amoretti*, 69. 13). But the word "purchase" does allow us to contrast Scudamore's purchase of Amoret by means of military activity with the conveyance perpetrated by the fraudulent Busirane.

If both Busirane and Scudamore have some claim to Amoret, the question is whose consideration is more valuable? Amoret seems to belong to Scudamore, of course, because she loves him. He had her first, he paid a price, and during her seven months of captivity, she refuses to yield to Busirane. He is a purchaser, while Busirane is a mere conveyor, a term that is usually associated with theft by Spenser. Yet just as a purchaser for value is helpless to void a fraudulent conveyance in the absence of an appropriate law, Scudamore is helpless to rescue Amoret until Britomart intervenes.

Scudamore plays the role of a purchaser who has not only been defrauded, but is also unrecompensed by any system of justice. It may seem that Busirane does not get away with his crime, because he loses Amoret. But he goes unpunished otherwise, while Scudamore continues to suffer from his loss. Although the lovers are joined in the original ending to Book III, the second installment of *The Faerie Queene* separates them, and they remain apart, or at least strangely reticent towards each other, for the rest of the poem. Scudamore's failure to recognize Amoret when they do come together (IV. ix) is often taken as one of Spenser's most obvious narrative lapses, but the inconclusive meeting actually works as an image of an unresolved dispute over property.

The legal correlative further suggests that Venus is as guilty as Busirane in arranging the fraudulent conveyance of Amoret. Scudamore's purchase occurs at the Temple of Venus (IV. x) when the goddess nods her approval and Scudamore seizes Amoret. But Venus also conveys Amoret to Busirane, for it is under her auspices, during the mask of Cupid (she is the mother of Cupid), that Amoret is kidnapped. The contorted syntax of IV. i. 3 suggests Venus's collusion. Grammatically Busirane conveys Amoret, but the passive construction of the last line, which says that Amoret is "conveyed quite away," allows the inference that Amoret was conveyed *to* Busirane, not *by* him. The ambiguity suggests that double-dealing Venus conveyed her, just as she earlier allowed Scudamore to purchase her.

The origin of the law to void fraudulent conveyances against purchasers points to the seller as the source of fraud. During the early debate over 27 Eliz., c. 4, one Member of Parliament named Mr. Birkit said "He would rather such a seller were punished as a felon."[19] If Venus has twice – thereby fraudulently – conveyed Amoret, she is the guilty party, rather than Busirane. This transfer of blame fits the perception of an older school of criticism, that Amoret's own susceptibility to the masque of Cupid explains her truancy with Busirane. Whether she is attracted to courtly, extra-marital love or fearful of the demands of marriage to Scudamore, her problem is venereal.

When Spenser added the second installment of his poem, he did not have to rewrite the story of Busirane's black magic in order to make the story work as an allegory of fraudulent conveyance. The poem is metaphorical enough to sustain both levels. The magician recites his incantations to make Amoret love him and then to restore her "perfect hole" (III. xii. 38)[20] again when, threatened by Britomart's sword, he reads his texts in reverse. Busirane's strange characters and magic books mimic legal proceedings to nullify a conveyance that otherwise has legal force.[21] Later Spenser associates Busirane with Lust when he says that Amoret is "conveyed" away by that allegorical figure in the forest (IV. vi. 47). Britomart, too, has a legal correlative. She operates like the queen's prerogative, voiding conveyances at will and reversing Busirane's documents with her own "gratious deed" (III. xii. 39).

The role of the queen raises the possibility of historical allegory. It was not unusual for Spenser to compose complex fictions by employing the sticks and fragments of reality. Scholars have already linked Amoret with Elizabeth's maid of honor Elizabeth Throckmorton, who infuriated the queen by marrying Ralegh. Amoret may also represent Mary Shelton, who similarly incurred the queen's wrath by marrying James Scudamore in 1574.[22] One more possibility hardly overburdens Spenser's capacity to create suggestive figures, and so Amoret may also be based on a third woman. I have not found her name, but she married a Scudamore and her brother, Francis Throckmorton, engaged in fraudulent conveyancing.

The real-life Scudamore and his wife were parties, innocently or not, to the fraudulent conveyances of Francis Throckmorton. A cousin of Elizabeth Throckmorton, Francis was the son of John Throckmorton, a lifelong Catholic. John had been Queen Mary's personal lawyer, and we have already seen him helping his brother-in-law George Puttenham convey away Margery Puttenham's manor of Heriard. As the twig is bent, so grows the tree, and John's son Francis conspired with the Spanish ambassador Mendoza to assist the other Mary – the Queen of Scots. He was caught and racked, made to confess, and executed in 1584.[23]

Not unexpectedly, there were rival claimants to Francis Throckmorton's estate. According to Pimb's Case, Francis Throckmorton committed his treason as early as

1576.[24] Between this first treasonous act and his later attainder, Throckmorton conveyed a use and a fine of certain lands to "a certain Scudamore" ("un Scudamore") and Scudamore's wife. The couple in turn sold the property for money to Pimb. The estate of a traitor would escheat to the queen unless it had been successfully conveyed. Legal arguments should have been based on the timing of Francis's conveyances.

It seems, however, that neither the facts of the case nor the law of fraudulent conveyancing was dispositive. No less personages than Edmund Plowden and John Popham told Pimb that the queen was entitled to all the land of a traitor before the time of his treason and after ("avant al temps del treason, ou puis"), which could only be true if the lawyers had 13 Eliz., c. 5 in mind. Elizabeth's statute voided fraudulent conveyances back to the beginning of the queen's reign, while the treason statute of Edward III only voided conveyances *after* the commission of a treasonable act. It is interesting that the case does not mention 13 Eliz., c. 5, however, just the queen's right to the land. The omission suggests that influential lawyers may have been convinced that 13 Eliz., c. 5 *should* have been available to void conveyances, but that opposing lawyers were able to undercut such a reading. What the lawyers told Pimb was that Throckmorton's treason destroyed the estate that Throckmorton had passed to Scudamore and his wife, which meant that Pimb had no claim to it. But Pimb seems to have been unconvinced. He sued the queen, probably on good advice, and she issued a patent to him for the land. The queen may have reasoned that Pimb was a bona fide purchaser, since he paid money. Or his lawyer may have successfully argued a traverse, the procedure by which someone who receives land from one indicted of a felony committed before the feoffment can "traverse" the felony because he is a stranger to it; by this means a late indictment would not bind the feoffee.[25] Pimb's Case ends quickly. Whether beaten at law or, more likely, exhibiting her own grace, Elizabeth allowed property to pass as if the conveyance were valid. The result was that she overlooked the role Scudamore and his wife may have played in Francis's fraudulent conveyance. The couple kept Pimb's money, but negotiators for the Crown may have sent a message that Scudamore and Francis Throckmorton's sister had cost the queen some income. Just so, *The Faerie Queene* brings Amoret and Scudamore together but then denies them a reunion.

Britomart's Timing

Britomart's involvement with and queenly control of conveyances picks up steam in Book IV. Having rescued Amoret, she then reaches an unnamed castle in the first canto where the "custom" is that only couples may enter. Here and elsewhere *The Faerie Queene* uses the motif of the strange custom of a castle to represent a clash of cultures, including the unsettled understanding of the law that Spenser complains about in the *View*. Those inside the castle represent one point of view, those who approach the castle another. As a general image the romance motif may apply to any number of issues. In this case, a "jolly knight" (IV. i. 10), by laying claim to Amoret, raises the problem of determining when a conveyance is fraudulent. His claim is patently false, since he has never met Amoret. The problem is that, as against Britomart, it has some validity, since she is not a man and therefore cannot claim a lady. They joust, and Britomart defeats him, making him "repent, that he had rashly lusted / For thing unlawfull, that was not his owne" (IV. i. 11). Nonetheless Britomart finds him "valiant" and takes it upon herself to help him enter the castle. At first Britomart, acting like a man, has Amoret admitted to the castle as her woman. She then reveals herself as a woman and has the knight admitted as her "debt" (IV. i. 12). Britomart controls the timing of the relationship, like a grantor who makes a revocable gift or conveyance. Poor jolly knight! The episode shows how difficult it is to claim property from an absent or invisible owner. At the end of the day, Amoret remains with Britomart, but the pairing is deceptive, since in reality she belongs to Scudamore. Even if the knight had defeated Britomart, his claim would have conflicted with that of Amoret's absent husband.

The situation of the jolly knight, besides depending on Britomart's control of timing, also corresponds to that of someone who is unaware of a previous contract or obligation. When Parliament debated the fraudulent conveyance law, the situation was mentioned wherein a man gifts his property to a son. Many felt that if the father then sold the property to a third party, the son might still have a claim, since he presumably exchanged his love and affection for his father's gift. The statute said that the son would have no claim if the wording of the gift gave the father the power to revoke. But in real life many gifts were made without legal writings, and the parliamentary debaters recognized both that fathers might change their intentions, and that there would also be cases where a son's ownership should be upheld. Typically that would occur when the son sold to a bona fide purchaser. Then who had the better right, the purchaser from the son, whose only consideration was love, or the purchaser from the father, who should have informed the buyer that the rights to the property were clouded?[26] The jolly knight acts like an innocent purchaser. Britomart's relationship to Amoret looks open. The knight thinks they are lovers and therefore, according to a convention of chivalric romance, he may try to win her. But he is deceived. First, since Britomart is a woman, within the heterosexual assumptions of the custom of the castle, she has no amorous or ownership relation with Amoret that she can pass to the jolly knight. Second, although her possession of Amoret is voidable, since she could admit she is female before fighting the jolly knight, Britomart's relationship to Amoret is not void, since she can maintain her possession of Amoret by maintaining her male disguise and defeating the jolly knight in combat, as she does. Britomart's intentions control the fortunes of the jolly knight. His quandary reflects, in romance terms, the dilemma of someone who pays value for an item that may have been given or sold to someone else.

The remainder of Book IV features a bewildering variety of knights who often appear, it seems, just to round out a foursome.[27] One explanation for the sudden appearance of otherwise unmentioned figures such as Sir Ferraugh and Sir Druon, as well as minor leaguers like Blandamor, is that they represent plaintiffs who appear out of nowhere with a claim to property against which putative owners must defend themselves. At the end of the first canto Sir Blandamor attacks Britomart in order to seize Amoret (IV. i. 35), and we are suddenly told – there is no hint of this earlier – that he hates Scudamore for having won her. Britomart defeats him, and he is tellingly said to be "convayd" away (IV. i. 37) by his friends, suggesting that his claim to Amoret is spurious. In Book IV, Blandamor gives Duessa to Paridell before jousting Britomart (IV. i. 35), precisely to avoid having to give up Duessa should he lose (as women were the normal prize demanded by knights who compete when traveling with ladies). Blandamor fraudulently conveys Duessa, just as one makes a gift to a friend to "delay, hinder, or defraud" a creditor, an impending creditor, or the queen. Later, in Book V, Duessa contrives with Blandamor and Paridell to destroy Mercilla (V. ix. 41), an episode that historically refers to the several plots of Mary, Queen of Scots, against Elizabeth. Part of their plot must have been the kind of fraudulent conveyancing that occurred as a prelude to rebellion in the north of England in 1571 and in Ireland during Spenser's service. Duessa represents not only Mary but also the rebels' estates. And Britomart represents both "creditors and others."

Unlike fictional stories, law cases for the most part settle issues on principle, not sympathy for a seeming victim. Most of the fraudulent conveyance cases one reads from the 1590s involve not the original parties, who may have been innocent or guileful characters, but their descendants and grantees, whose rights depend upon legal documents. This kind of moral cleansing seems to be one of the points of the brothers Priamond, Diamond, and Triamond, whose otherwise mechanical battles test the patience of readers of Book IV. The first two pass their souls to the third as they die, not only reinforcing Triamond's strength, but distancing him from their personal entanglements and foibles (IV. iii). It is hard to carry a moral grudge against a proxy. This strategy – which may explain why this trio appear under the name Telamond (perhaps their descendant?) in the title to Book IV – also explains why Blandamor enlists Paridell to fight for him against Scudamore, who never knows he is being attacked because of his claim to Amoret. The fight for property really is just business.

Friendship, not business, is the declared theme of the fourth book of *The Faerie Queene*, but these confusing encounters with pairing couples and foursomes just as often illustrate the downside of friendship, which is the appearance, to outsiders, of collusion or trust. Blandamor and Paridell collude to keep Britomart from winning Duessa in canto i and then again when Blandamor enlists Paridell as his proxy in canto ii. The pattern continues in canto ix, where Blandamor and Paridell join Druon and Claribell, previously unmentioned, in attacking Britomart and Scudamore, the two potential claimants to Amoret. By this time Amoret is traveling with Prince Arthur, a new figure of royal power, because Britomart has lost her to Lust. The claim of Busirane, the lustful ravisher, remains strong.

Aemylia's Consideration

The difficulty of writing a law voiding fraudulent conveyances against purchasers is that the law must sustain some frauds, and Busirane represents just such a hard case. Another example occurs after Satyrane's tournament, when Amoret notoriously steps away from Britomart to meet nature's call in some bushes, giving Lust the opportunity to snatch her up and throw her into a cave where he keeps Aemylia (IV. vii. 4–8). Their imprisonment associates the two women as victims of lust and imaginatively sustains Busirane's otherwise immoral pretensions to Amoret. Does Britomart (or any law) have the power to restore Amoret to Scudamore after Busirane conveys her? The question implicates the debate that took place in late sixteenth-century England over the extent to which laws were necessary to ensure what one parliamentary debater called "chevisance," a word that meant fair business practices but which Spenser recognized could be associated with chivalry.[28] Everyone agreed that fraud was bad, but it took time to craft rules capable of determining when fraud occurred.

Six years after the second installment of *The Faerie Queene*, Twyne's Case gave 27 Eliz., c. 4 a definitive reading when the Court of Star Chamber settled the problem of what constituted good consideration. Twyne's Case made clear that "good consideration" involved more than blood and natural affection. There had to be a payment that approached market value. Moreover, consideration of "nature or blood" did not defeat a precedent conveyance made by fraud or covin. Fraud and covin could only be defeated by a *valuable* consideration, for money. Nor was a fraudulent lease defeated by a bona fide loan made without a fine or rent reserved. A conveyance made with fraud and covin was "in equal degree" with a voluntary estate made with power of revocation. These rules had not been laid out in Spenser's day, but some of the precedent cases were being heard when he wrote and the issues must have been in the air, particularly for an author so personally concerned with conveyances of all sorts.

Just as one legal case may be decided by a holding in a similar one, Prince Arthur ultimately settles the claims of lust for the soul of Amoret by making a judicial decision in the case of Aemylia. At this point in Book IV, Amoret wanders away from Britomart while walking in the woods "for pleasure, or for need" (IV. vii. 4). Unprotected by the Knight of Chastity, Amoret meets Lust, who carries her to his cave. There she hears Aemylia, another prisoner of Lust (her name suggests she is Amoret's equivalent), tell her story: how she planned to elope with a squire of low degree, but when she reached the appointed grove, found Lust instead. Amoret escapes from the cave only to provoke Belphoebe's jealousy, which causes Belphoebe to banish Timias, another squire, from her presence. Timias and Belphoebe eventually reconcile (IV. viii. 17), and the story turns to Prince Arthur. He is traveling without his squire Timias when by chance he comes upon Amoret. She is with Aemylia (IV. viii. 19), who seems to have followed her out of Lust's cave. After fending off Slander, provoked by his accompanying two such women, Arthur slays Corflambo and rescues another squire whom this figure of lust had held in his grip. This young man's name is Placidas. He looks just like his friend Amyas, the squire of low degree with whom Aemylia had tried to elope. Placidas tells Arthur a longer version of Aemylia's story. He explains that Amyas failed to meet Aemylia because instead he met Corflambo (just as she was meeting Lust).

Aemylia's story, then, falls into two parts. First she tells her story in the cave, then Placidas tells what happened to Aemylia's lover Amyas. The first part sets up Aemylia as a property subject to competing claims, those of Lust and those of her squire of low degree. The issue of the second part of Aemylia's story is the relative value of non-monetary considerations. That is why, at the beginning of canto ix, the narrator asks which has more value, affection of kind, love of women, or zeal of friends:

> Hard is the doubt, and difficult to deeme,
> When all three kinds of love together meet,
> And doe dispart the hart with powre extreme,
> Whether shall weigh the balance downe; to weet

> The deare affection unto kindred sweet,
> Or raging fire of love to woman kind,
> Or zeale of friends combynd with vertues meet.
> But of them all the band of vertuous mind
> Me seemes the gentle hart should most assured bind.
>
> (IV. ix. 1)

The narrator suggests true friendship surpasses the other forms of love, and, indeed, the Aemylia–Amyas episode is usually read as an illustration of the virtue of friendship, because Amyas is assisted by his good friend Placidas. After Amyas finds himself imprisoned by Corflambo and then subjected to the wayward passions of Corflambo's daughter Poeana, Placidas intervenes to help his friend. The physical resemblance of Placidas to Amyas allows Placidas to join his friend in prison and deceive Poeana into making love to him instead of Amyas.

But the theme of friendship alone fails to account for several details of the second part of Aemylia's story. Finding no way to free his friend, Placidas does something very odd. He snatches up Poeana's dwarf, who holds the keys to the prison, and carries him away. Corflambo (that figure of lust) follows in hot pursuit, but Placidas refuses to drop the dwarf, "the purchase of my gotten pray" (IV. viii. 61–62). Placidas's reward for his theft of the dwarf – or is it asset management? – is that Arthur rescues him from Corflambo. Since Arthur is one of the heroes of the poem, he seems to approve of the deceptions of Placidas, who makes love to Poeana and calls his conveyance of her dwarf a purchase.

The deceptive stratagem of Placidas is then matched by a trick Arthur uses to rescue Amyas. He sets the dead Corflambo on his horse and has the dwarf lead him back into Poeana's castle. When an unsuspecting watchman unbars the gates, Arthur enters the castle. He captures Poeana, releases Amyas, and then attaches Corflambo's property on the grounds that it was gathered "by wrong and tortious power" (IV. ix. 12). The episode ends as Arthur divides the "purchast spoil" of the castle among the ladies after pairing off Placidas with a newly reformed and renamed Paeana. He restores Amyas to Aemylia. A general confusion of pronouns, however, makes it possible that Amyas switches his affection to Paeana and leaves Aemylia to his friend Placidas.[29]

Interpretations that force the episode into a pattern of strict friendship or a case study of the perils of Petrarchan love ignore the details and language Spenser chooses. These can be accounted for, however, by reading the episode as a free-for-all reflection of the contemporary debates over how much weight to give to different forms of consideration in determining what conveyances were fraudulent with respect to purchasers and which were not. What looks like theft or deception may be prudent action. It seems no accident that Placidas – and maybe Amyas – is called a "trusty squire" (IV. ix. 3). Secret trusts greatly complicated the forms of conveyance and led to the warning in Twyne's Case: "fraud is always appareled and clad with a trust, and a trust is a cover of fraud."

The moral ambiguity the episode imitates is further extended by the possibility, noted by critics, that Poeana marries Amyas, not Placidas. In that case Amyas would be one who transfers his affection, leaving Aemylia and marrying Poeana. Either way – and this may be the point – a revocable conveyance, as Justice Anderson pointed out in Twyne's Case, lies in equal degree with fraud and covin. The plot to deceive Poeana practiced by Placidas and Amyas is covenous in the legal sense: "a secret assent, determined in the hearts of two or more men to the prejudice of another."[30] But when Poeana switches her affection from Amyas to Placidas, she shows it is revocable. Her consideration is no better than theirs.

The Book of Friendship explores the line between acceptable collusion and illegal covin. Friendship is, naturally, a good thing, nor is it automatically unacceptable when used to deceive. In the phrase "fraud and covin," which judges looked for to determine guilt, fraud refers to the cheated party, covin to the collusion of two or more people to effect it. The law condemned collusion for the same reason Irenius complains about fraud among Irish jurors. But the flip side of collusion is friendship, and covin was a neutral term unless attached to fraud. The collusion of Placidas and Amyas, the conveyance of Poeana's dwarf by Placidas, the deceptive entrance by Arthur – all these are acts of friendship, but they could also be indicators of fraud.[31] The line *The Faerie Queene* seems to draw is that fraud and covin are acceptable as long as the right people obtain wealth in the long run. It was the same attitude that lies behind the *View*, whose attack on fraudulent conveyances is overtly political and, like Spenser's poem, tellingly omits specific legal recommendations. That Arthur seems to trick Poeana into opening her gates before he effectively seizes control of her assets suggests that her power resides not in force but fraud and that Arthur meets her in kind. She may even have some right on her side, figured by her singing, which "halfe rapt" the prince (IV. ix. 6). She saves at least half her property, either by conveying her affection from Amyas to Placidas, or submitting to Prince Arthur. For the daughter of Corflambo, she does not do badly.

Samient and Collusion

Arthur performs a very similar trick later in Book V, but this time the issue is fraudulent conveyances to deceive those political "others" suggested by 13 Eliz., c. 5, as well as the "purchasers" protected by 27 Eliz., c. 4. As in the Book of Friendship, Arthur uses deceit to enter a castle, this time to inflict justice on the wife of the Souldan. Here, too, he seizes the malefactor's property and redistributes it.

To a certain extent Arthur's actions reflect the experience of the Munster settlers. From the perspective of the 1590s, when Spenser wrote, the problem was no longer that of producing escheats. The problem was how the Munster settlers could protect their new properties from fraudulent claims. Lawsuits abounded, and in 1588 a commission, presided over by the chief justice Sir Edmund Anderson, was sent to Ireland to settle claims. The queen's men heard 82 bills presented against the undertakers, as the settlers were called. Most of the local claimants argued that lands had been wrongly seized. Some claimed they had not been in rebellion, others that lands thought to belong to rebels had only been leased, or that the claimants' ancestors had been quietly seized of lands that were falsely thought to belong to rebels. As Michael McCarthy-Morrogh points out, Anderson, who was "known for his rapidity in court and for skilful though harsh interpretations of the law," rejected every single claim, usually on procedural grounds or for want of evidence.[32]

The 1588 Commission was followed by another in 1592 and then a decade of legal wrangling – the period reflected by the *View* – that extensively restored to the locals lands that the attainder of the earl of Desmond had escheated to the Crown. As an undertaker himself Spenser tangled with Lord Roche, one of the more obstreperous petitioners. During the 1588 sitting at Cork, Roche was put in jail for choleric behavior after presenting what the court considered to be a number of "highly suspect witnesses." That did not stop him from engaging Spenser in court for the next five years, during which Spenser published the first installment of *The Faerie Queene* in 1590 and worked on the second.

As a literary reflection of Spenser's growing disillusionment and the increasing legal pressures on the Munster settlers, Arthur directly seizes property in the second half of the poem. In the first installment of *The Faerie Queene*, he rescues Red Crosse from Orgoglio's prison but does not appropriate Orgoglio's property (I. viii). He rescues Alma but leaves her house intact (II. x). In Book III he never goes near Britomart's home in Wales, nor does he approach the house of Busirane. In Book IV, however, he appropriates Poeana's castle, a gesture he repeats in Book V, when he gives Adicia's property to Samient, the handmaid of Mercilla, and again in Book VI, when he tricks his way into Turpine's castle and then takes possession of it.[33]

In Book V, which contains Spenser's crudest, or boldest, historical allegory, Arthur's intervention fits a backwards timeline of developing concerns about fraudulent conveyances.[34] Spenser, somewhat perversely, tends to reverse the events, perhaps to suggest that the path of Justice is always one of diminution: Astraea, goddess of Justice, rules the earth then leaves it. Lord Grey brings Justice, but then leaves Ireland. The Armada is defeated, and *then* the Spanish threaten Ireland with invasion. The figures of Detraction and Envy and the Blatant Beast at the end (V. xii) therefore represent the state of Ireland *before* Grey arrived. (He was backbitten from the beginning.) The Bourbon episode breaks the reversed chronology, because it refers to very recent events, yet it occurs in a later canto, and even there, Bourbon receives help, *then* he throws away his shield (V. xi. 54).

Such injustice is the subject of Arthur's encounter with Adicia (V. viii. 21–27). Her power precedes – and therefore by the reversed logic of the book, historically follows – the defeat of the Spanish Armada that Spenser portrays as a confrontation between Arthur and the cruel chariot of the Souldan, Adicia's husband (V. viii. 28–45). But Adicia is also active *after* the Souldan episode, since the arrival of the Armada was *preceded* by years in which a Spanish invasion of Munster was constantly expected. Agents like Nicholas Sanders and Thomas Stukeley were stoking the fires of resistance, Desmond eluded capture, and landowners were making the fraudulent conveyances that so troubled Spenser or, later, backdating documents to this period. The release of Adicia as a tiger into the savage forests (V. viii. 46–V. ix. 2) figures this period, as does the Malengine episode, in which Arthur uses Samient to expose the net-wielding, shape-shifting, Irish-looking shaggy-locked figure whose name suggests guile or fraud (V. ix. 3–19). Arthur and Artegall then witness the trial and execution of Duessa (V. ix. 20–50), who represents Mary, Queen of Scots. Her death in 1586 ended an era of intrigue that stretched back to the Northern Rebellion of 1569. Her episode therefore *follows* Spenser's allusion to the Armada of 1588.

Given the timeline of events in Book V, the language of fraudulent conveyance occurs where we would expect it, in the first of the adventures undertaken together by

Arthur and Artegall. These adventures correspond to the long legal aftermath of the Munster settlement; therefore they come early in the historical part of Book V. In the overall story, Artegall has just resumed his long-delayed mission to rescue Irena from Grantorto, when suddenly a woman being pursued by two paynims seeks his protection. He kills one pursuer. Arthur kills the other but then, "without discretion" (V. viii. 9), attacks his namesake Artegall. They joust and draw swords until Samient parts them. Samient identifies herself as the handmaid of Mercilla, who sent her to negotiate a peace with Adicia. The Sultan's wife, in turn, had been trying to subvert Mercilla by bribery and treachery and the promotion of false religion. These activities fit Philip II of Spain, who funneled money into England and Ireland, promoted Catholic missions, and supported both the Northern Rebellion of 1569 and the rebellions of Anglo-Irish discontents during the 1570s, 1580s, and 1590s. (The duke of Norfolk was finally executed in 1572 when his moneylender, named Ridolfi, inadvertently revealed the duke's correspondence with the Spanish king.) Samient uses the term "elf" to describe those of fairyland who accept the Souldan's bribes, a subtle cut at Artegall. The distinction between human and elf is not well defined in *The Faerie Queene*. Britomart is human; so is Red Crosse, although he was raised as an elf. Guyon is an elf, and so is Artegall. The term seems to apply to figures not wholly of the Fairy Queen's world; the historical manifestation would be a tinge too much of Catholicism or Anglo-Irish culture or even proneness to violence, such as Elizabeth's colonial administrators tended to exhibit.[35] In this series of episodes Arthur assuages whatever it is that creates Artegall's deficiency.

What looks like fraud to a creditor might seem like prudent asset management to a debtor. Who is to determine which of two bona fide purchasers has precedence? What is justice? Samient's name is usually glossed as "same." Her purpose is to identify Artegall, the knight of justice, with Prince Arthur, who wanders from book to book of *The Faerie Queene* – who, indeed, tells Artegall that "by the way unweetingly I strayd" (V. viii. 15) before he saw Samient pursued by a pair of paynims. The point of this identification is to grace, with the sheen of Arthur's higher purpose, the often dirty business of administering justice that clouds Artegall's deeds. The divinity that hedges Arthur is most obvious when he uses the brilliance of his magic shield to quell the Souldan, a reference to the historical fact of foul weather that defeated the ships of the Armada (V. viii. 37). It is less obvious when he uses deceit, but we know that Elizabeth often preferred to use tricky negotiations and deception rather than force in her foreign policy. Elizabeth also kept a wary eye on her foreign deputies, whom Artegall represents (he is not just Lord Grey). During the Northern Rebellion there were suspicions that Sussex, the lieutenant of the North, had Catholic sympathies. The duke of Norfolk turned against her, and even Leicester probably flirted with the possibility of marrying the Queen of Scots. No one could be fully trusted.

The necessity of deception makes sense of Arthur's plot to convey Samient back to Adicia's court. Before meeting Arthur and Artegall, Samient had failed in her mission to Adicia. The Souldan's wife thrust her out and then sent two agents in pursuit to dishonor her. Enraged by her story, Arthur and Artegall want to use "all their force to work avengement strong" (V. viii. 24) but think it best to use "counterfeit disguise" (V. viii. 25). Their use of deceit rather than force to defeat Adicia suggests that she, like Poeana, is a figure of fraud, in contrast to her husband the Souldan whose iron-hooked chariots and man-eating horses represent the sheer force of the Armada.

To fight injustice (the meaning of Adicia's name, from Greek *adikia*), the heroes decide that Artegall should disguise himself in the armor of one of the dead paynims and then "should as his *purchast prize* with him *convay*" Samient to the Souldan's court (V. viii. 25; my emphasis). Artegall does so, and then, exploiting the logic of a fraudulent conveyance to defeat a purchaser, Arthur appears at the Souldan's court and issues a defiant challenge to claim the damsel as his own, saying she is being held as a "wrongfull prisoner" (V. viii. 27). Two people claim the same property. How is the dispute to be resolved?

The resolution depends on our seeing the conveyance of Samient, the "purchast prize," as the problem of finding an adequate law against fraudulent conveyances in the period following 1588. The possibility of a Spanish invasion encouraged Irish rebellion and led local lords to craft fraudulent conveyances in the years before the Armada. The Souldan, who responds to Arthur's challenge, strangely represents the Armada itself. He attacks in his chariot, which his defeated horses wreck all over the countryside ("Through woods, and rocks, and mountains they did draw," V. viii. 41), recalling the wreck of Spanish ships all along the Irish coast. These wrecks were viewed and logged by the same commission of 1588 that was sent over to straighten out the first legal challenges to the Munster settlement.[36] Malengine (who appears after the Souldan episode, because Spenser reverses time) figures the earlier frauds.

If Samient stands for one and the same item claimed by two people – by Artegall in disguise and also by Arthur – the death of the Souldan, whom Artegall and Arthur had asked to judge their respective claims, leaves the issue undecided. Of course, injustice does not want the issue decided; that is why in the allegory Adicia tries to knife Samient, once she sees that Arthur has killed her husband the Souldan and hung up his armor. When Artegall, still disguised as Adicia's servant, frustrates her attempt, Adicia turns into a tiger, a poetical representation of Wrong armed with Might (V. ix. 1), and disappears into the countryside, while Artegall disperses "an hundred knights of name" who "maintain / That Ladies part" (V. viii. 50). Artegall's action allows him to open the gates of Adicia's castle to Arthur, which then becomes an image of the opening of Munster. At this point the language of one form of fraudulent conveyance law, that against purchasers, merges with the purpose for a better, more general law that would protect forfeitures to the queen. Arthur distributes the wealth of Adicia, which she had amassed not by force, but "through lawless power and tortious wrong" (V. viii. 51). His action works as an image of the redistribution of lands escheated during the Desmond rebellion, which happened *before* the Armada.

The logic of the law may be another reason for the reverse chronology of Spenser's historical pageant based on the Munster settlements. It is noticeable that Talus does not kill the hundred knights of Injustice (Adicia). They should not be identified in the historical allegory with those condemned by the bills of attainder of 1586, most of whom died during Desmond's rebellion, but they might represent cases based on those attainders that were heard by the courts and special commissions afterwards. The cases themselves were brought later, often by innocent heirs or purchasers, but the basis for most of those cases was in the past.

Guyon's Horse

Yet another image of fraudulent conveyance bridges the two installments of *The Faerie Queene* and reflects Ireland's legal crisis. In the opening canto of Book II, Sir Guyon, the knight of Temperance, encounters the dead body of Sir Mordant and his dying wife Amavia, two victims of the enchantress Acrasia, whom the Faerie Queene has assigned Guyon to defeat. Blood stains the hands of their appropriately named child, Ruddymane, either because it fell from his father, who is "besprinckled" with blood (II. i. 41), or because the baby has bathed his hands in the self-inflicted wound of his mother. When Guyon attempts to wash the baby's hands in a nearby lake, he finds that the water will not clean them because the lake memorializes a nymph who refused to be wrongly ravished. At the end of the episode, Guyon gives Ruddymane to his companion, the Palmer, to carry to the castle of Medina, where he will be raised. He himself takes up the armor of the dead Sir Mordant, but when he returns to where he has left his horse, finds it has been "convaide" (II. ii. 11). Three separate types of conveyance attend the baby's stains: ravishment, inheritance, and theft.

The episode of Amavia and Mordant is an allusive allegory that the poem's narrator fittingly calls a "pageant" because of its enormous complexity and the difficulty of accounting for all its details.[37] A line of critics read Ruddymane's stain that will not wash as a sign of original sin, the old Adam that condemns human flesh to temptation. But as eminent a critic as Rosemond Tuve refused to concede that washing was an allusion to the cleansing power of baptism.[38] If not baptism, Ruddymane's hands are nonetheless, in my view, an image of corrupt blood, an aspect of English law closely connected to the problem of fraudulent conveyances.

In what may have been the very last words he ever wrote Spenser identifies fraudulent conveyances as a means to avoid the consequences of "attainder."[39] The word attainder is cognate with tincture, or stain, because an attainted person is said to suffer from corruption of the blood. As a result, he loses the ability to inherit or to pass titles or property to heirs. As John Rastell's legal guide explains:

> Corruption of the blood, is when any is attainted of felony, or Treason, then his blood is said to be corrupt, by means whereof his children nor any of his blood, cannot be heires to him, or to any other ancestor, for which they ought to clayme by him. And if he were a Noble or Gentleman before, he and all his children thereby are made unnoble and ungentle, having regard to the Nobility or Gentry they clayme by their father, which cannot be made whole again by the King's Grant, without authority of Parliament.[40]

There were means for reversing corrupt blood, including one that sounds like the name of Ruddymane's father Mordant. One could appeal attainder by a writ of *mordancester*.[41] Just this possibility is suggested by the episode, since we never know what guilty deed doomed Mordant, or whether he committed one. Amavia is pregnant as she sets out for the Bower of Bliss to rescue her husband. She gives birth along the way, but when she finds Mordant, he is under the influence of the drugs of foul intemperance and essentially insane, since he does not know her or "his owne ill" (II. i. 54). She liberates him, but Acrasia, the enchantress of the Bower, casts a spell that kills him as soon as he drinks water. Our uncertainty about Mordant's guilt is repeated in the Palmer's humane decision to avoid looking too closely into whether Amavia killed herself. He declares that the baby's hands may signify guilt *or* innocence (II. ii. 10).

There is yet another source of ambiguity in the complex pageant of Amavia, Mordant, and Ruddymane. If Mordant's dead body sprinkled with blood represents his status as an attainted felon or traitor, it is therefore important to know whether Ruddymane was born before or after Mordant committed his guilty deed. The law was that if a man was attainted and should die before his son was born and during the lifetime of his ancestor, his younger brother, sister, or cousin would not be barred from inheritance, nor would his posthumous son's blood be corrupt.[42] A good lawyer might appeal Ruddymane's corrupt blood on the basis of timing, an important factor in the larger theme of Temperance.

Ruddymane's stain therefore represents neither corrupt blood nor innocence, but the possibility of either.[43] If we regard his father's armor as an image of his estate, it would be fraudulent to keep it from the queen. Guyon nonetheless hands it over to Medina, who takes Ruddymane, and his property rights, into wardship. The theft of Guyon's horse at this point may remind us that the financial penalties of wardships made well-heeled people avoid them, if possible, often by fraudulent and secret conveyances – "He [Guyon's horse] is convaide, but how or where, here fits not tell" (II. ii. 11). We seem to be left to our own theories, including what means should be used to keep a family estate out of the hands of the government. Two cantos later we learn that the horse was purloined by vain Braggadocchio, a lower-class character unfit for the aristocratic art of good horse management, according to the narrator, who suggests that riding is a "science / Proper to gentle bloud" (II. iv. 1). Fraudulent conveyancing was also an art that required a good lawyer not to do, but to do well.

Spenser's complaints about fraudulent conveyances in the *View*, and more so in the "Brief Note," help us to connect the problem of cleansing Ruddymane's hands with the difficulty Guyon has conveying the armor of Ruddymane's father without a horse. Reduced to walking, Guyon seems to be in a state of moral uncertainty until Braggadocchio's conveyance is finally undone, and Guyon's horse restored to him, in Book V. The agent of order is Artegall, who exposes another of Braggadocchio's frauds during a tournament held to celebrate Florimell's wedding. Braggadocchio falsely claims to have won, when the real victor is Artegall, who wears Braggadocchio's armor on the third day. At this point Guyon, who has been absent for more than two full books of the poem, arrives looking for his horse. He almost kills Braggadocchio and has to be restrained when he finds the vain villain with his steed (V. iii. 29). When Artegall wonders if he lost it by "might extort" or "slight deceaved" (V. iii. 30), Guyon answers by telling the story of Amavia and Mordant and how while he was busy with the "young bloodie babe," his horse "purloyned was by subtile traine." Artegall does not believe, or even seem to know, Sir Guyon, and requires a sign of his truth, just as the English courts would look for signs of truth in cases of fraud. Guyon satisfies the test by his ability to tame his steed, here named Brigador, but also by knowing about a black spot in his horse's mouth. Artegall therefore rules that the horse belongs to Guyon. The disappointed Braggadocchio then accuses the Faerie Queene's legal representative of injustice, which so provokes Artegall that he has to be restrained (V. iii. 36). But the iron man Talus – the executioner of justice, who seems to represent the dream of judicial efficiency – tears off Braggadocchio's armor, symbolically removing his pretense to nobility. He also defaces Braggadocchio's sidekick Trompart, whose name means "art of deception." Facial mutilation was part of the penalty for forging documents in both England and Ireland.

Unlike the fraudulent conveyance statutes, the English statute against forgery served word for word as the model for an Irish statute (f. 5 Eliz., c. 14 and 28 Eliz., c. 4 [Ireland]; the only change is that Star Chamber becomes Castle Chamber, a reference to Dublin Castle). With the strength of such a forgery statute, Talus could attack someone exposed by a black spot, reminiscent of the inky drop from a forger's pen, even though Arthegall – Spenser's nightmare of royal inefficiency – might be otherwise powerless against fraudulent conveyances.

Ralegh and the Lawyers

In conclusion, the jurisprudence of fraudulent conveyancing was actively developing in England when Spenser published the first installment of *The Faerie Queene* in 1590 and the second part in 1596, as well as when he wrote *A View of the Present State of Ireland*, probably in the 1590s, and registered it for publication in 1598. Several statutes were already in force and were finding their way into court cases for clarification and refinement. If the situation was unsettled in England, it was even cloudier in Ireland where Spenser lived and worked as colonial administrator. There the courts were ineffective either because the law was uncertain, their jurisdiction was in question or, as Spenser complained, they simply failed to execute justice.

Spenser blames political and cultural differences for the ineffectiveness of fraudulent conveyancing laws. At the same time, he urges reform of the law itself, and he had an audience. The lawyer and privy councilor Thomas Egerton owned and lightly annotated a manuscript copy of the *View*.[44] Egerton had extensive experience in Irish affairs, having been the main draftsman of the articles for the Munster plantation. His oldest son would die in Ireland during Essex's campaign in 1599. He and two other justices in Star Chamber participated deeply in the Munster plantation that colored Spenser's own ideas on transfers of property. One was Sir Edmund Anderson, Chief Justice of the Common Pleas, who led a commission to Cork in September 1588, in the first attempt to settle the claims and counterclaims that arose from disputes against and among plantation settlers in Munster. The other was Sir John Popham, the Attorney General, who was not formally part of the Commission, but also traveled to Cork. He was Speaker of the House in 1581, when Sidney would have heard debates about various forms of fraudulent conveyances. He heard the suit that Giles Allen brought against Cuthbert Burbage for tearing down the Theatre.[45] He was granted a seignory in Ireland, as were his sons-in-law, although he never succeeded in settling a plantation. Finally, Popham, Egerton, and Anderson, were the leading judges when in 1601 the Court of Star Chamber decided the single most important decision on fraudulent conveyancing in the history of English law.

Twyne's Case is a remarkable combination of political self-interest and dispassionate legal thought. As good servants of the queen, Egerton, Popham, and Anderson either extended, or confirmed, the application of 13 Eliz., c. 5 to forfeitures, making the statute available to the Crown in cases of treason and answering Spenser's complaint in the *View*. Like good lawyers, however, they also overcame the problem of intentionality by isolating what they called "badges of fraud," which remain the basis of determining fraudulent conveyances to this day. As we will see in the next chapter, the legal acumen of Twyne's Case seems remarkably free of politics, a truly universal standard for an area of law that tests the willingness of a society to restrict certain popular behaviors.

Fraudulent or not, conveyancing was something everyone did. Everyone with property, of course, which naturally included the elite audience for whom Spenser wrote *The Faerie Queene*. The example most on Spenser's mind was that of the earl of Desmond, who conveyed his property to associates within weeks of subscribing to a conspiracy of rebellion. This combination of events sufficed to demonstrate fraud even to the satisfaction of the Irish Parliament in 1586. Irishmen otherwise regarded conveyances as the proper procedure to ensure the inter-generation transfer of wealth, to counter the power of the state, and in a legal system that enforced corruption of the blood, to maintain self-identity.

Despite Spenser's shrillness on the subject, Desmond was only behaving like any Englishman of means. For example, a few years after Spenser died, his friend Sir Walter Ralegh prudently conveyed his estate to his son when challenged to a duel by Sir Amias Preston. He did so to protect his family property, since losing a duel meant possible death, as well as dishonor, corruption of the blood, and forfeiture.[46] Ralegh's duel never took place, but the paperwork served him, for a time, after his arrest for treason in 1603. King James wanted Sherborne, Ralegh's favorite estate, but it took a decade for the finest legal minds, among them the authors of Twyne's Case, including Sir Edward Coke, to discover a way to invalidate the conveyance. The king is said to have declared that "I maun ha' the land; I maun ha' it for Carr" (Robert Carr, his current favorite).[47] The lawyers could not attack it for fraud – could not claim that Ralegh had treason in mind when he made the transfer – but declared that the transfer itself, a complicated legal document, was invalid for technical reasons. A few key words, it turned out, were missing.[48]

Like piracy, tax evasion, and smuggling, conveyancing was a favorite practice, and some of this popular sentiment can be found in *The Faerie Queene*. Spenser never doubts what is correct, and nothing in the poem undercuts his ethical position. Ambiguity arises, however, because *The Faerie Queene*'s chivalric fiction imitates the process of sorting out competing values that lay beneath the debates over fraudulent conveyancing laws during this period. In conclusion, the history of the law helps us to appreciate Spenser's difficult poetic representations of the ethics of fraudulent conveyancing and to understand why he devoted so much discourse to the subject. Twyne's Case, we will see, also does this by turning to a related, and less politicized, area of fraudulent conveyances, those made to defeat purchasers, the subject of 27 Eliz., c. 4 (1585).

Notes

1 Ralegh to William Cecil, Letter 135 (1604), Edward Edwards, *The Life of Sir Walter Ralegh*, 2 vols. (London: Macmillan, 1868), vol. 2: *Letters of Ralegh*, p. 312.

2 For what is known about Spenser's life as well as accepted critical views of Spenser's work not otherwise footnoted, see *The Spenser Encyclopedia*, ed. A. C. Hamilton *et al.* (Toronto: University of Toronto Press, 1992) and Alexander C. Judson, *The Life of Edmund Spenser* (Baltimore: Johns Hopkins Press, 1945).

3 The text for Spenser's minor poems is that edited by R. E. Neil Dodge, *The Complete Poetical Works of Spenser* (Boston: Houghton Mifflin, 1908).

4   For arguments that no valid authority attributes the *View* to Spenser and even less authority makes him the author of "A Brief Note of Ireland," see Jean R. Brink, "Appropriating the Author of *The Faerie Queene*: The Attribution of the *View of the Present State of Ireland* and *A Brief Note of Ireland* to Edmund Spenser," in *Soundings of Things Done: Essays in Early Modern Literature in Honor of S. K. Heninger, Jr.*, ed. Peter E. Medine and Joseph Wittreich (Newark: University of Delaware Press, 1997), pp. 93–136.

5   W. L. Renwick, ed., *A View of the Present State of Ireland* (London: Scholartis Press, 1934), p. 36. Further page numbers are given in the text.

6   13 Eliz., c. 5 was extended by the Fifth Parliament in 1585 (27 Eliz., c. 11) and finally made perpetual in 1587 (29 Eliz., c. 5).

7   See *The Statutes of Ireland* (Dublin: Societie of Stationers, 1621).

8   Rudolf Gottfried, ed. *The Prose Works*, vol. 9 of *The Works of Edmund Spenser: A Variorum Edition*, ed. Edwin A. Greenlaw *et al.* (Baltimore: Johns Hopkins University Press, 1949), p. 300: "for example, the parliament of 1586 had to pass a special act providing that all conveyances made after 1579 by James Eustace, Viscount Baltinglas, and his brothers must be registered and that those made with treasonable intent be confiscated to the Crown (anonymous *History of Sir John Perrott*, pp. 252–66)."

9   The work of Stanford (the modern spelling) was often reprinted. I cite from *Les plees del corone* (London, 1607), p. 192: "Car pur terres, si tost que ascun de les offences avantdits soit perpetrat, maintenant est il restraine de faire done ou alienation de eux qui ne serra aniente apres sur son attainder, il ne fair ascun difference, mes que in lun cas & lauter, il serra relate al temps de loffence commise ... Mes pur biens, le temps est plus abridge. Car si un commit felony & est attaint, & mesne inter le felony & lattainder, il dona envoy ces biens, ce done est bone ... car pur biens ou chatelx, la forfaiture navera relation al temps del felony ou treason commise, eins al temps del forfeiture de eux." See also Abraham Fraunce, *The Lawyer's Logic* (1588; Menston, England: Scolar Press, 1969), p. 151, which summarizes Stanford's *Pleas of the Crown* using the logical format of Ramist dialectic and rather mysteriously cites lines from Spenser's *The Shephearde's Calendar* to illustrate certain syllogisms and "causes." See also *A Very Profitable Booke of Master John Perkins, Felowe of the Inner Temple* (London, 1555), s.v. Grantes, fol. 6: "Et quant a cest mater saches que atteindra de felony ou de murder &c. est communement dyt en troys maners, [that is] par utlage, par verdit, ou par confession, mes sur chescun de eux jugement covient estre don ou atremente ne serra dit atteindre. Et saches que atteinder par utlage avera relacion al *exigente* [the term means the first steps in outlawry] quant al terre et tenement issint que feoffemente del terre ou graunte del rente fayt devaunt in lexigent *agarde* [an award, or legal decision] par cesty qui est atteynt en tyel maner est bon. Et atteinder par verdsit avera relacion al temps del felonye fait solonque le suppose! del enditement quaunt al terre et tenement et issint avera atteinder par confession. Mes tout les atteynders quant al biens n'avera relacion forsque al iugement done issynt que done fait del biens par tiel home devaunt le iugement est bon, auxi la est atteynder par acte de parliament" (my emphasis).

A translation is given in *A Profitable Book Of Mr. John Perkins ... Treating of the Laws of England* (London, 1657), p. 10: "17   And as unto this matter, Know that Attainder of Felony, or of Murder, &c. is commonly said in three manners, that is to say, by utlagery, by verdict, and by confession. But upon every of them judgement ought to be given, otherwise it shall not be said an attainder. 18   And know, That Attainder by utlagery shall have relation unto the Exigent as unto lands and tenements, so that a feoffment of the Land or grant of a rent before the exigent awarded by him that is attaint in such manner is good: And Attainder by verdict shall have relation unto the time of the Felony committed according to the suppos al of the Endictment, as unto lands and tenements; and so shall have an attainder by confession. 19   But all the attainders as unto the goods shall have relation but unto the Judgement given. So that a gift made of goods by such a man before the judgement is good. Also there is an Attainder by Act of Parliament." The idea here is that the law distinguished lands from goods because a defendant needed to sustain himself until convicted. See William Roberts, *A Treatise on the Construction of the Statutes of 13 Eliz., c. 5 and 27 Eliz., c. 4, Relating to Voluntary and Fraudulent Conveyances* (Burlington, Vt.: Chauncey Goodrich, 1845), p. 582.

10   Spenser was secretary to Sir Thomas Norris, who represented Munster in Parliament. "As Spenser was much interested in the scheme of planting Desmond's escheated lands with English settlers, he was probably a frequent attendant of Parliament during this stormy session, which lasted from April 26 to May 14, 1586." Raymond Jenkins, "Spenser and the Clerkship in Munster," *Publications of the Modern Language Association* 47 (1932): 109–121, 116–117.

11   *Calendar of the State Papers Relating to Ireland, of the Reigns of Henry VIII, Edward VI, Mary, and Elizabeth*, ed. Hans Claude Hamilton *et al.*, 11 vols. (London, 1860–1872). See vol. 3: *1586–1588*, p. 63, for Wallop's letter to Burghley written on May 30, 1586.

12   A diary account of the parliament's reluctance to pass a fraudulent conveyance law can be found in F. J. Routledge, "Journal of the Irish House of Lords in Sir John Perrot's Parliament (3 May 1585–13 May 1586)," *The English Historical Review* 29 (1914): 104–117.

13   See *1 Henry IV* (II. iii).

14   *Calendar of State Papers of Ireland,* vol. 2: *1574–1585*, document 80.29, Sir Warham Sentleger to Burghley.

15   See Thomas Cromwell's journal for May 19, 1572, in T. E. Hartley, *Proceedings in the Parliaments of Elizabeth I*, 3 vols. (Leicester, 1981), 1: 361–362, 386–387, for this and the following quotations, from May 17 and June 3, respectively.

16   A. C. Hamilton, ed., *The Faerie Queene* (New York: Longman, 1977), I. ii. 24; II. ix. 32; book, canto, stanza numbers and sometimes year of publication, hereafter cited in the text. Spenser published the first half of his poem in 1590 then altered the ending of Book III when he added the second three books in 1596.

17   Lauren Silberman, *Transforming Desire: Erotic Knowledge in Books III and IV of The Faerie Queene* (Berkeley: University of California Press, 1995), p. 73, says Spenser changed the ending in order to provide a social context for Busirane's hostility, which is provoked by "the chastely loving wife" of Scudamore. I would argue that the hermaphroditic goddess of the Temple of Venus in Book IV resumes the symbolic merger of Amoret and Scudamore that ends Book III. It is part of Britomart's magic that the classical Venus overlaps with the Christian conception of the institution of marriage as the creation of "one flesh." See also C. S. Lewis, *Spenser's Images of Life* (Cambridge: Cambridge University Press, 1966), pp. 16, 38. Elizabeth Fowler "The Failure of Moral Philosophy in the Work of Edmund Spenser," *Representations* 51 (1995): 47–76, finds that Scudamore's "excessive reliance upon his own virtue" prevents him "from attaining Amoret's true consent" at the Temple of Venus (p. 66).

18   Spenser may have been following Sidney's identification of inter-class marriage as a form of fraudulent conveyance. In the first eclogues of the *Old Arcadia*, Artaxia is "conveyed in safety" (*OA* 61) to her home in Persia after her brother Otanes is defeated during his pursuit of Erona, who displeased her father by loving Antiphilus, a man of low-degree. Evil Artaxia then allows Antiphilus to fall in love with her, but does not reciprocate. Instead, she uses him to capture Erona, whom she hates, and has him tortured to death. See also David Quint, "Archimago and Amoret: The Poem and Its Doubles," in *Worldmaking Spenser*, ed. Patrick Cheney and Lauren Silberman (Lexington: The University Press of Kentucky, 2000), pp. 32–42, and Reed Way Dasenbrock, "Escaping

the Squires' Double Bind in Books III and IV of *The Faerie Queene*," *Studies in English Literature 1500–1900* 25 (1986): 25–45.

19   Thomas Cromwell's journal for June 3, 1572, in Hartley, *Proceedings* 1: 386.

20   The odd spelling of "hole" for "whole" may indicate a pun that alludes to Amoret's virginity.

21   Many of Spenser's chivalric images, aside from actual trials in the text, resemble or shadow legal procedures. The best example is probably Artegall's experience at Pollente's bridge; see my *Custom of the Castle* (Berkeley: University of California Press, 1997), p. 175n.

22   The husband may have been John, not James, Scudamore; see Linda Galyon's article in *The Spenser Encyclopedia*, s.v. Scudamore. The identification goes back to Upton. David Quint has related the change in the ending of Book III to Spenser's identifying Amoret with different personages: In the 1596 *Faerie Queene*, Amoret represents Elizabeth Throckmorton when Belphoebe catches her kissing Timias, who shadows Sir Walter Ralegh. To play this role, Amoret is no longer united with Scudamore. "Yet she has gone from representing one of Elizabeth's maids of honor to representing another, for in the poem's first installment of 1590 Amoret's story alluded to an earlier secret marriage between the queen's maid of honor, Mary Shelton, and James Scudamore in 1574. Queen Elizabeth had been angered on that occasion, too, so much so that she had broken Mary Shelton's finger. Spenser's poem had thus already invented the precedent and pattern for Ralegh's marriage before the marriage took place in 1591" ("Archimago and Amoret," p. 38).

23   See A. L. Rowse, *Sir Walter Ralegh: His Family and Private Life* (New York: Harper, 1962), p. 102; see also Conyers Read, *Mr. Secretary Walsingham and the Policy of Queen Elizabeth*, 3 vols. (Cambridge, Mass.: Harvard University Press, 1925), 2: 380–387.

24   Moore's Rep. 346. See Sir Francis Moore, *Cases Collect & Report* (2nd ed., London, 1688), p. 196.

25   See Sir Edward Coke, *The Third Part of the Institutes of the Laws of England: Concerning High Treason, and other Pleas of the Crown, and Criminall Causes* (London: M. Flesher, 1644), p. 230.

26   Thomas Cromwell's journal for June 3, 1572, in Hartley, *Proceedings*, 1: 386–387, particularly the remarks of Mr. Edgecome.

27   See James Nohrnberg, *The Analogy of The Faerie Queene* (Princeton: Princeton University Press, 1976), p. 604.

28   In a passage that has already been quoted, "Mr. Birkit said law was very necessary only to avoid frauds which the common law hath always condemned. The cause is not private but almost every man's case who hath lands. Very necessary to look back to do good and to punish fraud. He thinketh it good reason that he which selleth land and knoweth it to be encumbered with such former conveiance and will convenant to discharge the land of encumbrances should incur the danger. He would rather such a seller were punished as a felon. Good cause why the purchaser should be provided for. *The realm cannot stand without chevizunce.*" See Thomas Cromwell's journal for June 3, 1572, in Hartley, *Proceedings*, 1: 386. For Spenser's use of "chevisance," see *The Shephearde's Calendar*, April, line 143, and May, line 92, and *The Faerie Queene* II. ix. 8; III. vii. 45; and III. xi. 24.

29   For arguments for either pairing, see Walter F. Staton, Jr., "Ralegh and the Amyas-Aemylia Episode," *Studies in English Literature 1500–1900: The English Renaissance* 5 (1965): 105–114.

30   Fraunce, *The Lawyers Logike*, p. 60^v, cites Plowden, "Car covyn, solong; le vray definition de ceo, est un secreate assent, determine en les coeurs de deux ou plusors homes, al prejudice d'auter. Come si tenant pur vie voyle secretement conspirer avec un

auter, que l'auter recovera en prejudice de cestuy en reversion. Car per ceo son reversion serra toll."

31 Moreover, if the speculations of Richard Mallette, *Spenser and the Discourses of Reformation England* (Lincoln: University of Nebraska Press, 1997), are correct, the deceptions Placidas practices against Poeana include his sexual interest in his friend Amyas: "This episode depicts a strong homoerotic friendship, all the more pronounced because the story is largely narrated by Placidas, the friend with the greater degree of affection (p. 135). "Placidas claims wishfully (or defensively) that 'Aemylia will be lov'd, as I mote ghesse; / Yet greater love to me than her he did profess' (8.57) ... He also claims he is not able to accept the amorous advances of Poeana because 'I ... was not bent to ... love, / As was my friend' (8.60)." "Here is an obvious case of a homoerotic fondness transferred to a heterosexual alliance," says Mallette, and compares it to the "barely disguised incestuous attachment of Campbell to Canacee," a passion also suppressed, or dissolved, by a double marriage (p. 136).

32 Michael MacCarthy-Morrogh, *The Munster Plantation: English Migration to Southern Ireland, 1583–1641* (Oxford: Clarendon Press, 1986), pp. 98–99, for this and the following quotation in the text.

33 At Turpin's castle Arthur walks the fine line between local customs one must accept and those one must condemn, a theme suitable to the Book of Courtesy.

34 I owe the notion of reverse chronology in Book V to a paper titled "Apocalypse Then: *The Faerie Queene* 1590/96," written by James Nohrnberg and read by him at a program titled "Spenser 400" held at the Princeton University in 1990. Professor Nohrnberg has kindly supplied me with a copy of his unpublished remarks for this note: "If we don't count the supplemental Bourbon episode with its reference to 1593, the narrative order of the historical allegory in Book V is in exactly the reverse of the chronological and historical order – deeper and deeper into the past: the Armada, 1588 – canto viii; the Cadiz raid, 1587, and the Frotheringhay trial, 1586 – canto ix; the Netherlands campaign, 1585 – cantos x and xi; and Spenser's own experience in Ireland in 1582 and earlier – canto xii. The sequence is teleologically backwards, as it were nostalgic, regressing towards the poem's beginnings: even as it arrives at the sylvan settings of Book VI. *The Faerie Queene* sustains its great length upon the tremendous energies of the English Renaissance, but it terminates very abbreviatedly. On Acidale we catch a definitive glimpse of the poem's source in the beauty that flashes and evanesces through the woods of the poem as a whole, and yet that reveals itself – however lucid, lively, and lovely – in only brief intervals. The restoration of Adam, Verdant, and Amoret shows that the poem of 1590 celebrated the Elizabethan eighties as a rebirth indeed; but the poem of 1596 reflects elegiacally upon that interval as past and gone. Suddenly the heady eighties were ancient history, or an 'apocalypse then.'"

35 Andrew Hadfield, *Spenser's Irish Experience: Wilde Fruit and Salvage Soyl* (Oxford: Clarendon Press, 1997) notes that the distinction between English/Irish and civil/savage becomes tenuous in the second half of *The Faerie Queene*, and that Spenser came to oppose the indecisive policies of the aging queen. Although Spenser remained an advocate of reformation, there are traces of republican thought in his work. He was not "a penpusher in the service of imperialism" (p. 174).

36 On September 18, 1588, Sir George Carew wrote to Walsingham about the arrival of the "distressed Spanish fleet." Sixteen ships wrecked between Lough Foylle in Ulster and the Dingle peninsula in Kerry; five or six thousand men were said to be slain by sword or sea. See *Calendar of State Papers of Ireland*, vol 3: *1586–1588*.

37 Susanne Lindgreen Wofford, *The Choice of Achilles: The Ideology of Figure in the Epic* (Palo Alto, Calif.: Stanford University Press, 1992), notes that "The use of terms such as 'spectacle' and 'pageant' that in the late sixteenth century served also to designate the

effect of allegory is not fortuitous" (p. 249). See also Jeff Dolven, "Spenser and the Troubled Theaters," *English Literary Renaissance* 29 (1999): 170–200.

38 Rosemond Tuve, *Allegorical Imagery* (Princeton: Princeton University Press, 1966), p. 130, defines Spenser's temperance as misdirected allegiance, not excess. She takes issue with A. D. S. Fowler's "Emblems of Temperance in *The Faerie Queene*, Book II," *Review of English Studies* 11 (1966): 143–149. See also A. C. Hamilton, "A Theological Reading of *The Faerie Queene*, Book II," *ELH* 25 (1958): 155–162, and Carol Kaske, "The Bacchus Who Wouldn't Wash," *Renaissance Quarterly* 29 (1976): 195–209. Nonetheless, within the analogical structure of *The Faerie Queene*, the episode of Amavia, Mordant, and Ruddymane is usually read as a theological allegory: Ruddymane's *red hands* symbolize his condition as one who bears the stain of original sin. Typical is the view of Hugh MacLachlan, "The 'carelesse heavens': A Study of Revenge and Atonement in *The Faerie Queene*," *Spenser Studies* 1 (1980): 135–161, who thinks Guyon should "recognize that the bloody hands . . . represent the curse of original sin" (p. 141). Madelon S. Gohlke, "Embattled Allegory: Book II of *The Faerie Queene*," *English Literary Renaissance* 8 (1978): 123–140, makes the same point, that "Guyon nevertheless tries to deny the existence of an inherent blot in human nature by washing Ruddymane's hands" (p. 126). Harold Weatherby, *Mirrors of Celestial Grace: Patristic Theology in Spenser's Allegory* (Toronto: University of Toronto Press, 1994), pp. 175–178, has recently shifted the traditional interpretation that regards Ruddymane's red hands as representations of original sin by arguing that Mordant (the father), signifies Adam, while Ruddymane, because of his infancy, inherits only mortality, which the Law cannot remove (Ruddymane's hands remained stained despite attempts to wash them).

39 Citations for the "Brief Note" from Gottfried, *The Prose Works*; for its attribution to Spenser, see note 4 above.

40 John Rastell, *Les Termes de la Ley* (1525; London, 1624), p. 107, "corruption de sanke."

41 *Mort d'ancestor* was one of 75 writs existing by the end of Henry II's reign. Robert Dudley, the earl of Leicester, who was probably central to *The Faerie Queene* before he died in 1588, had his attainder falsified by a plea. See Sir Edward Coke, *The Third Part of the Institutes of the Laws of England Concerning High Treason, and Other Pleas of the Crown and Criminal Causes* (1817), p. 230.

42 Rastell, *Les termes*, p. 107, citing 32 Hen. VIII.

43 Red hands need not refer to original sin. Besides corrupt blood, the image can refer to bloody deeds, the bounty on Irish heads, mortmain, or, more positively in a hunting society, the washing of one's hands in the blood of a slain deer.

44 Christopher Highley, *Shakespeare, Spenser, and the Crisis in Ireland* (Cambridge: Cambridge University Press, 1997), p. 117, mentions the annotations. The Huntington Library manuscript EL 7041, the basis for the *Variorum* text, highlights Irish terms in the margins: Mantell, Glybbes, Bollykes, Armes, Language, Marriage, Bards, Jesters, Rathes, Cesse, Leases at wille, (46v), all in part 2. It uses block printing for the proverb "Better a mischiefe than an Inconvenience," the subject of a thoughtful essay by Judith Anderson, "'Better a Mischief than an Inconvenience': 'The Saying Self' in Spenser's *View*; or, How Many Meanings Can Stand on the Head of a Proverb?" in *Worldmaking Spenser*, pp. 219–233.

45 Charles William Wallace, *The First London Theatre* (1913; rpt. New York: Benjamin Blom, 1969), p. 163.

46 Whitney F. Bolton, "Riccardian Law Reports and *Richard II*," *Shakespeare Studies* 20 (1988): 53–66: "[A]s White [Edward J. White, *Commentaries*, 1913, p. 230] notes, in a trial by combat, 'if the accused was vanquished or killed . . . his blood was thereafter attainted, so that his heirs were cut off from inheriting from him, and all his posterity was made base and ignoble.'"

47 Edwards, *The Life of Sir Walter Ralegh*, 1: 469-470.
48 Ibid., 1: 468, notes that according to Sir Edward Coke, "the conveyance ought to have recited that the trustees '*shall and will from henceforth stand and be thereof seised*, to the uses, intents, purposes, and behoofs, in these presents specified, and to no other use, intent, purpose, or behoof'; and the essential words (here printed in italics) had been left out." Popham said he thought the problem was a clerical error. Roberts, *A Treatise on the Construction of the Statutes of 13 Eliz., c. 5*, p. 12, comments that Ralegh, "being possessed of a term of one hundred years, and intending to purchase the reversion in fee of the land, conveyed his term to his eldest son to prevent its being drowned, and afterwards purchased the fee, and a long time afterwards was attainted of treason, it was adjudged that the king should have the land in possession *discharged* of the lease, although *no fraud* was found in the case, but rather the contrary; but as it appeared upon evidence that Sir W. took the profits of the land, and held courts in his own name till the attainder, and as such assignment was apparently in trust, it was holden to be fraudulent and void against the king." A. L. Rowse, *Sir Walter Ralegh*, pp. 246–256, notes that Cecil stopped the dispersal of Ralegh's goods and chattels, which had been forfeit under his attainder to the Crown: they were now made over in trust for the maintenance of his wife and child. The suit over Sherborne ended in 1609, when it went to Robert Carr. James gave Bess Ralegh and her son £8000 as purchase money for their life-interest in the estate and a pension of £400 a year during her life and the eldest son's. The last word should be Ralegh's: In his "Discourse of War In General," in *The Works of Sir Walter Ralegh*, 8 vols. (New York: Burt Franklin, 1965), 8: 254, written while in the Tower, Ralegh reflected on the whole issue of private property and violence: "*But seeing our conveyances of land cannot be made so strong by any skill of lawyers*, without multiplicity of clauses and provisos, that it may be secure from contentions, avarice, and the malice of false seeming justice; it is not to be wondered" (my emphasis) that God's putting men over the things of the earth "hath bred much quarrel of interpretation."

Chapter 5

Coke, Collusion, and Twyne's Case (1601)

Crescit in orbe dolus

We now turn from literary representations of the features of fraudulent conveyancing law – from figures of speech, ethical dilemmas, the carrying away of women, and the protection of property – to the actual development of the law, not in Parliament, or in public opinion, but in court. Despite Glenn's assumption that Star Chamber heard Twyne's Case because of the political importance of the issue, its court was not yet the place of Stuart unpopularity. It issued fines, not indictments for felonies or treason; it used Chancery procedure; and it allowed the examination of witnesses at trial.[1] It was an arm of the Privy Council, part of the Queen's penal jurisdiction, but also a poor man's court and, although not a criminal court, it was charged with keeping the peace. As Shallow says in first words of *The Merry Wives*, after his keeper is beaten by Falstaff's men, his deer killed, and his lodge broken open, "Sir Hugh, persuade me not; I will make a Star Chamber matter of it" (I. i. 1).

Twyne's Case focuses on two key issues. First, it explains the badges of fraud. Second, it argues that a previous ruling on 27 Eliz., c. 4 should also apply to 13 Eliz., c. 5. The phrase "good consideration" should mean not just any amount. To prevent collusion it should be read to mean "valuable consideration." The case makes two other important points along the way. First, it shows why the penal clause in 13. Eliz., c. 5, which normally would require the strict construal of the statute, should be disregarded. This recognition, we shall see in the next chapter, informs Shakespeare's manipulation of the Alien Statute at the end of *The Merchant of Venice*. Second, Twyne's Case confirms Pauncefoot's Case in expanding the phrase "and others" to include the Crown. This reading confirmed what was not otherwise certain, that the statute allowed the government to receive forfeitures.

Badges of Fraud

Twyne's Case tells the story of a successful suit by a creditor referred to only as C. The creditor sought to attach the sheep of a man named Pierce in payment for a debt, but Pierce conveyed them to Twyne by deed. Because Pierce conveyed the sheep to Twyne to avoid his debt, the Court of Star Chamber declared the deed void and allowed the creditor to obtain possession of the animals. Coke's report instructs the reader that several indicators point to fraud: the gift to Twyne was made in secret, the sheep retained the owner's original mark, Pierce had no other assets, and the deed suspiciously proclaimed itself bona fide. Moreover, Pierce made the gift after a creditor filed suit. Timing alone was not sufficient to establish his intent to defraud. There was also a trust, the fifth badge of fraud the court lists: "Here was a trust between the parties, for the donor possessed all, and used them as his proper goods, and fraud is always apparelled and clad with a trust, and a trust is the cover of fraud" (*Ici fuit trust enter les parties, car le donor possesse tout, & use eux come ses biens propres, & fraud est touts soits apparel & clad [avec] trust, & trust est le cover de fraud*, 3. Co. Rep. 81a).

What the case means by "a trust" is not easy to determine. As proof of the trust, the case says that "the donor possessed all, and used them as his proper goods." But that statement merely repeats the second indicator of fraud, which says, more fully, that "the donor continued in possession, and used them as his own; and by reason thereof he traded and trafficked with others, and defrauded and deceived them" (*Le donor continue en possession, use eux come owner de eux, & per reason de ceo il trade & trafficke [avec] auters, & eux defraude & deceive*, 3 Co. Rep. 81a). The fifth rubric, "here was a trust made between the parties," leaves the distinct impression that by trust, Coke means collusion; or put another way, Pierce and Twyne were two friends who devised a plan to save Pierce's assets from ruthless creditors.

Several factors indicate a collusive friendship between Pierce and Twyne. First, Pierce owed money to Twyne as well as to C., but he chose to pay Twyne. The facts of the case say Pierce was indebted to Twyne for £400 and to C. for £200. He had goods to the value of £300, and these he deeded to Twyne. Second, when C. sent the sheriff of Southampton with a writ of *fieri facias* to levy on Pierce's goods, "diverse persons, by the command of the said Twyne" resisted him (*divers persons per commaundement del dit Twine [avec] force resist le vicount*, 3 Co. Rep. 80b).

In fact, Twyne and Pierce were probably not friends, but Coke leaves out facts that would undercut the story of trust and collusion he is telling. The same case is reported by Sir Francis Moore, serjeant of law, under the title "Chamberlain vers Twyne & auters."[2] Chamberlain (his first name is Brian) is therefore the unidentified C. of Coke's report, and we may speculate that Coke deliberately did not identify him. By only naming Pierce and Twyne he created a sense that the two were the dominant actors, working together. The use of Chamberlain's initial also seems to have allowed Coke to combine several creditors into one. Pearce (as Moore spells him) also owed £1300 to a man named Awdley, for which sum it seems Twyne was also obligated ("*Twyne fuit lye per obligacion anno 38 Reg. [avec] luy al Awdley*"). When yet another creditor, named Warburton, threatened to sue Pearce for yet another debt, according to Moore's account, Pearce had a scrivener named Proctor backdate a general deed of gift of all his goods. The deed purported to protect Twyne from the debt he owed Awdley ("*de saver luy harmless d'un vray & due debt*"). If it seems that Pearce was acting as a friend to Twyne, it is just as possible that Twyne insisted on the deed as a businessman, or as the facts in Moore's report suggest, that Twyne never knew about the conveyance. For the making and sealing of it was done in the absence of Twyne, the donee ("*Twyne ne fuit al feazance ne sealing de ceo, mes ceo fuit fait en son absence*"). Twyne never had possession of the deed, which was kept by Pearce's brother ("*Twyne nunqzs avoit possession del fait, mes ceo fuit gard per le frere de Pearce*").

Coke does not mention that Twyne himself was not present at the riot when the sheriff sought to impound the sheep ("*faire execucion*"), nor does he make clear that neither Pierce nor Twyne expressly ordered their servants to interfere with the sheriff. According to Moore, Twyne himself later sued Pearce for the debt owed to him. Such a suit hardly helped Coke make the case for a trust, and he left it out. In his version everyone is convicted of riot.

Moore's version stresses the role of the family in fraud, and the emphasis is on Pearce. It was Pearce who hired a scrivener and instructed him to backdate a deed and use all his skill to make it look legitimate (*"fuit antidated [avec] direction de faire son skill de preventer Warburton"*). It was Pearce's brother who held the deed, and Pearce's family that used the goods that by deed belonged to Twyne. Both versions list circumstances that indicate fraud. But only Coke includes "a trust between the parties." Coke tells a story of collusion, and he points a finger at Twyne.

Good Consideration

The explanation of what Coke means by trust occupies the second part of the report. Both versions of the case agree that the court ruled that even though the save-harmless deed was made on good consideration, because Twyne was owed money, the gift was fraudulent under 13 Eliz., c. 5. Moore goes no further. Coke, however, includes a long discussion of why "good consideration" was not sufficient to sustain the validity of Pierce's gift. (The term gift applied to a feoffment in fee that passed without conditions; a "gift" usually included a consideration, or payment.)[3] Coke's argument is legal in the strictest sense. It starts with the words of the final proviso of 13 Eliz., c. 5, in particular the word "and" before bona fide: "Provided also ... that this act ... shall not extend to any estate or interest in lands. ... had, made, conveyed, or assured, or hereafter to be had, made, conveyed, or assured, which estate of interest, is or shalbe upon good consyderation, and BONA FIDE." In Twyne's Case, Coke reminds readers of the significance of that word "and," which is that *both* elements of the final proviso must be met: "notwithstanding here was a true debt due to Twyne, *and* a good consideration of the gift, yet it was not within the proviso of the said act of 13 Eliz. ... for although it is on a true and good consideration, yet it is not *bona fide*" (*nient obstant que icy fuit [vraie] dett due al Twyne, & bone consideration del done, uncore ceo ne fuit deinz le provisoe del dit acte de 13 Eliz. ... car conit que est sur voier & bone consideration, unz nest BONA FIDE*, 3 Co. Rep. 81a). For Coke, collusion kept the conveyance from falling within that part of 13 Eliz., c. 5 (the "proviso") that allowed debtors to make certain transfers.

Good faith is the element missing when there is a trust. To illustrate his point, Coke creates a hypothetical case, which he addresses to the reader, to show how there can be good consideration and also bad faith. He posits the example of a man who owes several people £20 each. Holding goods to the value of £20, he makes a gift of the goods to one of the creditors. He does so with the understanding "that the donee shall deal favorably with him in regard of his poor estate, either to permit the donor, or some other for him, or for his benefit, to use or have possession of them, and is contented that he shall pay him his debt when he is able." Coke then declares that the man in the hypothetical shows bad faith for three reasons. First, when a debtor makes a preference of one creditor over another, it should be done in public, since secrecy is a mark of fraud. Second, goods and chattels should be appraised fairly. Third, Coke warns, be sure to take possession of the gift, since "continuance of the possession in the donor, is a sign of trust." Coke's hypothetical is obviously based on the facts of the main case, so much so that the story itself leaves out a detail crucial to the three-part moral. Coke forgets to say that the debtor paid his friend and made arrangements for lenient treatment *in secret*. His oversight is not uncommon among English Renaissance writers of prose fiction, who often forget where they leave things like characters, hats, and horses.

Having relied on the circular reasoning of a made-up story to illustrate lack of good faith, Coke turns to the other half of the final proviso of 13 Eliz., c. 5, which says that a gift is good if made with "good consyderation." He analyzes what, exactly, is meant by good consideration, starting with the distinction between good consideration and valuable consideration. "Good consideration" (*bone consideration*) is "consideration of nature or blood" (*Consideration de nature ou sanke*), while "valuable consideration" (*valuable consideration*), Coke's examples show, refers to money or the equivalent (3 Co. Rep. 81a–b). To make the distinction clear Coke resorts back to his hypothetical case and changes the story a little. Instead of coming to a secret agreement with one of his five creditors, this time the debtor gives all his goods to his son in consideration of "natural affection" (*natural affection*), so that the debtors all lose their debts. Although the statute clearly validates a gift made bona fide and with "good consideration," Coke says that "equity requires, that such gift, which defeats others, should be made on as high and good consideration as the things which are thereby defeated are" (*car equitie require que tiel done que defeat auts serra fait sur vy haute & bone consideration come le choses que son per ceo defeat sont*, 3 Co. Rep. 81b). In this case the "good consideration" of natural affection is not as "high and good" as the "valuable" consideration of an actual debt.

To shore up his hypothetical, Coke inserts additional information in the form of proverbial wisdom. He does so when he explains that no father makes a gift to his son without cause. "It is to be presumed, that the father, if he had not been indebted to others, would not have dispossessed himself of all his goods, and subjected himself to his cradle" (*& est etre presume que le pier sil navoit estre endebt al autres, ne voile dispossesse luy mesme de touts ses biens, & de subjecter luy meme a son cradle*). By cradle Coke means a man's child. He reads the statute according to his own conception of reason and tells a tale of moral philosophy about parents and children. (Ironically, 16 years later he lost control of a daughter, who was carried away by his estranged wife.)[4]

Buoyed by his hypothetical narrative and looking for ways to persuade the court to make "good consideration" in 13 Eliz., c. 5 mean "valuable consideration," Coke distinguishes expressed from implied trusts, or frauds as to creditors. An express trust appears from a writing; an implied trust "is, when a man makes a gift without any consideration, or on a consideration of nature, or blood only." Coke then associates the "trust" he finds between Pierce and Twyne – a trust that Moore does not mention – with the trusts that existed before 1535.[5] Coke recognizes that the persuasiveness of his argument turns not only on a story – his hypothetical – but on the court's accepting the moral of his story, that fraud is always on the increase and laws must be redefined to keep up with changing patterns of deception. To drive this home he steps back, ruminates on the work of Parliament, and draws on the Latin humanist tradition:

To one who marveled what should be the reason that acts and statutes are continually made at every parliament without intermission, and without end, a wise man made a good and short answer, both which are well composed in verse:

> Queritus, ut crescunt tot magna volumina legis?
> In promptu causa est, crescit in orbe dolus.
> [*If you ask why are there so many laws, the answer
> is that fraud ever increases on this earth.*]

And because fraud and deceit abound in these days more than in former times, it was resolved in this case by the whole court, that all statutes made against fraud should be liberally and beneficially expounded to suppress the fraud.

It should be clear by now that the report of Twyne's Case is not only the decision of the court, but the brief that Coke brought to court. That is why Moore does not mention most of this material and why it contains a huge hypothetical and the humanist distich on fraud. To make his case that the phrase "good consideration" should be read to mean not natural affection or blood but "valuable" consideration, it helped Coke to be able to show that a court had already crafted an expansive reading of 13 Eliz., c. 5.

One point of Coke's discourse, then, is to convince the judges that 13 Eliz., c. 5 should be broadly construed, not read narrowly the way penal statutes were interpreted. Two lines of cases showed how the courts had already widened the statute. First, the courts related it to the common law on fraud and did not treat it as a penal statute. Second, the cases had already given a broad reading of the phrase "and others." Mannocke's Case (1571), for example, which cites 13 Eliz., c. 5 within a year of its passage, illustrated the problems of an overly narrow reading of a law against fraud.[6] It relates to a common form of fraudulent conveyancing that occurred when the administrator of a deceased person's estate sought to deceive creditors of the deceased by conveying lands to friends and receiving profits himself. In this case a widow obtained administration of her dead husband's goods and chattels. She then sold them. After she died, a rival authority – the ordinary, not the Commissary – awarded her son administration of his father's estate. He sued a man, named Mannocke, who had purchased from his mother. The son was allowed to void the conveyance to Mannocke, but the court seems unhappy with its decision.

In Renaissance England, as in America until the reform of civil procedure, strict forms of a pleading often determined cases. The court pointed out that Mannocke could have won had he not pleaded that Nicholas, late Bishop of London, had committed the administration to the widow. He should have referred merely to an administration in general. The problem was that no notice of the assignment was found on the Bishop's Register, suggesting that the widow acted on her own and therefore defrauded the estate. Had Mannocke pleaded the former administration generally, the court would have found "a doubt" of the widow's guilt and ruled in his favor. By including this internal dissent against its own ruling the court indicated a conflict between the forms of pleading and the common law's traditional abhorrence of fraud.

Mannocke's Case (3 Dyer, 295a [1571]) helped open the door to a broad reading of 13 Eliz., c. 5 by including a list of similar cases where conveyances were voided even before passage of the statute. This list supports Coke's claim, in Twyne's Case, that the statute did not make new law but merely "declared" the common law's condemnation of fraud. In one of the earlier cases cited in Coke's report, "a man condemned" made "a gift of goods to delay execution, and he himself took the profits." In other words, he knew his conveyance would be voided but hoped that the law's delay would allow him to harvest his crops in the meantime, allowing him to earn money. Such a situation explains the inclusion of the word "delay" in the phrase delay, hinder, or defraud," which occurs in 13 Eliz., c. 5 as well as in modern statutes. Other cases are cited to show how debtors who took sanctuary were regarded as having delayed payment of their debts. In the same vein Mannocke's Case cites the much earlier case of Walter de Chyrton, a customer (that is, collection agent) of the king. Chyrton purchased lands with the king's money and passed the estates to his friends, keeping the profits for himself. He thus defrauded the king by direct and indirect means (language that arises in *The Merchant of Venice* when Portia accuses Shylock of contriving against Antonio's life "directly" and "indirectly"). These early cases show that statutes were not the only weapon available to fight fraud.

Penal statutes had to be strictly construed, every element proven, because they inflicted punishments, and 13 Eliz., c. 5 had a penal clause. Relying on the line of early cases against fraud, in 1591 the King's Bench observed in Gooch's Case that 13 Eliz., c. 5 provided that Acts of Parliament made in prevention or suppression of fraud ought to have "a favourable interpretation" (5 Co. Rep. 60). This ruling helped define the statute not as a penal law, which would require strict construction, but as a measure to prevent fraud, allowing a broad interpretation of the statute. The court held that because frauds were usually concealed, a plaintiff did not have to plead a feoffment. "To drive the plaintiff, who is altogether a stranger to it, to plead the foeffment (whereof he hath no knowledge) and that it was made by fraud, &c. would be mischievous and against law and reason."

Adding to these wider readings of 13 Eliz., c. 5, Pauncefoot's Case in 1594 explained, according to Coke, that the word "forfeiture" included "every thing which shall by law be forfeit, to the King or subject" (3 Co. Rep. 82b). That precedent allowed the court in Twyne's Case to hold that the phrase "and others" in 13 Eliz., c. 5 could be read to include anyone who had a cause of action that was hindered, delayed, or defrauded by a conveyance, including "all others who had cause of action, or suit, or any penalty, or forfeiture" (3 Co. Rep. 82a), *including* the Crown. If we trust Coke's account of Pauncefoot's Case, it therefore took 23 years for an English court to notice that 13 Eliz., c. 5 was available as a weapon against recusants. This delay fits the general trend of the times, which saw the greatest pressure being applied to recusants not back in 1571, but during the 1590s.

In fact, commercial concerns predominated in cases that cited 13 Eliz., c. 5 after 1571, many decided by men who would participate in Twyne's Case. The case of "Leonard *against* Bacon" (Cro. Eliz. 234) shows that although a tenant made valid gifts to different people, when those who had a cause of action in the same lands sued, his conveyances were "void against him."[7] Common Pleas heard the case in 1591. Sir Edmund Anderson presided as Chief Justice, Sir John Popham was Attorney General, and Sir Thomas Egerton was Solicitor General.

A third line of decisions, which limited plaintiffs to actual creditors, showed that these men respected what Parliament had written. In 1595, a jury determined that during his lifetime, one Craven "made a Deed of Gift of all his Goods to *Dixson*, and they found likewise that this Deed was to defraud Creditors, against the form of the Statute." Therefore the court found that the deed was void against Dixson when Kitchin brought suit against him as executor of Craven's estate.[8] The same year, in Packman's Case (6 Co. Rep. 18b) the court of King's Bench clarified the rule that if a "gift be by covin, it shall be void by the statute of 13 Eliz. against a creditor, but it remains good" against others (including, in this case, an administrator). The situation is similar to Mannocke's Case, as it involved the estate of an intestate (one who dies without a will) and two competing administrators. In Packman, the ordinary committed administration to a stranger, but at the request of the next of kin, the spiritual court repealed that administration. Meanwhile the first administrator sold the deceased's goods, seemingly a fraudulent conveyance against the next of kin. When the second administrator brought suit, it was resolved that the action did not lie, for the first administrator made the conveyance while he had the property in him, *before* it was revoked. The court ruled that although the gift would be void against a *creditor* by 13 Eliz., c. 5, it remained good against the second *administrator*.

Justice Anderson was also involved in "Upton *against* Basset" (Cro. Eliz. 445) a year later, which made the same point, that a fraudulent gift "is not fraud by the 13 *Eliz*., c. 5 against all, but only against his creditor."

Finally, in 1599 in "Bethel *against* Edward Stanhope," another case involving an executor, Francis Vaughan made a gift of his goods to his daughter before he died "with a condition [that] upon payment of 20s. that it should be void." The revocability of the gift indicates the fraud. The whole court held that the gift of the goods "is in itself fraudulent, as appears by the condition; and the covin is expressly found by the jury; and then it is utterly void against the creditors by the 13 *Eliz.* c. 5, and the intestate died possessed of them" (Cro. Eliz. 810). Even though the daughter took the goods, they remained as assets in the estate of the deceased "and the goods by law remained always in his possession" (Cro. Eliz. 811).

Coke worshipped the past, and past cases, as the source of the common law's greatness. He believed that the learning of the ages put the wisdom of the law above the knowledge or insight of any one man, including the sovereign.[9] Yet the logic of Twyne's Case is more sobering. Emotions aside, the important point is that a statute could be judicially construed to meet the challenges of the current times. A broad reading allowed the court to accept a redefinition of "good consideration," ignore the penalty clause because criminal statutes must be narrowly construed, and to let the whole statute be "expounded beneficially to suppress fraud."

Analogizing 13 Eliz., c. 5 and 27 Eliz., c. 4

The final section of Coke's reading of 13 Eliz., c. 5, as it appears in Twyne's Case, reinforces the argument, this time by analogy with 27 Eliz., c. 4, that a statute against fraud requires a broad reading. The holding is perhaps unclear, because the example involves a discussion of what constitutes "good consideration," which is relevant to but does not fully explain the course of Coke's larger argument against collusion. The first case cited is "Standen *against* Bullock," decided the year before Twyne's Case in Common Pleas, where Anderson was Chief Justice. The case involved a conveyance made with power of revocation, and then a bargain and sale. According to Coke's reading of 27 Eliz., c. 4, a voluntary conveyance with power of revocation should not "stand against a purchaser *bona fide* for a valuable consideration" (3 Co. Rep. 82b). The hitch in this case was that the statute seems to specify a *present* power of revocation, but the conveyance at issue included a *future* power of revocation ("as after the feast, or after the death of such one," Coke explains [3 Co. Rep. 82b]). Nonetheless, the case had shown that "the said Act should serve for little or no purpose, and it would be no difficult matter to evade it" unless this "small addition" were made to prevent an "evil intention" (3 Co. Rep. 82b). Coke did not miss the point: the court in "Standen *against* Bullock" had read 27 Eliz., c. 4 broadly to prevent fraud.

Coke cites a second case not just to define fraud or consideration but "on the same reason," to support his point that judges ought to construe a statute to fulfill its purpose. In Colshil's Case, decided in Common Pleas in 1596, where Coke next turns the reader's attention, a valid covenant to repay a sum of £300 occurred in an indenture (or contract) that was otherwise illegal because it violated a statute, 5 Edw. VI, c. 16, which restricted the deputation of office. The judges decided that the debt was void, because otherwise "the statute would serve for little or no purpose" (3 Co. Rep. 83a).

Having established the prerogative of the courts to give point to Parliament's statutes, Coke returns to "Standen *against* Bullock" and presents a hypothetical that apparently had been offered by the Court of Common Pleas in that case. Again his point is to show how the court had analyzed a statute in the past and should do so again. In his report on Twyne's Case Coke explains that 27 Eliz., c. 4 has two parts. The first makes void, as against any purchaser for "money or other good consideration," any conveyance made to "defraud and deceive." Otherwise the conveyance stands. The second part of the statute enacts that a conveyance made with power of "revocation, determination, or alteration" is void as against any conveyance made "*for money or other good consideration paid or given.*" The court in "Standen" apparently crafted a hypothetical situation to illustrate and resolve a possible conflict between the two sections. A conflict would arise if a valid purchaser took property that had been conveyed twice previously, once with power of revocation and once in a way that extinguished the power of revocation because there was intent to defraud. To resolve this complex conflict of interests, the court said that the valid purchaser should take the property. By the first clause of the statute, the conveyance that extinguishes the power of revocation is void because the defendant made the conveyance with intent to defraud. The second clause of the statute made a conveyance with power of revocation void as to a valid purchaser. Coke then concludes, "And it was said, that the statute of 27 Eliz. hath made voluntary estates made with power of revocation, as to purchasers, in equal degree with conveyances made by fraud and covin to defraud purchasers" (3 Co. Rep. 83a). Something had to give.

What is the force of Coke's comment that follows from the hypothetical, not the facts of the case? Its purpose is rhetorical, persuasive, to help Coke dismiss the objection that despite the appearance of fraud, Twyne should go free because he gave good consideration (he was owed money) for the goods Pierce conveyed to him. The phrase "and it was said" indicates that the judges realized there was some anomaly in a statute that equates a voluntary estate made with power of revocation, a common practice, with a conveyance made by fraud and covin. The hypothetical shows not that the two conveyances are in fact equivalent, but that to make the statute work to prevent fraud, they should be considered so. Coke then cites "Upton and Basset" again to make the point that the statutes only make the conveyances void as against the purchaser, that they are otherwise valid. Since the purchaser took a lease "without fine or rent reserved," he was not a purchaser, and therefore could not void the previous lease, even though it was made by "fraud and covin" (3 Co. Rep. 83a).

The rest of Coke's report on Twyne's Case considers instances where a purchaser is not a purchaser in the sense required by the statute. Coke proceeds at length because what "Upton *against* Basset" decided for 27 Eliz., c. 4, that good consideration must mean valuable consideration, is the very point that Coke wants to prove with regard to 13 Eliz., c. 5. Yet he cannot argue the analogy directly. He cannot say that "good consideration" should mean the same thing in 13 Eliz., c. 5 as it now does in 27 Eliz., c. 4. As a penal statute, 13 Eliz., c. 5 should have been narrowly construed. But having made the case for a broad reading of 13 Eliz., c. 5 as a statute to prevent fraud, Coke now uses the differentiation of purchasers to rehearse the logic that the court should apply to redefine "good" consideration.

In Upton the court distinguished what was paid from what was given. Although 27 Eliz., c. 4 twice – once in the preamble and once in the body of the statute – refers to "money or other good considerations" *paid* by a valid purchaser, in the portion concerning power of revocation, a revocable conveyance is void as against another conveyance made "for money or other good consideration *paid or given*" (Twyne's Case [3 Co. Rep. 83a] summarizing "Upton *against* Basset" and correctly citing language in 27 Eliz., c. 4; my emphasis). The additional words "paid or given" establish the point Coke wants. The Upton court apparently read the phrase correlatively, attaching "money" to "paid" and "good consideration" to "given." But whereas "good consideration" traditionally referred to "considerations of nature or blood, or the like" (3 Co. Rep. 83a–83b), that meaning had to be excluded from 27 Eliz., c. 4, because – and here is the telling point – nature and blood cannot be "given." One does not hand over kinship and family. It is, we may say, always already there. Coke concludes that the phrase "money or other good consideration paid or given" (3 Co. Rep. 83a) was "intended only of *valuable* consideration which may be given" (3 Co. Rep. 83b; my emphasis). The logic of the law lies in the chiasmus. Good consideration does not mean good consideration. It means valuable consideration.

Next Coke supports the point that purchasers can be of different quality by referring to Nedham and Beaumont's Case. Although determined in 1590, the case considered facts dating back to 1566.[10] A man named Babington covenanted with a Lord Darcy, whose sister was Babington's wife, to settle a certain manor on his children, but then by "fraud and covin, to defeat the said covenant," he made a lease of the manor to someone else. His children were purchasers "in vulgar and common intendment" of a right to their settlement (3 Co. Rep. 83b). (The children were purchasers because they were given rights to the manor by the covenant; they did not inherit the rights. A purchaser is one whose property right comes by any means other than inheritance, including gift, sale, forfeiture, theft, or shipwreck.) But they were not purchasers in the sense that would apply to 27 Eliz., c. 4, because "natural affection is good consideration but not such good consideration which is intended by the statute of 27 El" (3 Co. Rep. 83b).

Finally, Coke returns to a last point made by Anderson in Common Pleas in the case of "Upton *against* Basset." Because Coke makes it sound as if the point refers to an actual case, his reference is hard to understand. Fortunately we possess a fuller account of Upton (Cro. Eliz., 445) and can see that the case is actually a hypothetical made up by Anderson to demonstrate that a purchaser is not necessarily a purchaser under the statute, even where he pays consideration. He is not a "purchaser" under the statute, for example, when he operates unlawfully. The law will not recognize as a "purchaser" one who buys from a seller of "small understanding." The case report ends there. Where Anderson had redefined the term "purchaser" on moral grounds, Coke's lengthy case report uses Anderson's own precedent of redefining a term to support the redefinition of "good consideration." Twyne's consideration was "good" but not good enough. Coke's arguments about collusion and a broad reading of a statute were necessary to make 13 Eliz., c. 5 effective.

Conclusions

Like any good appeals court lawyer, Coke uses past decisions – particularly those handed down by the judges he faces – to support his argument. He also tells some good stories, only his literary form is not romance or comedy, but the case report. One of his stories sounds like something Sidney would write, the triumph of reason as the law slowly developed sound rules to control the passions of men. Another involved questions similar to those raised in the Aemylia episode in Book IV of *The Faerie Queene*, which asks what is worth more, "The deare affection unto kindred sweet, / Or raging fire of love to woman kind, / Or zeale of friends combynd with vertues meet" (IV. xi. 1). Spenser made his point in a story that cries out for elucidation, as do so many of his pageants and spectacles, and they do so because they are presented as riddles that have more than one answer, part of a poetic tradition that was obviously influenced by medieval schools. Poetry and the law have a common root in logic and rhetoric. But where the poet used a story to raise questions about competing values, Coke used hypothetical stories to make sharp points, to resolve contradictory statements by the law.

A third narrative strand finds Coke appropriating the very bone and fiber of Anderson's earlier decisions and applying them to a similar statute. In so doing, he behaves like that protean imitator of language and manners, Falstaff. Twyne's Case ends with an action on a riot, for "by the judgment of the whole court Twyne was convicted of fraud, and he and all the others of riot." That is where *The Merry Wives of Windsor*, written in the same years, begins: "The Council shall hear it, it is a riot" (I. i. 35). It is strange that Pierce – the villain in Moore's account – is for some reason not convicted of fraud, or at least not mentioned. Strange, too, that Windsor society forgives Falstaff his trespasses.

A final story sounds like *The Merchant of Venice*, because the law regarded what might be considered an act of friendship – Twyne's helping Pierce – as a form of collusion that jeopardized creditors. Was Twyne doing a good deed? Was Shylock?

Coke portrays Twyne as a colluder, attacks him for being a good friend, when it may be he was merely a victim of Pierce's frauds. Similarly, as the next chapter shows, Shylock looks bad but his debtor Antonio is no saint.

Notes

1. See G. R. Elton, *The Tudor Constitution* (Cambridge: Cambridge University Press, 1960), p. 101, and his *Star Chamber Stories* (London: Methuen, 1958), p. 16.
2. See *Cases Collect & Report per Sir Fra. Moore Chevalier, Serjeant del Ley* (London, 1688), p. 638, cited by lawyers as Moore 638.
3. See R. B. Pugh, *Calendar of Antrobus Deeds Before 1625* (Devizes, 1947), p. v.
4. On July 12, 1617, Coke charged his wife, Lady Haton, with "conveying away her daughter *clam et secrete*." See Catherine Brinker Bower, *The Lion and the Throne: The Life and Times of Sir Edward Coke (1552–1634)* (Boston: Little, Brown, 1957), p. 404. The king ordered her return.
5. Coke writes only 27 H. 8., but he must have in mind 27 Hen. VIII, c. 10, "An order for Uses and Wills." The preamble to that statute tells how once lands passed by "livery and seisin ... made *bona fide* without covin or fraud," but now "divers and sundry imaginations, subtle inventions and practices" allow conveyances that create "secret uses, intents and trusts, and also by Wills and Testaments, sometime made by *nude parolx* and words, sometime by signes and tokens." Such "fraudulent feoffments, fines, recoveries, and other like assurances to uses" have disinherited many lords, who have lost their "wards, marriages, reliefs, heriots, escheats, aids *pur fair fitz chivaler et pur file marier*, and scantly any person can be certainly assured of any lands by them purchased." The king has lost the lands of "felons attainted ... to the utter subversion of the ancient common Laws of this Realm." For more on uses and fraud, the mechanics of which are beyond the scope of this book, see A. W. B. Simpson, *A History of the Land Law* (1961; 2nd ed., Oxford: Clarendon Press, 1986), pp. 183–184.
6. Michaelmas Term, 12 & 13 Eliz., Dyer 295a. See *The English Reports* (Abingdon, Oxfordshire: Professional Books, 1979), vol. 73, pp. 661–664. Sir James Dyer, a justice under Queen Elizabeth, kept reports of some of his cases that were published as *Cy ensuant alcun novel cases* (London, 1585).
7. The text is that of Sir George Croke, a justice of the King's Bench and Common Pleas, who published reports of some of his cases.
8. Gouldsborough 116. See *Reports Of that Learned and Judicious Clerk J. Gouldsborough, Esq. ... His Collection of choice Cases ... With Learned arguments at the Barr, and on the Bench, and the grave Resolutions, and Judgements, thereupon, of the Chief Justices, ANDERSON, and POPHAM, and the rest of the Judges of those times ... With short Notes in the Margent ... By W. S. of the Inner Temple, Esq.* (London, 1653), p. 116. Gouldsborough was a justice of the Court of Common Pleas and other courts from 1586–1602.
9. For a good introduction to Coke's conception of the roots of the common law, see J. G. A. Pocock, *The Ancient Constitution and the Feudal Law* (New York: Norton, 1967).
10. See *Les Reports du Treserudite Edmund Anderson Chivalier, Nadgairs, Seigniour Chief Justice del Common-Bank. Des mults principals Cases argues & adjuges en le temps del jadis Roign Elizabeth* (London, 1664), p. 233.

Chapter 6

Shylock's Penalty

> "I confess fraud is to be detected, detested, and punished. But as that is an ill medicine, which cureth a disease and breeds ten worse in the body, so this bill."
> Member of Parliament, 1572[1]

The dilemmas of *The Merchant of Venice* allusively relate to the development of fraudulent conveyance law during the period between 1571 and 1601 as well as to antecedent works of English literature that we know Shakespeare read: Sidney's *Arcadia* and Spenser's *Faerie Queene*.

Long the subject of investigation by lawyers, *The Merchant of Venice* in recent years has also been a key text in the law and literature movement.[2] Two approaches may be distinguished, one narrow and one broad. The more closely focused scrutinists have been mainly concerned with the trial in Venice at which Shylock, having refused Antonio's belated offer of payment, demands the penalty of a pound of flesh according to his bond. They tend to agree that the trial has little basis in legal reality.[3] Those who take a broader perspective, however, tend to argue that Shylock's trial raises the larger questions of equity. They see the Duke's court as groping its way to a just solution. Portia's wit saves Antonio's life, and if her means are suspect, they are justified by the need for mercy.[4]

Each approach raises problems. However absurdly run, Shylock's trial is not inconceivable, or there would be no need for trained lawyers to debunk it. And of course the pleasing notion that equity dictates a fair solution is undercut by the forced conversion of Shylock and the financial penalties imposed on him by the court.[5] *The Merchant of Venice* is usually classified as a problem play just because one cannot help believe that Shakespeare wants us to feel the justice of Shylock's cause even as the plot of the play undercuts it.

While a great deal of legal attention has been paid to theories of contract and equity, few commentators discuss Portia's prosecution of Shylock or the penalty she imposes. Portia charges Shylock with the equivalent of attempted murder. She then imposes a punishment based on a provision that imitates the penal clause that both characterized and clouded the working of 13 Eliz., c. 5. Neither her charge of attempted murder nor Shylock's penalty occurs in the old story of the debtor bond. Shakespeare added them to his source because the *Merchant of Venice* asks us to look beneath the veil of a Venetian statute against attempted murder to engage with the deeper debate of the day. That debate concerned the shifting balance of power between debtors and creditors, including the state, that animates the history of the law against fraudulent conveyance.

The Law of Fraudulent Conveyance

Insofar as the penalty provision of Portia's Alien Statute resembles that of the 1571 statute of fraudulent conveyance, it could not have been popular in the eyes of Shakespeare's audience. For despite the law, in England anyone in debt – a class that included almost everybody at one time or another – might also practice some form of conveyance to defeat creditors, potential creditors, or the interests of the state. Aristocrats and commoners concealed assets. Shakespeare's friends the Burbages conveyed their property whenever they went into debt. Sir Walter Ralegh assigned all his assets to his son before he was arrested for treason. The courts hesitated to prevent the practice, strictly defining the times during which a criminal could or could not convey property.

Then as now, there was a fine line between fraud and what modern lawyers like to call careful asset management. It was a line that would not be reasonably well drawn until 1601, a few years after Shakespeare wrote *The Merchant of Venice*. At that time the Court of Star Chamber laid out what it called badges of fraud. Using these guidelines a judge could attempt to gauge whether a debtor intended to make any particular transfer of property for a sound commercial purpose or to defraud a creditor. The statute of 13 Eliz., c. 5 had tried to resolve the moral ambiguity of a transfer of property that left a debtor unable to pay what he or she owed. It looked not to the effect of the transfer but to the debtor's intention. If the transfer was made with the intent "to delay, hinder, or defraud creditors and others," then a court could declare the transfer "clearly and utterly void, frustrate, and of no effect." But intention is difficult to prove, since we cannot read people's minds. Therefore the court in Twyne's Case finessed the question by listing facts that indicated fraudulent intent. The judges asked, Was the transfer made in secret? Did the transferor maintain use of the property even though he conveyed away title? Did he receive an equivalent amount (that is, good consideration) in exchange for the transfer? Did the transfer leave the debtor insolvent? Twyne's Case affirmed the commercial character of the fraudulent conveyance statute, judiciously ignoring parts of the bill and precisely outlining the circumstances when fraud might be presumed.

Listing badges of fraud helped obscure the political origins of the law. The problem with the 1571 statute, the legal scholar Garrod Glenn has argued, is that it was intended as a political act. Its purpose was not to provide a necessary remedy for commercial creditors, but to provide a legal tool that could be used to raise money for the state, particularly when the government sought to seize the property of recusant Catholics. Recusants were often liable to ruinous fines, or even driven to rebellion.

Although the motives behind the 1571 statute were probably commercial as well, what gives away the government's hand is the inclusion of a *qui tam* provision, one that awarded part of the value of the fraudulent conveyance to the queen. That is, who ever sought to defraud a creditor was liable to

> the penalty and forfeiture of one year's value of the said Lands, Tenements, and Hereditaments, Leases, Rents, Commons, or other profits, of or out of the same, and the whole value of the said goods and chattels, and also so much money, as are contained in any such covenous and feigned bond: the one moiety whereof to be to the Queen's Majesty, her heirs and successors, and the other moiety to the party or parties grieved by such feigned

and fraudulent feoffment, gift, grant, alienation, bargain, conveyance, bonds, suits, judgment, executions, leases, rents, commons, profits, charges and other things.

In the Renaissance, the government typically used a *qui tam* law as an instrument to combat fraud. Then as now its use was controversial. The Latin phrase "qui tam" means "who as well. . ." It describes a cause where the plaintiff sues for himself *as well* as the state, under a statute that authorizes that part of the penalty shall go to the person who brings the civil action while the remainder goes to the state.[6] This form of action was not uncommon in Elizabethan England, which lacked a regular police force and so depended on citizens to enforce its laws. The comments of Members of Parliament attest to the controversial nature of *qui tam* laws. Most members had a low opinion of the kind of person who would make a living pursuing such suits.[7]

Once passed in 1571 and published as a matter of record the statute of 13 Eliz., c. 5 could easily have been something Shakespeare knew about. Parliamentary statutes were constantly reprinted, and unlike the overwhelming mass of federal, state, and local law passed today, statutes were few enough that they could be read easily, even by a non-lawyer. Moreover, everyone with property knew about fraudulent conveyancing, the way we know about itemizing deductions. Whether or not Shakespeare actually read 13 Eliz., c. 5, the striking fact is that the statute contained a penalty provision that was instantly recognized as inept. The case history of the next 30 years, until just after Shakespeare wrote *The Merchant of Venice*, shows that the courts ignored the *qui tam* provision. They probably recognized its unpopularity and impracticality.

Fraudulent Conveyance Laws in Italy

It is no accident that the resolution of Shylock's trial, including the Alien Statute and the disposition of Shylock's property, raises issues associated with the law of fraudulent conveyance. Two hundred years before Elizabeth's parliament put an odd penalty clause in a fraudulent conveyancing bill, the Italian city-state of Florence grappled with the larger problems of politics and the need to protect creditors in order to encourage commerce. The source story of Shakespeare's *Merchant of Venice* derives from this period of Florentine history. It may be found in a collection titled *Il Pecorone*, attributed to Ser Giovanni. The story tells about a Jewish moneylender who loses his suit for the value of a bond when a judge rules that the law does not allow him to draw blood or to take any more or less than an exact pound of flesh.[8] The unnamed moneylender tears up his contract and departs, unpaid but also unpunished. Shakespeare's play begins with this Italian story, but it also adds the Alien Statute. Portia's citation of this law leads us into the problem of finding the grounds for Shylock's guilt and pondering the justness of his punishment. In contrast to the source story Portia does not release Shylock. Instead, she charges him with a felony attempt on the life of Antonio, thereby putting Shylock's life and all his property at risk.

The legal debate over how to balance the rights of debtors and creditors flourished to a remarkable degree in Florence, beginning in the thirteenth century.[9] Statutes, some of which incorporated laws dating back to 1252–1286, were passed in 1322,

1355, 1408, 1421, 1458, and 1467. These Florentine laws typically required the registration of loans. They made businessmen or family members liable for the debts of a partner or relative. They controlled the repudiation of an inheritance or the emancipation of minors. We can do no more than glance at this legislation here, but one case holds our attention because it allows us to see how Shakespeare shaped the Alien Statute to fit the themes of the rest of the play. It shows how a desperate debtor, like Antonio, could be rescued by a court willing to allow a quibble to control the law.

The registration of bonds and other instruments required by the statutes of Florence often had limited effectiveness because debtors might employ highly paid lawyers to defend them. Tuscan advocates could construct arguments based on Roman law, which Florentine statutory law took for granted. They could cite the statutes of Florence. Or they could rely on a set of circulating opinions called *concilia*. These were used by an institution known as the *consilium sapientis*, "where a judge, often a political appointee with little or no knowledge of the law, sought the opinion (*consilium*) of a lawyer (*sapientis*) and then aligned his verdict with it."[10] In Florence and other Italian city-states, the *consilium* often reconciled the civil law with local customs, statutes, and usage.[11] It resolved conflicts between theory and practice, between the letter of the law and its application.

Portia's ruling on the meaning of Shylock's bond, after she enters the Venetian courtroom disguised as a learned jurist, depends on such a *consilium*. Thomas Kuehn, who has written a history of the development of the law of fraud for Florence in the fourteenth century, including various forms of fraudulent conveyance, has discovered a remarkable example that, I believe, illustrates the issues and procedures of the source story of the pound of flesh. The case concerns two Florentines, who went to court to cut off the reach of a creditor. According to the law, an unemancipated minor was liable for his father's debts. In 1467 Antonio Strozzi and Bartolomeo Sozzini, with the help of two lawyers from Perugia, argued that Francesco, the son of Antonio della Luna, should not be liable for the debts of his father, who had gone bankrupt, even though Francesco had not been emancipated at the time. They claimed that the word "emancipated" implied a choice, but where the son was *infans*, there could be no choice. Since the governing statute spoke only of those sons who could receive emancipation, the son, although not emancipated, was also not unemancipated in a sense that would make him liable for his father's debts.

In fact, as Kuehn points out, an *infans* could be emancipated. The argument carried conviction, however, because the lawyers used public policy to buttress it. Arguments from public policy usually occur where laws conflict or changing circumstances threaten to undermine their purpose. Strozzi and Sozzini argued that the statute was odious because the civil law created the category of *infans* and gave it privileges that should not be overridden by a local statute. Nor should the son suffer for the sins of his father.[12] Because these local laws conflicted with the civil law, the lawyers argued, they should be read restrictively.

The problem of emancipation shows that the law is not confined to statutes but also includes narrow legal arguments, even where there is a whiff of the ingenious or even the fraudulent about them. It was only by quibbling over the meaning of "emancipation" that Strozzi and Sozzini could fling public policy back into the teeth of a law that everyone knew was designed to ferret out fraudulent attempts to harm legitimate creditors. In a similar way, English courts read penal laws restrictively, a practice that helps justify Portia's reading of Shylock's bond, since it contained a penalty clause. At the same time, laws against fraud were broadly construed, as they are today. A balance had to be found between the rights of debtors and creditors, and a quibble serves the purpose, if necessary.

In both the *Pecorone* and Shakespeare's play, Portia's character is said to present the learned opinion of a famous judge when she rules that Shylock can have his pound of flesh, but that he must take exactly one pound, no more or less, and no blood. Terry Eagleton claims that Portia's "ingenious quibbling" would be ruled out of order in a modern court. The *Variorum* says Portia's ruling is based on a "miserable quibble." Kornstein calls her ruling "a transparent and absurd quibble," yet Kuehn's example shows just how far Florentine courts could go in entertaining such fine distinctions, especially where the individual was pitted against an unpopular law.[13] Neither Shylock, Antonio, nor the Duke is a *sapiens*, and their arguments that equate maintaining the bond with the validity and reputation of the law of Venice do not carry the weight of Portia's learned *concilium*. "To do a great right, do a little wrong," Bassanio beseeches the Duke (IV. i. 216), and it may be that Portia, disguised as Balthasar the judge, does just that when she rests her decision on the legal opinion she has brought from the great lawyer Bellario.[14]

The Alien Statute

After Portia settles the problem of Shylock's bond by learnedly construing the meaning of a pound of flesh, she moves to the penalty phase of her proceeding. She first invokes the Alien Statute and then again uses her cunning to craft a penalty based on that statute. Insofar as we can glean its wording from what Portia pronounces, this Venetian law sounds like a treason statute, only instead of preserving the life of the sovereign, it protects every citizen. It punishes foreigners who attempt to murder a Venetian citizen, and it does so by appropriating the malefactor's property and putting his life in jeopardy.

> It is enacted in the law of Venice,
> If it be proved against an alien
> That by direct or indirect attempts
> He seek the life of any citizen,
> That party 'gainst the which he doth contrive
> Shall seize one half his goods; the other half
> Comes to the privy coffer of the state,
> And the offender's life lies in the mercy
> Of the Duke only, 'gainst all other voice.
> (IV.i.348–356)[15]

What Portia describes sounds like a treason statute because the contrast between alien and citizen resembles the division between a subject and a sovereign. In practice, however, the category of alien was fairly fluid in Shakespeare's London, if not in his fictional Venice. There was a middle category of "denizens" who had the freedom of the city and certain privileges.[16] Moreover treason is an act against the state by one who owes it his allegiance. One cannot be an alien and also owe allegiance. Treason also depends on identifying the interests of the state with the interests of a person, usually the king, and not a citizen. A treason law would not give Antonio the power to take or spare Shylock's life. Yet he suggests that in exchange for the clemency the Duke has already granted, Shylock be forced to convert to Christianity. The Alien Statute distinguishes a citizen from the state by dividing the offender's property between the victim and the government. This provision is typical of a *qui tam* law.

If the Alien Statute does not fit comfortably within the guidelines of a treason statute, however, neither does it quite work as a *qui tam* statute. In both cases the problem is the separation of the victim from the state. In a typical *qui tam* case, the government is threatened, and a private citizen brings suit. In the case of the Alien Statute, however, an individual – Antonio – is threatened, and the state, in the guise of Portia, brings suit to protect him. Portia represents the state because she is the agent of the jurist Bellario, for whom the Duke sent. The situation is different in Shakespeare's source, where Portia's equivalent character impersonates a mediator whom the parties agree to and pay. Because Portia takes over Antonio's suit, it has appeared to commentators that she suddenly shifts Shylock's case from a civil action for debt to a criminal proceeding based on a charge of attempted murder. The key idea seems to be the notion that Shylock is guilty if he "doth contrive" against the life of Antonio.

Portia's word "contrive" might suggest that Shylock is guilty of conspiracy. According to Sir James Stephens, the common law defined attempt and conspiracy, and provided in general that "incitements, attempts, and misdemeanors are conspiracies."[17] But a conspiracy, as Staunford noted in *Les plees del corone* (1557), cannot be committed by a single person; there must be at least two ("*conspiracie ne peut estre commise per un person solement, eins deux almeins*").[18] Coke agrees with this definition.[19] Although Twyne's Case considered the possibility of collusion, Elizabeth's 1571 statute against fraudulent conveyances "devised or contrived" to "delay, hinder, or defraud" creditors does not list conspiracy among the synonyms like "feigned, covenous, and fraudulent" actions done with "malice, fraud, covin, collusion, or guile." The language of the statute is meant to cover actions by a single person without requiring proof of evil intent. Shakespeare usually uses the words "conspiracy" for the actions of a group such as the assassins who conspire against Caesar, or Caliban and his confederates, who conspire against the rule of Prospero.[20] Shylock, however, operates alone.

It is not obvious that Shylock conspires with anyone else to kill Antonio. It may be that Shylock is somehow punished for contriving with Tubal or even, in a sense, with Antonio himself to commit murder. A live production might exploit these possibilities. Motives and morals can shift from moment to moment. If there is a conspiracy in the play, however, it arises from the network of friendship, kinship, and honor that Shylock finds himself facing before the Duke. The key figure in this conspiracy is Portia, disguised as a learned jurist. Since the work of A. W. Moody, modern criticism has generally seen Portia as more worldly than nice.[21] She may signal Bassanio which casket to choose.[22] She manipulates Shylock in court and turns a quibble on flesh and blood into good law. She is related to the best friend of Shylock's adversary.[23] Most importantly, she accuses Shylock of contriving to murder Antonio, despite the absence of a conspiracy and the absence, in English common law at least, of a crime of attempted murder.

Attempted Murder

The Alien Statute, which allusively mimics a treason statute, creates a crime of attempted murder when an alien commits the crime against a citizen. In modern criminal law, the category of attempt has two elements: the intent requisite for the main crime and a first step toward the commission of that crime. But legal scholars have not been able to agree on the first step or act that makes Shylock culpable. Mark Edwin Andrews, in his 1935 legal analysis of the play, claimed that Shylock's indirect attempt occurs at the inception of the bond when Shylock feigns humility and good will and calls the bond a "kindness." The direct attempt occurs when Shylock whets his knife and says "A sentence! / Come, prepare."[24] Yet Andrews cites no historical law of attempt to back up his opinion. George W. Keeton, in 1967, said of the Alien Statute that there was "a similar law in England, as the audience very well knew," against "anyone attempting the life of a citizen," but he does not cite a law either. He believes that Shylock's direct attempt occurs when he whets his knife, but he offers no reason to support his assertion that this action is "clearly a criminal attempt."[25] O. Hood Phillips, in *Shakespeare and the Lawyers*, is summarizing Keeton when he writes that "the criminal attempt by Shylock was not the bringing of the judicial proceedings but the attempt to exact the penalty by force himself."[26] Marc Shell believes that a charge of attempted murder makes sense, because Shylock seeks revenge for the loss of his own flesh and blood, Jessica; as law he cites the *lex talionis*, an eye for an eye. But that law can only be applied metaphorically, since Jessica does not die.[27] Daniel Lowenstein concludes that Shylock's repeated insistence that he will take the pound of flesh, his enforcement of the legal proceeding, and his refusal to accept money in court "are easily sufficient to constitute a direct or indirect attempt to take Antonio's life." He bases his reasoning on the definition of attempt in America's Model Penal Code because, he admits "the common law . . . apparently was somewhat murky."[28]

In fact, as Lowenstein suggests, there was no clear law against attempted murder in English common law. The most convincing evidence that English law did not include a charge of attempted murder can be found in *The Lawyer's Logic* (1588) by Abraham Fraunce, which admits the oddity of this feature of the law. Fraunce first cites the medieval compiler Bracton, who appears to allow a conviction for attempt in the case of extreme battery:

> Suppose a man, planning to kill another, wounds him so grievously that he leaves him for dead. Then it happens that the man revives. Nonetheless, the first man committed a felony, because he openly intended murder. His intention appears from his deed, and as Bracton says, "In maleficiis spectatur voluntas et non exitus, & nihil interest utrum quis occidit, an causem mortis praebeat" [the intention can be discerned from the criminal act, not the outcome; it does not matter whether the man die, since the cause of murder occurred].

Shylock, of course, never touches Antonio, so this law would not have applied anyway in an English court. But Fraunce then goes on to show that despite Bracton's reasoning, there is no crime of attempt. The victim must die before the crime can be judged a felony. These days, Fraunce muses, a man can rewrite the text of Bracton and say that the outcome determines the crime, not the intention. Tucked away within the legal French and Latin of *The Lawyer's Logic* is the surprising rule that no felony is committed unless a victim dies: "Car il doyt morir en fayt, avant que il serra aiudge felony." Fraunce is as amazed as we are at what was once the law.[29]

There was no crime of attempted murder. English law provided for the registry of a sealed bond and the means to enforce a judgment. Therefore it is not likely that Shakespeare's audience would have imagined Shylock's guilt under the Alien Statute as arising either from his including a life-threatening clause in the bond or from his waving a knife. These two actions are usually taken to be the "indirect" and "direct" attempts on Antonio's life that Portia charges Shylock with committing. In fact, the debate over whether Shylock's guilt lies in the formation of the contract or his drawing his knife in court rests ultimately on a misunderstanding of the legal meaning of the terms "direct" and "indirect." They are not two separate actions, but two aspects of a single act of deception. The terms occur in the 1351 Star Chamber case of Walter Chirton, who conspired to cheat the king by a fraudulent conveyance.[30] Cited in Twyne's Case, it was well known to lawyers in Shakespeare's day. Walter took £1800 from the king and used it to buy lands. The charge was that he "by covin had caused the Vendor to enfeoff his friends in fee to defraud the king, and notwithstanding took the profits himself." He was sent to the Fleet, a prison in Southwark, for debt. The king took possession of the land, "for in the case of the king, an act done by covin, *per obliquum*, shall be equal to an act done *de directo*, to the party himself ... but be it the one way or the other, no subterfuge that the party can use, can defeat or defraud the king." Walter's conspiracy formed an "oblique" act, which insofar as it had a victim, the king, was also "direct." With regard to the king, therefore, "de directo" harm is not an alternative to harm "per obliquum," but the legal equivalent to it, for the law holds that indirect harm may be considered to be direct harm. It is a device that allowed the king to void Walter's conveyances and re-seize his property. The general rule follows, that where a thing is forbidden by law, "the prohibition extends to every circuitous mode of effecting the same." In *Magdalen College* (11 Rep. 74a), it was noted that an act being general for the suppression of fraud shall bind even the king.[31] Portia's words similarly indicate that Shylock is guilty of fraudulently manipulating the power given to him by his bond. His guilt lies not in how he worded the bond – Antonio seems to have written it – or in waving his knife, but in stubbornly construing its meaning in defiance of Portia's will and the power of the state.

The odd tense of Portia's phrase "doth contrive" supports the interpretation that she finds Shylock guilty for his stubbornness, not his bond or his knife. It is certainly reasonable to think that Portia punishes Shylock for his role in the formation of the penalty clause and contract, but it is even more reasonable, I think, to conclude that she punishes him for misconstruing the contract, and doing so in court. "Sir Thomas Elyot wrote a good deal about deceit, and his principal examples were contractual; even a man who wilfully misconstrued a contract, according to Elyot, committed a 'damnable fraude, beinge as playne agayne justice as if it were enforced by violence.'"[32] Shylock's crime is fraud in the most basic sense of a false representation intended to injure another party. Once Portia rules that the plain meaning of the contract limits Shylock to flesh, not blood, and to one pound exactly, not more or less, then it follows that Shylock has attempted to deceive the court by misreading his bond.

Shylock's Guilt

The Alien Statute, under which Shylock is accused of "indirectly, and directly" contriving against the "life" of Antonio, creates a back shadow that gives the impression that Shylock has sought Antonio's life all along, but it is an impression that the play carefully avoids confirming. Shakespeare's Italian source says that the Jewish lender offers the penalty of the pound of flesh because he wants the merchant to die. The Italian version of Shylock openly announces his plan to kill the merchant "in order to be able to say that he had put to death the greatest of the Christian merchants."[33] The motivation of Shakespeare's Shylock is much harder to fathom. Unlike his Italian counterpart, Shylock never claims to want Antonio dead. Instead, he suggests a "merry bond" of a pound of flesh as a substitute for usury. It is only during the court scene, when Portia reads the bond aloud, that we first learn that the pound of flesh Antonio must forfeit is the fatal pound nearest his heart.

If Antonio seems certain that he will die from his loss, it is at least in part because he created the condition that threatens his life. During their negotiations, Shylock and Antonio reach an oral agreement about the bond after Shylock says that the penalty should be a pound of flesh, "to be cut off and taken / In what part of your body pleaseth me" (I. iii. 150–151). Shylock then tells Antonio to meet him at "the notary's," where Antonio should give the notary "direction for this merry bond." There is a rule of construction – Francis Bacon mentions it – that the wording of a contract should be strictly construed against the party who wrote it.[34] Since Antonio seems to be the one who instructs the notary, he is most likely responsible for the addition of the phrase "nearest the heart." He is the one responsible for making the loss of a pound of flesh more life threatening than it would be if Shylock could, at his discretion, cut somewhere else. Shylock would be responsible for the words in a bond with his seal on it, but insofar as they are ambiguous – and they do not specify that Antonio must die – they would not be strictly construed against him. Moreover, physical mutilations, such as the loss of an eye or a limb, were not unknown in either Italy or England, and they were not equated with a capital sentence.[35]

Throughout his financial troubles, Antonio presumes that he will lose not only his flesh, but also his life. But he is a melancholy man whose malaise is matched only by that of Portia. He is half in love with easeful death, as many have noted. The addition of the phrase "nearest the heart" fits Antonio's character. Shylock, by contrast, seems motivated by the desire to humiliate Antonio, not kill him. Typically, Antonio claims that Shylock seeks his life, when, in fact, Shylock only has him arrested before his bond is due (III. iii. 36). London law allowed a creditor to request an arrest before the due date of bond to keep the debtor from absconding.[36] Antonio's arrest is a matter of course in a debt case, not necessarily a prelude to murder. Antonio's fears are exaggerated.

Moreover, when news of Antonio's troubles first reaches Belmont, Salerio and Jessica believe that what is at stake is not a life but Shylock's "envious plea / Of forfeiture, of justice, and his bond" (III. ii. 282–283). It is Antonio who raises the possibility of his own death in a letter that Bassanio reads aloud to Portia and others. In that letter Antonio claims that it is impossible for him to pay a pound of flesh and "live." Yet his complaint is somewhat undermined by his worry that his other creditors "grow cruel." Why should he worry about other creditors if he is going to die? It is hard to escape the conclusion that Antonio fears death because he is something of a coward.

Antonio's character carries over into his trial. There he is ever ready to dramatize his worries, as when he calls himself "a tainted wether of the flock / Meetest for death" (IV. i. 114–115). He alone first raises the possibility that the incision may kill him, not for loss of blood, which concerns Portia, but "if the Jew do cut but deep enough" (IV. i. 280). That "if" implies that Shylock may, perhaps, not cut deep enough. Everyone present at the trial objects to Shylock's cruelty, but no one else really expects Antonio to die. Portia thinks Shylock should provide Antonio with a surgeon, but she seems not so concerned that he will bleed to death that she orders one herself.

Because the law of attempt was undeveloped, and because the play suggests that the threat to Antonio's life may have been as much a product of Antonio's imagination as any deliberate plot by Shylock, the charge of attempted murder does not stick. Antonio does not die, nor is he harmed. It is only with difficulty that Shylock can be said to have committed a crime.

The Penal Clause

The Alien Statue resembles but is not the same as a treason statute. It creates a crime of attempted murder, whereas none existed in England for ordinary citizens, nor is it easy to argue that Shylock would be guilty under such a law. We have seen that it also has certain features of a *qui tam* statute, but with a difference. Antonio is not suing on behalf of the state. Rather, the Alien Statute provides an analogue to the strange situation where the state sues for a private citizen and then divides the proceeds with him. This situation occurred in the statute against fraudulent conveyancing that was passed in the thirteenth year of Elizabeth's reign. By awarding Antonio half of Shylock's estate, the Alien Statute rewards him as if he were a private citizen who undertakes the burden and expense of a prosecution in the interest of the state. The problem is that Antonio has no such role in *The Merchant of Venice*. He comes into court not as a plaintiff, but as the defendant. Nor, as noted earlier, is the state a principal. No one is defrauding the Duke (although an issue is made about the reputation of Venice for fairness).

Portia's Alien Statute imitates a *qui tam* law while failing to achieve its purpose. And it too raises the question, Why should the state of Venice receive half the penalty? Why should Antonio? It is not enough to say that in English law the property of a convicted felon escheated to the state. After a successful prosecution, the state received *all* of a felon's property. The victim's satisfaction extended no further than the corporal or capital punishment of the malefactor. If the Alien Statute were a true criminal law, Antonio would receive nothing. But the Alien Statute does not quite fit the pattern of either a criminal or a *qui tam* law. Like the 1571 law, its purpose seems to be political, to seize land from the enemies of the state, while at the same time, in practice, it also gives the public what it wants.

Portia's Decision

Shakespeare's play prefigured Twyne's Case by offering a dramatic resolution to a similarly political or misguided penalty clause in the Alien Statute. The punishment Portia invokes is stern – death unless the Duke commutes Shylock's sentence, loss of half Shylock's goods to the state and the other half to "the party 'gainst the which he doth contrive." That is, the Alien Statute initially gives half Shylock's property to the state and half to Antonio. The Duke, however, spares Shylock's life and then reduces his half to a fine. At this point Antonio makes two requests to alter the punishments. He asks that Shylock be forced to convert as a *quid pro quo* for the Duke's having spared his life. And he also creates a set of conditions by which Shylock's wealth will be preserved for his daughter on his death. By the end of the trial it is possible that Shylock may receive the same benefits that could be achieved by the kind of fraudulent conveyance that was popularly practiced in England before Twyne's Case swung the pendulum in favor of creditors. His daughter will be the beneficiary.

The Alien Statute produces a dramatic shock at first, but as Shylock is relieved of its worst consequences, the shock wears off. At Antonio's request the one half of Shylock's fortune, or what is left after the Duke's fine, will go to Jessica when Shylock dies. To assure this transfer, the Duke orders Shylock to prepare a deed of gift. In so doing the Duke seems to recognize that the state does not just punish a malefactor when it appropriates a man's estate: it also punishes his family. The amount the Duke will fine Shylock is not specified, but the Duke's ordering of the deed of gift implies that it will not be ruinous. The Duke himself therefore winks at the conveying of value away from the state.

The other half of Shylock's original estate belongs to Antonio. What his legal title will be is not altogether clear, but the bottom line seems to be that Antonio intends to take the income from the estate while preserving the corpus for Lorenzo, Jessica's husband. Thus Jessica (assuming Lorenzo allows her access to her inheritance) is guaranteed at least half the value of Shylock's present estate, plus whatever Shylock might add to his own holdings during his lifetime. There is no real fraud against the state, since the Duke is aware of what he is giving up, but there is still a sense that Antonio's adjustments to the penalty manipulate the outcome to produce a fairy-tale result for Jessica. English debtors and others in trouble with the law practiced fraudulent conveyancing to keep property away from the state and within the family. Portia, Antonio, and the Duke negotiate adjustments to Shylock's punishment that leave Jessica in approximately the same position she would have enjoyed had Shylock done so himself.

Moral Resolution

Portia's manipulations remind us that fraud, including fraudulent conveyances, could be good or bad, depending on one's view. As Kuehn points out in his history of Italian law, fraud could be an affair of honor. It showed that the debtor had some skill. It gave him prestige by freeing him from the claims of others, including the power of the state and its statutes.[37] In a world that was presumed to be hostile, kinship and friendship created welcome opportunities for fraud, collusion, conspiracy, false deeds, and trusts. "So the very Florentine who feared fraud in others could and did give advice on how to commit fraud."[38] The English were no less adept at practicing asset management.

To counter the machinations of debtors who lacked a "modicum of decency," creditors required patronage and kinship. Loners were often in a precarious position. Shylock's shrill, sometimes tragic demand for his bond expresses the difficulties of small creditors who faced powerful debtors. "Those who stood to lose were mainly the middling element in society, the small shopkeepers and artisans. Simple refusal to pay or well-established methods of legal chicanery left creditors deceived and deprived."[39] It is an indication of Shylock's powerlessness that even with a formal bond, he must go to court before receiving a judgment.

The problem of defining what behavior is acceptable in a commercial situation is directly connected to the last element of the punishments that arise from the Alien Statute and the modifications Antonio proposes.[40] One of the meliorating features of *The Merchant of Venice* is that Shakespeare leaves Shylock's religious fate uncertain. In fact, the play's bittersweet quality depends on permitting Shylock the possibility of deception at the end to balance the collusive behavior of the principals in the main plot. Antonio calls for Shylock's conversion, along with the redistribution of his wealth, but we never quite know what Shylock does. The language of the comedy may be read to suggest that Shylock dissimulates in response to the Duke's demand to know if he accepts the terms of Antonio's proposal. Shylock's answer, "I am content," echoes the slight self-deprecation Antonio assumes when he first proposes his modifications to the Duke. "I am content," Antonio says, meaning that he will not contradict the Duke's mercy so long as the Duke imposes some additional conditions, including Shylock's conversion. The phrase "I am content" is the same one that Petrucchio uses when Kate entreats him to stay in Padua for dinner after their wedding, although Petrucchio has declared they must leave at once.

> Petrucchio: I am content.
> Katherine: Are you content to stay?
> Petrucchio: I am content you shall entreat me stay,
> But yet not stay, entreat me as you can.
> (*Taming of the Shrew*, III. ii. 201–202)

It is possible that Shylock no more means what he says than Petrucchio does, and that when he seems to accept Antonio's offer, he means to conform outwardly while remaining true to the faith in his heart.[41] His punishment is the subject of public discourse; we are not sure about his private beliefs.

Notes

1. In T. E. Hartley, *Proceedings in the Parliaments of Elizabeth I*, 3 vols. (Leicester, 1981), 2: 207, speaking on a draft of 27 Eliz., c. 4, on the complaint that proceedings under the bill would be referred to Star Chamber.
2. The difference between a legal analysis of the play and a law-and-literature analysis is that between positivism, an earlier form of scholarship that hunted for actual laws and the

legal meaning of various terms, and more modern Cultural Studies, which seeks a broader perspective on the social practices that shape the law and literary expressions. Law and literature, which gathered force as an academic discipline in the 1980s, seems to have outlasted the more radical project of the Critical Legal Studies movement, perhaps because of the centrality of the trial to western culture, a fact recognized by Richard Weisberg's *The Failure of the Word: The Protagonist as Lawyer in Modern Fiction* (New Haven: Yale University Press, 1984) and the work of David Papke, for example, "The American Legal Faith: Traditions, Contradictions and Possibilities," *Indiana Law Review* 30 (1997): 645–657.

Having provided an answer to the legal question of whether a modern court would enforce Shylock's bond, law professors now tend to engage much larger cultural themes – for example, Paul W. Kahn, *The Cultural Study of Law: Reconstructing Legal Scholarship* (Chicago: University of Chicago Press, 1999) – while the job of historical analysis has fallen to English professors versed in the law. Here the work of Don Wayne, Luke Wilson, and Charles Spinosa connects the changing nature of contract in English law to the cultural transition critics typically find in early modern literature: the transition from feudalism to capitalism or the crisis in patriarchy revealed by the exchange of gifts. On contract and intention, see Don Wayne, "Drama and Society in the Age of Jonson: An Alternative View," *Renaissance Drama* 13 (1982): 103–129; Luke Wilson, "Ben Jonson and the Law of Contract," *Cardozo Studies in Law and Literature* 5 (1993): 281–306, and "*Hamlet*, Hales v. Petit, and the Hysteresis of Action," *ELH* 60 (1993): 17–55; and Charles Spinosa, "The Transformation of Intentionality: Debt and Contract in *The Merchant of Venice*," *ELR* 24 (1994): 370–409, and "Shylock and Debt and Contract in *The Merchant of Venice*," *Cardozo Law Review* 15 (1994): 65–85 (another version of his *ELR* article). On the relation between social class and commerce, see Walter Cohen, "*The Merchant of Venice* and the Possibilities of Historical Criticism," *ELH* 49 (1982): 765–789, and Frank Whigham, "Ideology and Class Conduct in *The Merchant of Venice*," *Renaissance Drama* 10 (1979): 93–115. On the role of gift giving, see Ronald Sharp, "A Gift Exchange and the Economies of Spirit in *The Merchant of Venice*," *Modern Philology* 83 (1986): 250–265; Karen Newman, "Portia's Ring: Unruly Women and Structures of Exchange in *The Merchant of Venice*," *Shakespeare Quarterly* 38 (1987): 19–33; and Jyotsna Singh, "Gendered 'Gifts' in Shakespeare's Belmont: The Economies of Exchange in Early Modern England," in *A Feminist Companion to Shakespeare*, ed. Dympna Callaghan (Oxford: Basil Blackwell, 1999), pp. 144–159.

3   Those who scrutinize procedure and contract include Mark Edwin Andrews, *Law and Equity in The Merchant of Venice* (Boulder: University of Colorado Press, 1965); George W. Keeton, *Shakespeare's Legal and Political Background* (New York: Barnes & Noble, 1967), pp. 132–150; O. Hood Phillips, *Shakespeare and the Lawyers* (London: Methuen, 1972), pp. 91–118 (Phillips provides a useful survey of what lawyers have said about the play); E. F. J. Tucker, "The Letter of the Law in *The Merchant of Venice*," *Shakespeare Survey* 29 (1976): 93–101; Richard Posner, *Law and Literature: A Misunderstood Relation* (Cambridge, Mass.: Harvard University Press, 1988), pp. 91–99; and Daniel J. Kornstein, *Kill All the Lawyers? Shakespeare's Legal Appeal* (Princeton: Princeton University Press, 1994), pp. 65–89. Among their points is that the judge is a woman in disguise who is related to one of the interested parties. Neither Antonio nor Shylock are represented by lawyers. The case begins as a civil suit brought by Shylock and ends as a criminal proceeding against him. Portia's decree that Shylock may have neither more nor less than a pound of flesh and her decision not to allow Shylock to take any blood with Antonio's flesh violate the principle that where the law allows a remedy, it allows the means to that remedy. Then again, it is held, no court would recognize a penalty clause whose enforcement would entail the death of the defendant.

4   Those who analyze the trial scene broadly do so in terms of justice and mercy. See E. M. W. Tillyard, "The Trial Scene in *The Merchant of Venice*," *Review of English Studies* 2 (1961): 51–59; Barbara Tovey, "The Golden Casket: An Interpretation of *The Merchant of Venice*," in *Shakespeare as Political Thinker*, eds. John Alvis and Thomas G. West (Durham, NC: Carolina Academic Press, 1981), pp. 215–237; William Chester Jordan, "Approaches to the Court Scene in the Bond Story: Equity and Mercy or Reason and Nature," *Shakespeare Quarterly* 33 (1982): 49–59; Alice Benston, "Portia, the Law, and the Tripartite Structure of *The Merchant of Venice*," *Shakespeare Quarterly* 30 (1979): 367–385; Richard Weisberg, *Poethics: and Other Strategies of Law and Literature* (New York: Columbia University Press, 1992), 94–104; and Theodore Ziolkowski, *The Mirror of Justice: Literary Reflections of Legal Crises* (Princeton: Princeton University Press, 1995), pp. 174–176. Related to the broad scheme of justice and mercy is the conflict between the social order and the instability of language; see Terry Eagleton, *William Shakespeare* (Oxford: Basil Blackwell, 1986), pp. 35–48.

5   Richard Weisberg questions the identification of mercy with the Christians in "Antonio's Legalistic Cruelty: Interdisciplinarity and *The Merchant of Venice*," *College Literature* 25.1 (Winter 1998): 12–20. See also Tucker, "The Letter of the Law," refuting the link between equity and the Court of Chancery.

6   Examples of *qui tam* laws can be found in Ferdinando Pulton, *An Abstract of All the Penal Statutes* (London, 1596). To take one instance: under 23 Hen. VIII, c. 16 and 1 Eliz., c. 7, a party could arrest someone guilty of the felony of selling a horse into Scotland without a license from the queen "and he shall have one moiety of the price of the horse, and the Queen the other." A *qui tam* action overrides the general rule that one must be personally affected by a crime in order to have standing to bring suit before a court. In 1863 Abraham Lincoln himself wrote a law that empowered private citizens to combat fraud against the government and, at the same time, enrich themselves by taking a percentage of treble damages and steep civil penalties that might be awarded. See Steve France, "Qui Tam Pop Quiz," *ABA Journal* (February 2000): 32.

7   For the lack of a bureaucracy for law enforcement, see Penry Williams, *The Tudor Regime* (Oxford: Oxford University Press, 1979), pp. 149–151. He cites William Lambarde, who calls informers "flies that feed on the sores of diseased animals." See Lambarde's *Archeion: Or, A Discourse upon the High Courts of Justice in England*, ed. Charles H. McIlwain and Paul L. Ward (Cambridge: Mass.: Harvard University Press, 1977), p. 151. For the opinion of Parliament, see Hartley, ed. *Proceedings*, 1: 201, where informers (in this case, those who must punish non-attendance in church) are called "the worst sort of men." A good overview of the system can be found in M. W. Beresford, "The Common Informer, the Penal Statutes and Economic Regulation," *The Economic History Review* 10 (1957): 221–237.

8   I follow the version of the story translated in Geoffrey Bullough, ed., *Narrative and Dramatic Sources of Shakespeare*, vol. 1: *Early Comedies, Poems, Romeo and Juliet* (New York: Columbia University Press, 1957), pp. 463–476.

9   See Thomas Kuehn, "Multorum Fraudibus Occurrere: Legislation and Jurisprudential Interpretation Concerning Fraud and Liability in Quattrocento Florence," *Studi Senesi* 93 (1981): 309–350; *Emancipation in Late Medieval Florence* (New Brunswick, NJ: Rutgers University Press, 1982); and "Law, Death, and Heirs in the Renaissance: Repudiation of Inheritance in Florence," *Renaissance Quarterly* 45 (1992): 484–516.

10 See Kuehn, *Emancipation,* p. 123.

11 Ibid., pp. 123–124.

12 Kuehn, "Multorum Fraudibus," pp. 334–335.

13 Eagleton, *William Shakespeare*, p. 37; Kornstein, *Kill All the Lawyers?*, p. 70. For complaints made by nineteenth-century German critics about the "miserable quibble," see

Furness, ed., *A New Variorum Edition of Shakespeare*, vol. 7: *The Merchant of Venice* (Philadelphia: J. B. Lippincott, 1895), p. 410.
14 Tucker, "The Letter of the Law," p. 100, defines equity not as mercy but as the application of reason to actual cases and readings of statutes, broadening or narrowing the sense of words: "Portia's judgment reflects an equitable diminishment of the letter of the law according to the reason and intent of true justice."
15 Citations to act, scene, and line here and elsewhere in the text are from *The Riverside Shakespeare*, ed. G. Blakemore Evans (Boston: Houghton Mifflin, 1974).
16 James Shapiro, *Shakespeare and the Jews* (New York: Columbia University Press, 1996), p. 181, has shown how a patchwork of competing jurisdictions allows Portia to shift Shylock from the category of Jew to that of alien, to his detriment.
17 Sir James Stephens, *The History of the Common Law*, 2 vols. (London: Macmillan, 1883), 2: 189.
18 Sir William Staunford, *Les plees del corone* (1557; rpt. New York: Garland Publishing, 1979), p. 173.
19 Sir Edward Coke, *The Third Part of the Institutes of the Laws of England: Concerning High Treason, and other Pleas of the Crown, and Criminal Causes* (London: M. Flesher, 1644), p. 143. See also *A Collection in English, of the Statutes now in force, continued from the beginning of Magna Charta . . . under Titles placed by order of Alphabet* (London: Thomas Wight and Bonham Norton, 1598), s.v. "conspiracie."
20 *Julius Caesar*, II. i. 77; *The Tempest*, II. i. 301. Shakespeare also has Gloucester use the word to describe what he believes is Edgar's evil plan to kill him. Since Edmund reveals the plot to Gloucester by showing him a letter Edgar supposedly wrote to enlist Edmund's help, the term seems to apply where two people are involved but only one is guilty (*King Lear*, I. ii. 55).
21 A. W. Moody, *Shakespeare: The Merchant of Venice* (London: Edward Arnold, 1964), pp. 10, 53. Lawrence Danson, *The Harmonies of The Merchant of Venice* (London: Yale University Press, 1978), takes the opposite approach, finding the morality of the play more trouble-free than most critics do.
22 Marc Shell, *Money, Language, and Thought: Literary and Philosophical Economies from the Medieval to the Modern Era* (Berkeley: University of California Press, 1982), pp. 57–58.
23 Inherent in the Italian story is the potential for fraud that this legal arrangement offered. It was a rule that specialist courts of appeals and fiscal matters were presided over by judges who had to be foreigners. Ferrara law, for example, forbade such an official from "entering any relationship (for example, matrimony) with local inhabitants that might betoken obligation." See David S. Chambers and Trevor Dean, *Clean Hands and Rough Justice: An Investigating Magistrate in Renaissance Italy* (Ann Arbor: University of Michigan Press, 1997), p. 49. In practice, a podestà would often link himself with members of the local elite, often by means of his wife. Ariosto's father married into one of the better families of Reggio while he was captain of the citadel there, serving the duke of Ferrara. More commonly the wife of an official would have friends whose needs might reach her husband's ears with her help. The taint of fraud hangs over the lady in *Il Pecorone* not only because she is a woman in disguise then, but because of her close relationship with the Jew's adversary. Like Portia, the lady is related by friendship and, since she is married to the merchant's protégé, by kinship to one of the parties in the dispute. It adds realism to the proceedings by hinting to attentive readers of the possibility of corruption in the courts.

Moreover, central administrators in Venice, Ferrara, Mantua, and other cities in the Po valley would often assign to their satellite towns a podestà, a kind of tribune or functionary, who stood for the power of the Doge, duke, or prince to control legal proceedings, issue orders for arrest, decree punishments, or use torture. This appointee might assist a local magnate, who often had no legal training, in administering justice. He would therefore combine the advice of a *sapiens* and the power of the state. The lady in *Il Pecorone* slips into a double role when she appears before a "tribunal appointed for such cases" (Chambers and Dean, *Clean Hands*, p. 7). She speaks for the merchant Ansaldo, but she also has the power to call in an executioner with his block and his axe to threaten the Jew should he spill one drop of blood.

24 Andrews, *Law and Equity in* The Merchant of Venice, p. 70.
25 Keeton, *Shakespeare's Legal and Political Background*, p. 145.
26 Phillips, *Shakespeare and the Lawyers*, p. 117. The Cambridge editor also follows Keeton, without further evidence. See M. M. Mahood, ed., *The Merchant of Venice* (Cambridge: Cambridge University Press, 1987), p. 18.
27 Marc Shell, *Money, Language, Thought*, p. 61.
28 Daniel Lowenstein, "The Failure of the Act: Conceptions of Law in *The Merchant of Venice*, *Bleak House*, *Les Misérables*, and Richard Weisberg's *Poethics*," *Cardozo Law Review* 15 (1994): 1167. "Attempted murder," Lowenstein writes, "would probably be anachronistic" (p. 1168, n. 130). Joan Ozark Holmes, *The Merchant of Venice: Choice, Hazard, Consequence* (New York: St. Martin's Press, 1995), p. 201, says that Shylock's words "specified in the written bond, as they were not in his oral offer, indicate that he desires to take the flesh from a life-threatening place," yet insofar as the play attributes the phrase "nearest the heart" to anyone, it is Antonio, who goes to the notary to have the bond prepared before Shylock arrives. Her opinion is that Shylock indirectly attempts to murder Antonio at that moment when he refuses to provide a surgeon, and that he directly attempts to carve the flesh at the moment when, his knife poised in mid-air, he hears Portia say, "tarry a little." These suggestions fit the modern definition of attempted murder, which is the commission of a first step toward a crime with the requisite intent, but they have no historical basis. Theodore Ziolkowski, *The Mirror of Justice*, p. 182, is contradictory, noting that "no crime has been committed" by Shylock but that Portia dispenses with "justice" (that is, with equity) in applying the Alien Statute and gives it "the strictest possible construction."
29 It is always hard to prove a negative, like the absence of a law against attempt. Some of the murkiness felt by commentators lies in the nature of criminal jurisprudence. The criminal law consisted of oral proceedings based on a written indictment. Since no records were kept, no jurisprudence could develop. Jury verdicts also precluded the development of reasoned opinions, since jurors were not asked to explain their decisions. See Louis A. Knafla, ed. *Crime and Criminal Justice in Europe and Canada* (Waterloo, Ont., Canada: Wilfrid Laurier University Press, 1985), p. 2. What legal principles existed probably developed, according to J. H. Baker, *The Third University of England: The Inns of Court and the Common Law Tradition* (London: Selden Society, 1990), p. 20, in the inns of court, from which early writers like William Fitzherbert, William Staunford, and Edward Coke drew their material. Baker notes that "the earliest readings on homicide, for instance, contain discussions of accident, duress, negligence, insanity, automatism, drunkenness, abortion, and other problems that do not surface in the law reports until long afterwards." See also J. H. Baker, "English Criminal Jurisprudence," in Knapfla, *Crime and Criminal Justice in Europe and Canada*, pp. 26–27. Routine cases did not employ criminal counsel, and even a record-keeper like Justice James Dyer did not take his notebooks with him on circuit. J. H. Baker, *Reports from the Lost Notebooks of Sir James Dyer*, vol. 1 (London: Selden Society, 1994), p. xcii. Baker notes that the judges usually traveled on circuit for two or three weeks in the counties of Northampton, Warwick, Coventry, and Leicester (p. xciv), and that no counsel were employed in routine criminal cases (p. xcv).

Often common law crimes were "not proscribed by statute but punished by the courts anyhow," according to John Langbein, *Torture and the Law of Proof: Europe and England in the Ancient Régime* (Chicago: University of Chicago Press, 1977), p. 46. It is not impossible that attempted murder fits this category, despite the absence of records. It may be significant that in one of the few studies we have, Barbara Hanawalt, *Crime and Conflict in English Communities: 1300–1348* (Cambridge: Cambridge University Press, 1979), p. 101, found "no cases of people being tried for attempted suicide" in fourteenth-century England.

Nonetheless, English criminal law gave inordinate power to judges to pronounce guilt and hand out sentences. As J. H. Baker, *An Introduction to English Legal History* (London: Butterworth, 1979), p. 411, has noted, "the only substantive question which could arise on the record was whether the accused was charged with a known offence." Since criminal defendants were not allowed counsel, the average person rarely challenged the technical correctness of the charge against him or her. It was therefore historically accurate for England that Shylock does not have counsel. It also would have seemed realistic that he and others are unaware of the legal language or force of the Alien Statute, and that they accept the law as pronounced by Portia. Although the use of a jury to decide criminal charges was a unique feature of English law, that uniqueness made it historically accurate for Portia, presiding in a fictional Venice, to issue a verdict without the advice of a panel.

In exceptional circumstances an English judge could convict for a crime committed in his presence, a feature that seems to be behind the common belief that Portia convicts Shylock for raising his knife to Antonio. Wielding a weapon in court could be a crime, but not a capital one. It allowed the judge to do what was necessary to keep the peace – fine, imprisonment, pillory. According to Baker, *An Introduction to English Legal History*, p. 419, "At common law, summary trial (that is, without indictment or jury) was permitted only in respect of offences, such as contempt, committed in the view of the judges sitting in open court." London had a statute to preserve the peace, ordering a fine of half a mark or 15 days in Newgate for anyone "who shall draw a sword, misericorde [a dagger with a thin blade], or a knife, or any arm, even though he do not strike." But no felony punishment was available, in the absence of harm, for attempt alone. See *Liber Albus: The White Book of the City of London* (London: Richard Griffin, 1861), p. 408. (The *Liber Albus* was compiled in Latin and legal French in the last mayoralty of Richard Whitington, 1419. In 1582 a transcript and translation was made of an original found in the Guildhall.) There could be no murder without a corpse, no battery without a wound to the body. Michael Dalton's *Countrey Justice* (1618), p. 244, tells us that it was no felony to hunt deer or conies in a park, or with disguises, "where the offenders killed no Deere," rabbits, or hares. Except in the case of treason or heresy, a speech act was not sufficient to constitute a crime. Where the charge was sorcery, a felony could lie on the second offense on the basis of "the intent to hurt any person in their body, though it be not effected." See Dalton, *The Countrey Justice*, p. 243; and also Coke, *The Third Part of the Institutes*, p. 45. The first witchcraft statute was enacted in 1542. For the legal background to later prosecutions, see Alan Macfarlane, *Witchcraft in Tudor and Stuart England* (New York: Harper & Row, 1971), pp. 16–22. Although Jews were associated with witches in the popular imagination, actual prosecutions of Jews for witchcraft were practically non-existent. See Anna Foa, "The Witch and the Jew: Two Alikes that Were Not the Same," in *From Witness to Witchcraft: Jews and Judaism in Medieval Christian Thought*, ed. Jeremy Cohen (Wiesbaden: Harrarrsowitz, 1996), pp. 361–374.

Although in 1615 it was held to be treason to say that it would be lawful to kill the king, Baker, *An Introduction to English Legal History*, p. 428, argues that "in most ages the court required an overt act." Even the developing jurisprudence of intent depended on the identification of an overt act from which intent could be inferred. It is not particularly surprising, then, that scholars are unable to agree on what constituted Shylock's direct or indirect acts, since there was no law that required an action or "first step," as we say today, to establish "attempt."

30   Walter Chirton, Trin. 24 Edw. III, Rot. 4 in Saccario. The case is cited in Mannocke's Case (3 Dyer 295a) and by Coke in *Ford and Sheldon's Case* (12 Co. Rep. 2 [1605]) – see Sir Edward Coke, *The Twelfth Part of the Reports of Sir Edward Coke* (London: Henry Twyford and Thomas Dring, 1658), p. 3, Wing STC C4970; also *The English Reports*, vol. 77 (Abingdon, Oxfordshire: Professional Books, 1979), p. 1286. Here and elsewhere I regularize spelling and punctuation.

31   See William Roberts, *A Treatise on the Construction of the Statutes of 13 Eliz. c. 5 and 27 Eliz. c. 4, Relating to Voluntary and Fraudulent Conveyances* (1800; 3rd American ed., Burlington, Vt.: Chauncey Goodrich, 1845), p. 586.

32   J. H. Baker, *The Reports of John Spelman*, 2 vols. (London: Selden Society, 1977–78), 2: 230.

33   See Bullough, *Narrative and Dramatic Sources of Shakespeare*, 1: 463–476.

34   Francis Bacon, *Maxims*, in *The Works of Francis Bacon*, ed. James Spedding, Robert Leslie Ellis, and Douglas Denon Heath, 14 vols. (London: Longman, 1861; New York: Garrett, 1968), 7: 333. Compare the argument made by one of the king's Serjeants in *Reniger* v. *Fogossa*, 1 Plowden 11, in *English Reports*, vol. 75: *The Commentaries or Reports of Edmund Plowden* (Abingdon, Oxfordshire: Professional Books, 1979), pp. 16–17: "And there is a principle or ground in the common law for the exposition of words, clauses, or sentences, viz. (i) that in every grant or gift, if the words are ambiguous and doubtful, they shall be taken most strongly gainst the grantors or donors, and most beneficially for them to whom the grant or gift was made."

35   The punishment for fraud and deceit was the pillory and a fine. See Baker, *Reports from the Lost Notebooks of Sir James Dyer*, p. 114.

36   See *Liber Albus*, p. 194: "Item: when a debtor is bound within the said city by an obligation to pay a certain sum on a certain day to come, the which debtor was held to be sufficient at the time when he entered into such obligation, but has since become ... non-sufficient"; then the creditor can bring four or six persons to testify that the "debtor wishes to withdraw himself and to remove his goods from the City," and the Mayor can "arrest the debtor, even though the day named in the obligation had not yet arrived, and to detain the said debtor in prison." A similar text can be found in *The Ancient Customes and Approved Usages of the Honourable City of London* (n.p., n.d. [early seventeenth century]), p. 53.

37   Kuehn, "Multorum Fraudibus," p. 344.

38   Ibid., p. 342.

39   Ibid., p. 348.

40   Antonio displays a notable lack of compassion in setting the condition of conversion, thereby undercutting Portia's earlier catechism on the quality of mercy, Richard Weisberg argues in "Antonio's Legalistic Cruelty." For a good historical and theoretical survey of the problems raised by Shakespeare's choice of a Jewish villain, see John Gross, *Shylock: A Legend and Its Legacy* (New York: Simon and Schuster, 1992), who concludes, "Exactly where the play now stands depends on one's wider reading of European history. I personally think it is absurd to suppose that there is a direct line of descent from Antonio to Hitler, or from Portia to the SS, but that is because I do not believe that the Holocaust was in any way inevitable. I *do* believe, on the other hand, that the ground for the Holocaust was well prepared, and to that extent the play can never seem quite the same again. It is still a masterpiece; but there is a permanent chill in the air, even in the gardens of Belmont" (p. 352).

41 Norman Rabkin, *Shakespeare and the Problem of Meaning* (Chicago: University of Chicago Press, 1981), p. 13, notes that there is no mention of Shylock's salvation: his "conversion is dictated as part of a settlement that is otherwise entirely fiscal."

Conclusion

The interplay between debtors and creditors is usually told as the historical ebb and flow of sympathy from one figure to the other. According to the conventional wisdom, Shylock represents the old medieval hatred of the powerful creditor. Where creditors are villains, debtors and conveyers like Antonio and Bassanio are heroes. If there is a little fraud, as in Portia's ruling in court, Antonio's adjustment of Shylock's punishment, or even Portia's demand that her husband give her a ring she knows he is pledged to keep, it is for a good cause. Usury laws, dating from the thirteenth century, encouraged a popular image of creditors as villains, often an outsider, as in the image of the Mediterranean Jew found in Shakespeare's play and his source. But the culture was shifting even as Shakespeare wrote. Usury laws were relaxed during Elizabeth's reign, and new bankruptcy laws helped create a picture of the debtor merchant as "an elusive social deviant." A few years later after *The Merchant*, Thomas Dekker's satiric portrait of Sir Politic Bankrupt, who borrows freely and ruins other men by not repaying them, illustrates the growing Renaissance distrust of dissolute debtors. Dekker's play *The Seven Deadly Sins of London* (1606) condemns the man who borrows other men's gold or merchandise, then absconds or barricades himself in his house and offers cheap composition to his helpless creditors.[1] The real issue in both plays is not who was a bad person. It is to what extent frauds, deceptions, concealments, and conveyances would be legal to protect property from creditors, including the state.

Fraud ever increases in the world – *crescit in orbe dolus* – and had been doing so long before changes in the English property laws and the Statute of Uses complicated matters. In *Clouds*, by the Greek playwright Aristophanes, a debtor named Strepsiades hires a witch of Thessaly to charm the moon from the sky, because the custom of the Greeks was to settle debts monthly at the new moon. If the moon should happen not to rise, Strepsiades will not have to pay. His strategy provokes his creditor into hiring a second witch, however, not only to keep the moon in heaven, but to speed its rising so he can obtain his money sooner.[2] Thomas Wilson, who sat in Parliament and was of the queen's Privy Council during the period discussed in this book, cites the play in his *Discourse Against Usury*.

As the law of fraudulence conveyance developed in the period from 1571 to 1601, the connection between the rights of creditors and the needs of the Crown created a broad field of play for Sidney, Spenser, and Shakespeare. Garrard Glenn believed that 13 Eliz., c. 5 was passed solely for political reasons, to persecute Catholics. This conclusion is unwarranted; nonetheless, the crown had a role in the development of the law. For centuries the kings of England sought to protect their own interests against citizens who evaded taxes, wardships, escheats, and forfeitures. Yet they also helped protect families against those who would carry off women for marriage. The fiction writers do not represent the law directly: we never see an escheator, or a creditor, argue that a court should void a conveyance. But the writers we have considered do offer literary representations of what was a general cultural practice in Renaissance England. Moreover, each of these men witnessed the formation of the law and knew people who used deceitful conveyances to protect their estates. As citizens they understood the ethical issue that makes fraudulent conveyancing a concern even today: the problem of balancing moral precepts against personal circumstances and responsibilities. As authors they knew how to invent metaphors based on the problems of debtors and enrich their texts with the language of conveyancing.

After 1601, and the clarification of the law by Twyne's Case, debate over the law grew less intense. In 1603, between the Quarto and Folio versions of *Merry Wives*, King James's First Parliament made a fraudulent conveyance an act of bankruptcy (the law applied only to merchants).[3] The next act of this legal history occurred in 1623 when James's new bankruptcy bill (21 Jac., c. 19) incorporated the specific language of 13 Eliz., c. 5 and Twyne's Case, which survives to this day in many US states ("to delay, defraud, or hinder" creditors and others). The bill limited the fraudulent conveyancing provision to amounts of £20 or more, uncannily echoing Falstaff's debt to Brooke in *The Merry Wives*. The bill also set a threshold amount for litigation, saying a debtor's obligations must be £100. This provision also echoes Shakespeare's play, since it is the amount that Fenton offers the Host to help him convey away Anne Page. Finally, the bill provided that if the debtor did not reveal the transfer on examination, he should suffer the pillory and loss of one ear – the legal equivalent to the pinches the fairies inflict on Falstaff when he dresses himself as Herne the Hunter. Whatever its influence – I would not want to insist on a direct connection – Shakespeare's play accurately reflects English economic life.

Fraudulent conveyance laws did not change much in England or in the colonies for the next several centuries. Although later cases fine-tuned the badges of fraud and extended the reach of laws to protect purchasers, the foundation laid in the period between 1571 and 1601 remained firm. The growing complexities of commerce and the development of contract law led to the Statute of Frauds in 1677. But that famous landmark is really about when some kind of written document is required, not the problem of discerning an intent to deceive. By the eighteenth century, overt politics no longer hovered over the fraudulent conveyance statute: Lord Hardwicke, Chancellor from 1737 to 1756, simply believed that the phrase "and others" was inserted to cover those who became creditors *after* a conveyance.[4] For the most part the struggle to craft fair rules ended with Twyne's Case.

Although the written law was fixed, it remains true that the fine line between prudent self-protections and deceitful practices will never be completely stable. "The fraud of men was ever so" – so goes the refrain in *Twelfth Night*, which applies to debtors as well as lovers, and those who are both. Falstaff will not be the last word, but an inimitable reminder that Shakespeare lived and worked in a great age for fraudulent conveyances.

Notes

1 Robert Weisberg, "Commercial Morality, the Merchant Character, and the History of the Voidable Preference," *Stanford Law Review* 39 (1986): 3–138, 16, draws attention to this passage as well as to changing conceptions of debtors and creditors.

2 Thomas Wilson, *Discourse upon Usury by Way of Dialogues and Orations* (London: Augustus M. Kelley, 1963), p. 339.
3 The issue in Elizabethan times was the trade rule in bankruptcy, which was added to the 1543 statute in 1571. After 1571, courts gradually clarified what manufacturers of tangible goods could be covered by bankruptcy law: shoemakers in 1592, drapers in 1610, dyers in 1621, bakers in 1623, and carpenters in 1688. See Weisberg, "Commercial Morality," pp. 22–24. Much later the issue would become discharge or the modern "fresh start."
4 William Roberts, *A Treatise on the Construction of the Statutes of 13 Eliz. c. 5 and 27 Eliz. c. 4, Relating to Voluntary and Fraudulent Conveyances* (1800; 3rd American ed. Burlington, Vt.: Chauncey Goodrich, 1845), p. 13, citing Lord Hardwick in *Taylor* v *Jones*, 2 Atk. 601.

Index

Alien Statute 7, 26 n.34, 101, 114–124, 128 n.28, 129 n.29
Allen, Gyles ix, 17, 29, 48, 92
Anderson, Edward 106–107, 111 n.10
  involvement in Ireland 92
  judge in Twyne's Case xi, 85–86
Arcadia 43–69
  composition of 52, 63, 67 n.51
  conveyancing of women in x, xii, 5, 57, 95 n.18
  ending of 60–62
  plot summary 56
  source for Sidney and Shakespeare xii, 6, 62, 113
attainder 29, 75
  bills of 6, 35, 37, 39, 43–46, 49, 72–73, 77, 89
  defined 46, 90
  penalty for conveying women 58
  See also O'Neill, Shane; Desmond, earl of
attempted murder 7, 118–121, 128 n.29

Bacon, Francis 19, 55, 121
Bacon, Nicholas, Lord Keeper (father of Francis) 36, 38
badges of fraud xi, 6, 9 n.23, 76, 78, 92, 101–103, 114
  continuance of possession 104
  power of revocation 32, 107
  See also consideration, collusion, good faith, secrecy, timing
Baker, J. H. 128 n.29
bankruptcy xi, 19, 30–31
  fresh start 20
  in Roman law 22
  See also English Statutes
bona fide. *See* good faith
building on another man's land 5, 12, 16–19, 24 n.10
Burbage, James ix, 17–18, 25 n.21, 29
  his son Cuthbert 24 n.21, 48, 92, 114
Burghley. *See* Cecil, William

cases, law
  Bethel *against* Edward Stanhope (1599; revocability of gift indicates fraud) 107
  Chamberlain vers Twyne & auters (1601; version of Twyne's Case) 102–103
  Gooch's Case (1591; 13 Eliz., c. 5 not subject to strict construction, despite penal clause) 106
  Leonard *against* Bacon (shows commercial purpose of 13 Eliz., c. 5) 106
  Mannocke's Case (1571; common law condemned fraud) 20, 105
  Nedham and Beaumont's Case (1590; statutory meaning of "purchaser" requires valuable consideration) 109
  Packman's Case (1595; conveyance voidable only by creditor) 2, 107
  Pauncefoot's Case (1594; meaning of forfeiture) 106
  Standen *against* Bullock (1600; revocable gift not equivalent to purchase for valuable consideration) 107–108
  Upton *against* Bassett (1596; gift fraudulent only against creditor) 107, 109–110
  Walter Chirton, case of (1351; direct and indirect fraud) 25 n.34, 106, 120, 130 n.30
catachresis 61–62
Catholics 81
  and fraudulent conveyancing laws 29–31, 55, 74
  persecution of and recusancy ix, 5, 36, 51, 67 n.49, 72, 106, 114
  Philip Sidney's attitude toward 50, 53
  supported in Ireland by Philip II, 88
  under Mary Tudor 46
  See also Northern Rebellion
Cecil, William, Lord Burghley 31–45, 53, 75–76
  death of 64
  "grave" 77
  lord treasurer 40 n.6
  made an earl 36

137

138 Index

role in passing 13 Eliz., c. 5: 32, 38, 76–77
his son Robert Cecil 64
chevisance x, 84, 96 n.28
coign and livery 47
Coke, Edward 111 n.9
  arguments against collusion 107
  his report of Twyne's Case xi, 2, 6–7, 30–31, 49, 101–111
  prosecutor of Walter Ralegh 93
collusion 75–78, 80, 83, 86, 102–103, 110, 118, 123
comedy xiii, 11, 19
concealed lands 63–64, 68 n.66, 77
consideration 6, 77–79, 82
  allegory of 84–85
  construing good consideration to mean valuable consideration 72, 101, 103–104, 107–108
  definition 77
  natural affection in exchange for a gift 104
conspiracy 67 n.63, 72, 76, 93, 118–119, 123, 127 n.19
constructive fraud xi, 5, 17–18
construction, rules of 121. *See also* fraud, penalty
conveyance, conveyancing
  definitions of 2, 12, 15, 78
  See also women, carrying away of
corruption of the blood 46, 91
definition 90
"creditors and others" 2, 6, 29–41, 72, 83, 113–114
difficulty of phrase 38, 41 n.26, 134
crescit in orbe dolus 101, 105, 133
custom of the castle 81–82

Dante 22
debt 2
  and marital obligations ix
"delay, hinder or defraud" 2, 106, 114, 118
Desmond, earl of 6, 46, 50, 55, 73
  conveyances by 75–76, 93
  forfeitures following his rebellion 71, 73, 77, 87, 89
dilapidations 1, 38
direct and indirect fraud 14, 26 n.34, 106, 120, 128 n.28, 129–130 n.29
  and Alien Statute 117
Dudley, Robert, earl of Leicester 52–53, 71, 88

Dyer, James 31–32, 63, 111 n.6, 128 n.29, 130 n.35
Dyer, Edward 52, 62–64, 65 n.33

Egerton, Thomas 106
  his foster mother a recusant 67 n.49
  interest in Irish affairs 92
  judge in Twyne's Case xi, 49
elves, in *Faerie Queene* 88
Elizabeth, Queen 43–44, 46, 51, 53, 62–63, 66 n.41
  allegories of in *The Faerie Queene* 83
  excommunicated 36, 55
  interest in finance and property 3, 34, 39, 46, 48, 81
  and Ireland xiii, 6, 33
  petitioners to 33
  prerogative 77
  suspicious of her deputies 88
Elyot, Thomas 120
English Statutes
  Act of Uniformity (1559) 30
  early conveyancing statutes 7–9, 14, 31, 58, 67 n.53, 75, 111 n.5
  13 Eliz., c. 3 (against overseas fugitives) 37, 74, 77
  13 Eliz., c. 4 (agents of Crown liable for their debts) 48
  13 Eliz., c. 5 (1571; voids fraudulent conveyances) xi, 29–41, 48, 56, 73, 77, 81
    commercial purpose of 5–6, 106
    construal of 31, 72, 74, 101–111
    penal provision 30–31, 107, 114
    political purpose 122
    proviso for transfers for good consideration and bona fide 103–104
    restatement of common law 74, 106
    source of modern statutes ix, 30
    See also "creditors and others"; "delay, hinder or defraud"; Twyne's Case
  13 Eliz., c. 7 (bankruptcy provision for tradesmen) 31
  13 Eliz., c. 10 (dilapidations) 38
  13 Eliz., c. 16 (Percy estate preserved) 43
  13 Eliz., c. 26 (attainder) 35–36
  14 Eliz., c. 11 (extension of 13 Eliz., c. 5) 74
  18 Eliz., c. 4 (fraudulent conveyances by rebels in the North) 35–36, 43
  23 Eliz., c. 1 (due obedience bill containing fraudulent conveyance clause) 55–56

27 Eliz., c. 4 (1585; against fraud of purchasers), 8 n.7, 9 n.22, 30, 56, 72, 84, 86, 93, 107–108. See also *The Faerie Queene*
1 Jac. I, c. 15 (1603; fraudulent conveyance constitutes bankrupty) 30
21 Jac. I, c. 19 (1623; Bankruptcy Act) 30
Statute of Frauds 134
escheats, escheator 6, 23 n.6, 47, 67 n.49, 77, 87, 89, 122, 133
estate tail, definition of 14

Falstaff x, 11–27, 29, 101, 134
  conveyed to Thames in buckbasket ix, 5, 12, 16–17
  expenses 19, 21
  horses conveyed 5, 11–12, 21–22, 26 nn.35 and 37
  legal acumen of 4, 17–19, 25 n.32, 26 n.42, 110
  moral ambiguity of 3, 22
  See also intention
The Faerie Queene 2, 6, 25 n.26, 72, 77–99, 113
  Aemylia episode as allegory of contemporary debates over relative value of non-monetary consideration 78–79, 83–85, 110
  allegory of bona fide purchasers and comparative consideration 79, 83
  allegory of moral ambiguity in confusion between Amyas and Placidas 85
  Amoret conveyed by figures of lust 78–84, 95 n.17
  Arthur and allegory of applying a legal holding 84–85
  Arthur and problem of preventing fraudulent conveyances 87–89
  Britomart and custom of the castle as allegory of timing 82
  Britomart and allegory of the power of the law to void fraudulent conveyances 83
  Busirane as ravisher and fraudulent conveyor 78–80, 83
  foursomes and forms of fraudulent conveyances 82–83, 86
  friendship and allegories of collusion 86
  Guyon's conveyed horse as image of uncertainty about the law 91
  historical allegory 80–81, 87–89, 96 n.22, 97 n.34
  and Ireland 72, 83
  Ruddymane as allegory of corruption of the blood 90–91
  Samient and use of fraud to fight fraud 88–89
  Scudamore as purchaser 78–81
  Trompart and allegory of forging documents 91
  See also Edmund Spenser; elves
fee, definition of 13
fine and recovery (or common recovery) 12–15, 24 n.10
forfeiture 6, 46, 67, 71–72, 121
  law on forfeitures during war 34
  timing of 75
  See also escheats; corruption of the blood; attainder
fraud 13–14, 84
  admirable 22, 124
  allegorical figure of 22, 29 (see also *The Faerie Queene*)
  definition 120
  no bright line test for 44
  reading fraud statutes broadly 105, 117, 120
  See also direct and indirect; English Statutes: Statute of Fraud
Fraudulent conveyance
  case law 2, 61
  definition xii, 1
  ethical and moral uncertainty of ix, xiii, 1, 2, 4, 5, 11, 32, 48, 51, 56–61, 73–74, 85, 88, 91, 93, 123–124, 134
  of family assets xii, xiv, 4, 13, 19, 49, 59, 85
  Italian laws 115–117
  jurisprudence of x–xi
  legal history of 1, 11, 13–14, 17, 19, 46–49, 111
  other literary examples xiv, 1, 4, 133
  and metaphoric language 4–5, 11–13, 15–17, 57–59, 61, 80
  against purchasers 30, 82–83
  ravishment as romance and pastoral form 57–59, 62, 93, 96 n.21
  and society's values 12, 29, 34–35, 43, 81
  and Tanastry 46, 49
  and United States law xii–xiii, 2, 19
  See also cases; comedy; English Statutes; fine and recovery; law and literature; property law; manumission; waste; women, conveyancing of
Fraunce, Abraham 94 n.9, 96 n.30, 119–120

Glenn, Garrard 2, 6, 7 n.3, 29–30, 37, 39, 55, 101, 114, 133
good faith (bona fide) 78, 83–84, 111 n.5
 badge of fraud 101
 proviso in 13 Eliz., c. 5 103
 purchasers 88
Gresham, Thomas, founder of the London Exchange 3, 30, 39
Greville, Fulke 51, 53, 63, 67 n.51

Howard, Thomas, Fourth Duke of Norfolk 32, 36, 40 n.6, 45
 his brother Northampton 63, 69 n.70
 execution 88
Hunsdon, Lord 33–35, 39

intention xi, 5–6, 12, 17, 20, 22, 102, 108, 114
 See also constructive fraud; looking backward; Falstaff; badges of fraud
Ireland xiii, 3, 28, 39, 72–78, 86
 bills of attainder 39
Irish statutes
 of year 1310 against fraudulent conveyancing 29, 31, 48, 74
 28 Henry VIII, c. 1 (attainder of earl of Kildare) 48
 11 Eliz., c. 11 (attainder of Shane O'Neill) 43
Italian law 6, 115–117, 127 n.23
 See also Kuehn, Thomas

Jonson, Ben 1, 13
Johnson, Samuel 22
Justinian 22, 25 n.30, 26 n.41, 27 n.45

Kuehn, Thomas 116–117, 123, 126 nn.9–10

Lambarde, William 3
law and literature ix, xii, 4–5, 7, 9 nn.18 and 20, 17, 29, 80, 93, 96 n.21, 113, 123, 134
 and cultural studies 124 n.2
 Henry Sidney's literary style 47–48
 love and debt 61
Leicester, earl of. *See* Dudley, Robert
looking backward xi, 77
 See also intention

manumission 19
Mary Tudor, Queen of England 44, 62, 75

Mary, Queen of Scots 32, 36–37, 80, 83, 87–88
Merchant of Venice 6, 110, 113–131
 Alien Statute 114, 116–117, 122
 and Italian source x, 6, 115–117, 121
 penal provision in 31
 and Twyne's Case 123
Merry Wives of Windsor ix, xiii, 4–6, 11–27, 110
 and middle class life 11, 29
 versions of 5, 21, 23 nn.3–4
moral philosophy 52
mutual mistake 19

Neale, J. E. 8 n.6, 20, 48, 54–55
Neville, Charles, earl of Westmorland 32, 36–37, 39, 39 n.4,
Norfolk, Duke of. *See* Howard, Thomas
Northern Rebellion of 1569 5, 30–36, 39 n.6, 40 n.7, 43, 55, 83
 costs involved 40 n.13
 supported by Spain 88
Nohrnberg, James 96 nn.27 and 34
Northumberland, earl of. *See* Percy, Thomas

O'Neill, Shane 43, 47–50, 61
overseas fugitives 38, 73–74

Page, Margaret
 use of legal language ix, 12–16
Parker, Patricia 5, 9 n.19, 11, 22 n.1, 23 n.9
Parliament, English, 31, 36, 54, 66 n.45–46, 74–75, 115
 debates of fraudulent conveyance laws 30, 37, 39 n.2, 48, 56, 61–62, 72, 77–78, 83–84, 113
Parliament, Irish 75–77, 95 n.10
penalty 58
 provision of 13 Eliz., c. 5: 7, 30, 113
 restrictive reading 116
 See also *Merchant of Venice*; Alien Statute; *qui tam*
Percy, Thomas, earl of Northumberland 32, 36–37, 39
 his younger brother Henry 35, 43
physical mutilation 91, 121
Pimb's Case 80
Pistol 20
Plautus (Roman playwright) 1
Plowden, Edmund 81
Popham, Sir John 48, 54, 65 n.18, 81, 92

as judge 106
Posner, Richard 4, 9 n.20, 17, 125 n.3
power 7, 29, 123
  of fraud 86
  and public discourse ix–x, xiii, 93, 113
property law 13–15, 17–18, 46–47, 83
purchase, purchasers 8 n.7, 9 n.22, 72, 85, 88
  defined 79, 109–110
Puttenham, George, 61–62, 80

qui tam law 114–115, 118, 122, 126 n.6
  See also penalty

Radcliff, Thomas, viscount Fitzwalter (or Fitzwater), earl of Sussex 32–35, 40 n.6
  career in Ireland 45
  made earl, 45–46
Ralegh, Walter 26 n.37, 52, 80, 92, 93 n.1, 99 nn.47–48, 114
Roberts, William 2, 8 n.11, 135 n.4
Roman law 19, 22, 116
Rowse, A. L. 8 n.13; 9 n.17, 63, 67 n.49, 68 n.61, 69 n.70, 96 n.23, 99 n.48

sanctuary, or safe haven from debt 1, 19, 31, 38
secrecy 101
Shakespeare, William 6–7, 113
  five years old during Northern Rebellion 39
  friends who were fraudulent conveyors, ix, 18, 24 n.21, 114
  knowledge of law 4–5, 11, 29, 115
  other plays 4, 124, 127 n.20, 134
  1, 2 Henry IV 19, 21–22, 75
  sonnets 16
  See also Merchant of Venice, Merry Wives of Windsor
sheep
  asset in Twyne's Case, xi, 20, 101–103
  and Scotland 1, 4
Shylock 3, 7, 110–111, 113, 115, 121–124, 130 n.40
Sidney, Henry, Lord Deputy of Ireland, 3, 5–6, 43–50, 62
Sidney, Philip x, 43, 50–71
  Astrophil and Stella 52–54
  his brother Robert 52, 61–62
  in Ireland 50
  not opposed to fraudulent conveyancing 5–6
  at Oxford, 39
  in Parliament 54–55
Spain 46, 76, 87–88
Spenser, Edmund x, xiii, 2, 7, 63, 71–99
  and Anglo-Norman rebels, xiii, 71
  attitude to fraudulent conveyancing 6, 30, 46, 64, 72–73, 91
  estates 73, 87
  Mother Hubberds Tale 71
  See also The Faerie Queene; View of the Present State of Ireland
Star Chamber 11, 58, 92, 101, 114, 120
stare decisis 110
  See The Faerie Queene: Arthur and allegory of applying a legal holding
Staunford, William *Les plees del corone* (1560) 75, 94 n.9
surrender and regrant 47
Sussex, earl of. *See* Radcliffe, Thomas

Tanastry. *See* Fraudulent Conveyance: and Tanastry
Throckmorton, John 62, 80
theater ix, 16, 92
timing 75–78, 81–82, 91
  badge of fraud 102
  See also forfeitures
trust, trusts 15, 104
  See also collusion
Two Gentlemen of Verona 4–5
Twyne's Case (1601) x–xi, 2, 20, 30, 74, 78, 93, 101–111, 114, 123
  date of 5, 11
  defined good consideration 84, 86
  extended 13 Eliz., c. 5 to cover forfeitures to the state 72, 92
  facts of 101–102
  justices for 48
  legal French text of xix, 9 n.23
  See also badges of fraud; Statutes, English: 13 Eliz., c. 5

United States
  civil procedure reforms 105
  Constitution of 46
  See also Fraudulent Conveyance: and United States laws

View of the Present State of Ireland 6, 30, 33, 72–78, 87, 92
  authorship of 94 n.4

Walsingham, Sir Francis 52, 96 n.23, 98 n.36
waste 12–13
Weisberg, Richard 4, 9 n.20, 125 n.5, 130 n.40
Westmorland. *See* Neville, Charles
wills and trusts 15
Wilson, Thomas 133
Worden, Blair 65 n.16, 68 n.54

women
  carrying away of x, xii, 1, 5–6, 56–58, 133–134
  and interclass marriage 79, 95 n.18
  Jessica 7, 119
  statutes 58
  See also *The Faerie Queene*: Amoret conveyed by figures of lust